Introduction to Research

TYRUS HILLWAY
Colorado State College of Education

Introduction

to Research

HOUGHTON MIFFLIN COMPANY
Boston   The Riverside Press Cambridge

condemnation of mere opinion . . .

EPICTETUS

CONTENTS

PREFACE

Why This Book Was Written

The author's experiences in teaching and advising a large number of graduate students have led him to the belief that many aspects of the scholarly life are, at first contact, extremely perplexing to the young scholar. Approaching specialized study and research for the first time, the beginner frequently fails to understand what is expected of him and finds questions rising in his mind for which the answers are far from easy to obtain.

What methods are acceptable in research? How are suitable problems for study chosen? For what purposes are graduate schools organized, and how do they differ from undergraduate colleges? Why do the standards for a research report differ from those of the course paper or the scholarly essay? How should the report of a piece of original research be organized and written? How does one go about the business of publishing his discoveries? These and scores of other questions on principles and procedures may remain unanswered in the young scholar's mind for many months after he has begun his training in advanced scholarship.

To furnish reliable answers to such questions in a straightforward way is the object of this book. The author has tried to avoid unessential details, technical terms, and complicated explanations. It is his hope that the information he has provided will make the principles and methods of research clearly understandable, and hence will make research itself easier and more effective.

The book is divided into four parts. Part One is introductory; it considers the meaning and importance of research in modern life, as well as the problems that face the graduate student about to undertake a research project of his own. Part Two briefly describes the general processes of research and the way a trained investigator plans and begins a study. Part Three examines in some detail the various methods of finding and analyzing data and drawing conclusions from them. Part Four deals with matters connected with preparing the written report and securing its publication.

All the facts and ideas given have been tested and found helpful in actual work with first-year graduate students and others who were learning to conduct research projects. The book is intended as an orientation to research in all fields, for knowledge is a seamless whole. Although the subject matter and research materials of one department of study may differ from those of another, the basic principles of research remain the same. The author believes, therefore, that, for the beginning student of research, mastery of the specific techniques in one subject field will be less useful than a thorough understanding of the fundamental principles of research as applied in all fields. The problems of young scholars in the various fields prove upon close examination to be remarkably alike. It is assumed that, if these common problems are solved and if the basic ideas and methods of research are understood, the young scholar will then be able constructively to apply what he has learned to his own special field.

For many of the underlying ideas presented here, the author owes a long-standing debt of gratitude to the excellent scholars who have been his teachers, including especially Professors Chauncey B. Tinker and Stanley T. Williams of Yale University and Hyder E. Rollins of Harvard University, as well as a host of more recent colleagues and friends, particularly Professor Ben D. Wood of Columbia University. For the most useful thoughts in this book, the suggestions and — more important — the inspiration received from such men as these may well deserve the full credit. For the form in which these thoughts are here given, however, and for any aberrations from the principles which these wiser men have instilled in him, the author must accept complete responsibility.

Special acknowledgment should be made also to the many friendly and stimulating students in the author's classes who saw these materials in their preliminary form and who offered many helpful criticisms and suggestions for their improvement. If he has been able to gather together information which will make more meaningful and beneficial the early stages in the training of young scholars, the author will feel satisfied that he has done a useful thing in writing this book.

TYRUS HILLWAY

PART ONE

Research and
Graduate Study

1

THE ROLE OF RESEARCH

IN MAN'S RISE FROM

BARBARISM

Progress as we know it in the modern world would be impossible without research. Each year new products, new facts, new concepts, and new ways of doing things come into our lives as the result of it. Our national government as a regular policy now spends huge amounts of money to support research that will develop new weapons of war (like the hydrogen bomb) for the defense of our country against attack. Manufacturers carry on research to discover new products (like television in color) for the modern consumer. Agricultural experts perform experiments to find or develop new species of plant life or new breeds of cattle that will supply larger yields at smaller cost or that will prove immune to destructive diseases. Archaeologists are digging into the ruins of ancient cities to learn how our remote ancestors lived and conducted their affairs. Research is going on at this moment which no doubt will provide us with better and faster transportation, more comfortable and cheaper housing, medicines to cure our most critical illnesses, improved methods and materials for educating our children, a more thorough understanding of past history and of the times before recorded history began, more effective controls over our men-

3

tal processes — in fact, one could go on almost endlessly predicting the numerous benefits which will certainly result if research continues at its present rate in the years to come.

Who Carries on Research?

Perhaps we are prone to believe that the progress of research will continue indefinitely and that a steady increase of our knowledge and powers can be taken for granted. But research cannot go on or learning advance unless men and women are constantly being trained for this vital work.

The advancement of knowledge does not just happen; on the contrary, it requires constant effort by intelligent and highly trained people who spend their lives pushing back the boundaries of human ignorance. It is no exaggeration to say that nearly all the worthwhile discoveries and improvements in our present civilization came about through planned research. This was not always true, however, in man's history. The principles and methods of research that we now employ so effectively have been available to us only within comparatively recent years — recent, that is, in terms of man's long struggle to rise out of barbarism. What we now accept as a necessary and even routine part of modern civilized life — the techniques of research and the benefits resulting from them — could never have been dreamed of by our primitive forebears, though even they must have had within them that vital spark of imagination, that speculative power which has grown into the marvelous tool of learning we call research.

Everyone learns new facts and ideas in the ordinary ways, which are *chance, trial-and-error,* and *generalization from experience.* Man's first knowledge about fire, for instance, probably came to him by chance, through accidental means. Other things he undoubtedly learned by deliberately trying them out; for example, he may have discovered that certain herbs are poisonous merely by tasting them and then noting the after-effects. After a time, the things learned through chance or trial-and-error were very likely transmitted to other men, so that they became common knowledge. Thus began the building up of a permanent body of useful information about the world.

The accumulation of a general body of knowledge must have involved the drawing of broad conclusions from specific incidents of past experience. Perhaps this is how some of the early religious taboos originated. If it was observed that a number of persons in a tribe had been made ill by eating shellfish at the wrong time of the year, a little thinking about the matter might result in a prohibition against eating shellfish at any time. The kind of generalization we get from experience will depend very much upon the kind of experience we happen to have.

These three elementary methods of adding to the sum total of human knowledge (chance, trial-and-error, and generalization from experience) appear to be used by nearly everyone. But a great many people can also employ the method of *logic*, which is considerably different. By logic we "reason things out." Not only do we generalize from our experiences and from those of others, but with logic we can arrive at certain conclusions based upon our previous generalizations. Thus the logical method represents a step forward in man's development of the means by which he learns new things.

But going far beyond the elementary methods of chance, trial-and-error, and generalization from experience, and even beyond the more advanced method of logic, is that method of seeking truth which we call *research* or *scientific inquiry*. The greater part of this book is devoted more or less to the definition of research, to descriptions of its many forms, and to extensive discussions of how its results are accomplished. It will be enough here, however, to describe research briefly as a method of study by which, through the careful and exhaustive investigation of all the ascertainable evidence bearing upon a definable problem, we reach a solution to that problem. Research is an instrument which mankind has perfected very slowly over a period of several centuries, and it seems to be at present our most reliable means of advancing our knowledge. Its purpose, like that of all the other methods, is to discover facts and ideas not previously known to man.

Earlier Methods of Adding to Knowledge

Before we can fully appreciate the tremendous advantages of research as a method of learning new truths, we must understand something of the customs of thinking which preceded it. So far as we can tell, men have always tried in one way or another to learn more about themselves and the world in which they live. Curiosity has impelled us to probe the secrets of nature, even when such knowledge might not necessarily have any practical application. It is enough that we desire to know. Even small children exhibit in a remarkable degree this quality of curiosity. They are constantly asking questions. What are those tiny points of light in the sky which we call stars, and why do they move across the heavens? What makes the grass grow? Why is the grass green? How big is the earth? What makes people ill? How far away is the moon? Such questions as these, which we hear asked by children, probably were asked in a remoter day by our earliest ancestors upon the earth.

Until mankind had built up a considerable body of knowledge as a common heritage for educated men, these questions could not be answered in any manner that we should now consider reasonable. Primitive man could satisfactorily explain unusual facts or incidents only if he attributed them to magic and to the influence of some supernatural power. Thus objects of nature sometimes came to be regarded as the dwelling places of spirits who caused certain things to happen according to their whims. The sun in its journey across the sky, for example, could be explained as a chariot of fire driven by a god. A belief in magic provided a convenient means of accounting for anything which did not fit the pattern of understandable everyday experience. Even today, when some unusual event or coincidence occurs, there are people who are still willing to ascribe it to magical or supernatural influences without looking for a natural cause. Gradually, however, as man acquired more knowledge, many things formerly believed magical grew familiar, and natural explanations were found for them.

Appeal to Authority

Mankind seems to have developed very early a sense of reliance upon authority. When a tribe was attacked, when it was struck by a pestilence, or when a river flooded the arable lands after heavy rains, people wanted to know why such a thing had happened to them. They would go for an explanation to their priests or wise men. The priest might account for the visitation as punishment for sins or for failure to propitiate some god. Frequently the advice of the priests and the wise men was good advice, and men came to trust their chosen authorities implicitly.

Out of this age-old reliance upon authority seems to have grown the idea that the great thinkers of the past were able to discover the truth for all time and that man even today can best learn to know himself and his world by studying their writings. In Western civilization, the great period of reliance upon authority was the Middle Ages, when the teachings of the ancients (Plato, Aristotle, the early Christian Fathers, and others) had far higher standing as creditable sources than did first-hand observation and analysis of facts. For this reason, mistaken theories of early writers on medicine continued to be put into practice (because these writers were accepted authorities) long after experience had proved them wrong. Veneration for authorities led medieval scholars to adopt the attitude that copying, translating, or commenting on earlier works ranked as more important and respectable than personal investigation and original thinking. Truth, it was assumed, had been fully discovered and proclaimed by the scholars of the past; hence, to learn the truth about anything, one would need only to study the works of the right authority.

Nor did the practice of relying blindly on authority die out with the Middle Ages. In Soviet Russia today, to cite one example, the writings of Marx and Lenin on history, politics, economics, and other subjects are supported officially by the government as fixed and unalterable truth. It would be dangerous in Russia not to believe in these authorities, even when their teachings clearly do not agree with observed fact.

Since even the best authority can be wrong, the dangers of reliance on authority seem obvious. Sometimes, however, we find that a problem does not lend itself to scientific investigation. In such a case, the most nearly reliable *opinion* as to a solution may be that of a person who has had long experience with that problem and who has studied and thought much about it. We may assume that such a person's opinion on the subject would be worth more than that of someone chosen indiscriminately. We should call such a person an authority. In a court of law, the expert opinion of a man who is recognized as an authority upon some subject may be accepted as testimony (or evidence) in a trial, especially when the question at issue depends upon opinion. What we are saying is that, when factual evidence that will solve a problem cannot be obtained, we may have to rely upon authoritative opinion for the time being as the only possible avenue to a solution. In such a case, the point at issue becomes the "authoritativeness" of the authority.

The Triumph of Reason

Perhaps no other people contributed more than did the ancient Greeks toward the development of mental tools by which man may approach the problems of the universe. In devising and using logical and mathematical methods to ascertain facts and principles, the Greeks dealt a death blow to explanation by magic. Largely through their speculations Western man arrived at the concept of the universe as an ordered cosmos, in which everything happens according to definite laws of cause and effect. Beginning with a belief in the natural order of things, the Greeks set out to learn the characteristics of this natural order. They succeeded remarkably well.

Greek thinkers like Aristotle reasoned from the known to the unknown by a deductive process whose basis is the syllogism. The syllogism provides a means of testing the validity of any given conclusion or idea. To use a familiar example, we may state a given proposition as follows:

1. All men must die;
2. Socrates is a man;
3. Therefore, Socrates will die.

In this example, if the two preliminary statements (premises) can be shown to be true, it follows that any reasonable person must accede to the third statement (conclusion). By the rules of Greek logic, a conclusion properly deduced from reliable premises is itself inevitably reliable. Of course, this presupposes that every element in the argument has been carefully examined and all unrelated materials discarded, so that the premises are sound and an unbreakable chain of argument results.

Unfortunately, the method of deduction, however useful, sometimes deceives the user by its tendency to interest him in mental processes and skillful argumentation instead of keeping him on the path to truth. During the Middle Ages the followers of Aristotle's methods neglected his plain emphasis upon the direct observation of nature and formed the habit of deriving conclusions and generalizations by means of logic alone. Using the syllogism, they deduced both facts and principles from certain selected statements of approved authorities, often without checking upon their accuracy and reliability. By the clever use of this instrument and the appropriate selection of premises, they were able to "prove" almost anything. But such distortion of the method must be regarded as a mere *tour de force*, and it does not invalidate deductive logic as a mental tool. The great weakness of the syllogism, of course, lies in the possibility that one of the premises may be erroneous or that the premises may be unrelated; thus, unless each of the premises is carefully tested and the relationship shown, the conclusion may be wrong. Another serious weakness of the syllogism, as the study of semantics has recently shown us, is its dependence upon verbal symbolism.

Inductive Reasoning vs. Deductive Reasoning

As we have seen, the Greeks developed through the use of reason alone a superb methodology of intellectual discovery which added many treasures to the wealth of human knowledge. The advances they made, particularly in geometry and the physical sciences, were not materially improved upon until the sixteenth century. They never succeeded, however, in developing and applying widely the idea of the scientific experiment. This did not arise until comparatively recent times.

We have also seen that the syllogism, which the Greeks invented, fosters *deductive reasoning*. That is, one deduces a specific, or particular, fact or conclusion from the relationship of two or more general facts or principles. In the late sixteenth century Francis Bacon broke with the tradition of his times and attacked this method of reasoning as unsound. He also severely criticized Aristotle and the followers of Aristotle for first deciding upon a conclusion and then deliberately selecting facts and principles tending to support it. This is the method sometimes used in debating. When two opposing debaters marshal the arguments on both sides of a question, each is likely to be more interested in winning the debate — proving his side right through the power of logic and eloquence — than in finding the true answer. But Bacon was being a little hard on Aristotle, for the latter seems to have insisted on the necessity of basing generalizations upon facts. The followers of Aristotle in the Middle Ages, however, undoubtedly neglected this part of his teachings and adopted the habit of deriving their conclusions from generalities and from statements of presumed authorities.

Bacon — and, for that matter, Leonardo da Vinci before him — stressed the need for basing general conclusions upon specific facts through direct observation. This, of course, is what we know as *inductive reasoning* — that is, going from the particular to the general, rather than, as in deductive reasoning, from the general to the particular. Bacon advised the scholar to ignore authorities, to observe nature closely, to experiment, to draw his own inferences, to classify his facts in order to reach minor generalizations, and then to proceed from the minor generalizations to greater ones. He especially warned against formulating any hypothesis (or probable solution) until all the facts have been gathered. This system of reasoning has been termed mechanistic, because every step of the process is based on provable fact rather than on speculation or logic.

The plain truth is that many scholarly problems cannot be solved by inductive reasoning alone, as Charles Darwin found when he attempted zealously to follow Bacon's advice. For years he collected fact after fact in his biological researches, hoping that the facts themselves would lead to an important generalization. Fact-gathering, however, proved as unproductive of results as gathering bricks for a house when there is no architectural plan for building it. Not until Darwin stumbled upon a possible solution to the problem of how evolution takes place and began to test it by making deductions from it was he able to see how his facts could be put together to form a workable theory. He describes this event as follows:

> My first note-book [on evolution] was opened in July 1837. I worked on true Baconian principles, and without any theory collected

facts on a wholesale scale, more especially with respect to domesticated productions, by printed enquiries, by conversation with skillful breeders and gardeners, and by extensive reading. When I see the list of books of all kinds which I read and abstracted, including whole series of Journals and Transactions, I am surprised at my industry. I soon perceived that selection was the keystone of man's success in making useful races of animals and plants. But how selection could be applied to organisms living in a state of nature remained for some time a mystery to me.

In October 1838, that is, fifteen months after I had begun my systematic enquiry, I happened to read for amusement 'Malthus on Population,' and being well prepared to appreciate the struggle for existence which everywhere goes on from long-continued observation of the habits of animals and plants, it at once struck me that under these circumstances favourable variations would tend to be preserved, and unfavourable ones to be destroyed. The result of this would be the formation of new species. Here then I had at last got a theory by which to work. . . .[1]

In other words, having gathered a considerable body of data, Darwin made a shrewd guess (derived from reading Malthus) as to what the data might mean. He formulated in his mind a tentative explanation of the facts he already knew and then proceeded, with his theory (or hypothesis) as a guide for further investigation, to see whether his idea would be supported or proved wrong by the additional evidence which could be gathered. Thus Darwin used both inductive and deductive reasoning to arrive at his final conclusions. This is a good example of how modern research works.

The Scientific Method

The system Darwin used in seeking an explanation of biological evolution is often called the method of scientific inquiry. This method, of course, is effective not only for studies in the physical and biological sciences but for studies in any field.

Most modern research is conducted in accordance with the same method. Scientific inquiry as a method of learning new truth differs, as we have already seen, from the methods of chance, of trial-and-error, of generalization from experience, and of the syllogism. It also

[1] Francis Darwin, ed., *The Life and Letters of Charles Darwin*, 2 vols. (New York: D. Appleton and Co., 1899), I, 68.

differs from a way of learning often claimed by creative artists and
by many scientists too — that of intuition. We should not rule out
the possibility that valuable advances in knowledge may sometimes
be the result of "unearned grants of insight," to borrow the phrase
of Walter B. Cannon. Many an important idea has arrived as a
flash of intuition, like Athena springing from the brow of Zeus. But
these insights that overleap methods are most likely to come to the
scholar who has worked long and hard on a project, and he will subject them to the rigorous tests of the scientific method before he accepts them as truth. Intuition must be regarded as a fortuitous
glimpse of truth which comes as the result of no conscious effort or
plan. Intuitive insight, moreover, cannot be relied on without careful consideration of its applications; it can be wrong as easily as it
can be right. Since the intuitive recognition of truth cannot be objectively analyzed, and since it cannot be controlled, we shall not
here discuss it in detail; our concern is with the conscious method
or planned procedure that has proved most useful in modern research.

A great research institution recently described the process which
is used for all studies made by its staff. The process consists of
several very definite steps. These are: (1) identification of the problem to be investigated, (2) collection of essential facts pertaining
to the problem, (3) selection of one or more tentative solutions of
the problem, (4) evaluation of these alternative solutions to determine which of them is in accord with all the facts, and (5) the
final selection of the most likely solution. In general, these are the
steps most commonly followed in all modern research. They are
discussed in considerable detail in later chapters of this book.

What are the distinguishing characteristics of this method? In
the first place, it is based upon the belief that a natural explanation
can be found for every observable phenomenon. It assumes that the
universe is an ordered cosmos in which there is no result without a
cause. Whereas primitive man ascribed anything unusual that he
might see or hear to the special intervention of the gods, modern
man looks for natural causes. Although there still remain many areas
of knowledge that have resisted scientific investigation, we have had
remarkable success in applying this fundamental assumption of the
scientific method.

In the second place, this method rejects reliance upon authority and substitutes the idea that conclusions are valid only when supported by evidence. The modern scholar does not accept the word of Aristotle or anyone else as authoritative unless he has confirmed it by an inspection of the facts. This entails both direct observation and experiment. Galileo reportedly investigated the rate of acceleration of falling bodies by dropping cannon balls of various weights from the leaning tower of Pisa in 1589. He did not satisfy himself by merely *reasoning* or by consulting authorities on the matter, but actually studied the facts by experimental means. Until his time it had been commonly assumed by thinking men, following Aristotle, that a heavy object naturally would fall to the ground faster than a lighter object. This assumption appears perfectly logical and reasonable to anyone who thinks about it without taking the trouble to test it by experiment. Galileo refused, however, to accept either authority or logic as the basis for his conclusions and so learned, perhaps to his own surprise, that the cannon balls he dropped, except for minor differences caused by the resistance of the air, would all fall at the same rate of speed.

Galileo's experiment also illustrates a third way in which the scientific method is unlike others. This is in the substitution, wherever possible, of actual observation for logic. Ideas and facts, whether arrived at through logic or taken from some authoritative source, must be tested and shown to be either true or false.

What we have said in the preceding paragraphs does not mean, of course, that either logic or authority can be entirely dispensed with in research. The statements of experts upon some subject may be useful when other evidence is lacking, and especially when we have no contrary evidence. Yet reliance upon authority does not in itself constitute scientific investigation, and it may lead the investigator astray. We must also say that arguments advanced in the support of any conclusion should always be logical. In other words, the conclusion ought to be consistent with the evidence and with known facts and experience within the field of study. Logic may be thought of as the language of reasoning (relating to quality), just as mathematics is the language of measurement (relating to quantity or size). The use of logic, therefore, is essential to scientific inquiry.

The Development of Research

To write a complete history of research would be a considerable undertaking. A perspective may be gained, perhaps, by mentioning a few of the most important milestones in the development of our present proficiency in this type of activity.

We have no very clear idea of any point in human history at which we can say research began. While much of what man learned in the primitive cultures undoubtedly was the result of chance, trial-and-error, and generalization from experience, probably a few men even in very early times made a conscious and systematic effort to discover new knowledge. No doubt one of the first products of such an effort was the calendar. By the use of a calendar it became possible to predict the seasons and thus to know when the crops could be planted. The custodians of such information were the first scholars. And because this knowledge appeared mysterious and even sacred to the ordinary person, it was recorded and guarded by the priests. In Egypt, for example, the priests became versed in mathematics and invented surveying, so that proper land boundaries could be restored after the annual floods of the Nile. Certain medical data were also recorded; we can still find, carved on stone in hieroglyphics, instructions regarding the cure of several diseases and advice on dental surgery.

Agriculture and medicine may well have been the earliest fields of research, with astronomy close behind as the ancient astronomers learned to use mathematics as a tool in their studies. When Ptolemy explained the motions of the stars, he did so in mathematical terms. He broke with his predecessors in refusing to ascribe the movements of heavenly bodies to supernatural causes — a great heresy in his day and an important step in the direction of modern research.

Following the example of the priests, the men who conducted early research by the use of mathematics or logic in science, literature, ethics, and other fields often regarded their discoveries as almost mystical and as not to be shared with the common run of their fellow-beings. Thus the followers of Pythagoras are said to have murdered one of their number who had betrayed some of the principles of geometry to the general public in a speech he had given.

This attitude is a far cry from that of today's scholar, who looks upon his discoveries as a contribution to the world's knowledge and not as a private possession.

Great advances in the principles of research were made by the ancient Greeks. Building partly upon previous discoveries recorded by the Egyptians and Babylonians, the Greek thinkers delved particularly into astronomy, medicine, physics, and geography, and some of them explored literature and ethics. A few instances will illustrate the scope and the fundamental importance of their contributions to the sum of human learning. Among the earliest whose names we know were Thales and Anaximander (about 600 B.C.), whose principal work was done in astronomy. Pythagoras, living at nearly the same period, studied physical geography and notably furthered the growth of mathematical and philosophical speculation. Democritus (about 400 B.C.) proposed the atomistic theory to explain the structure of matter, though he had no means of investigating the problem experimentally. Hippocrates, often called the "father of medicine," was a pupil of Democritus who revolutionized medical knowledge and practice by insisting upon exact and careful diagnosis and the study of the body and its functions. Aristotle (fourth century B.C.), though best known as a philosopher and logician, added much to our knowledge of many fields, including animal anatomy. Theophrastus, a follower of Aristotle, established a systematic method of studying botany. Archimedes (third century B.C.) worked with physics. Strabo, who settled in Rome about 20 B.C., developed geography as a science. Ptolemy (second century A.D.) was an Egyptian who used Grecian and Egyptian mathematics and science to devise the first satisfactory theory to account for the movements of the planets.

The Romans were the heirs and perpetuators of Greek learning, but their own genius was more for practical application than for the pursuit of knowledge for its own sake. They were lawmakers and engineers rather than speculative thinkers. After the decline of the Graeco-Roman civilization and the break-up of the Roman Empire, not only the methods of research but many of its accumulated fruits were for a time virtually lost to Western Europe. Early Christians tended to avoid pagan books and art. Moreover, the search for secular knowledge appeared far less worthy than preparation of the soul for eternity. In the Mohammedan countries, on the other hand, the tradition of research persisted. Chemistry began to be studied by the Arabs, from whom it spread to medieval Europe as alchemy, a pseudo-science based upon the futile search for a method of transmuting base metals into gold. In somewhat the same way, early astronomy degenerated into astrology, another pseudo-science, which attempted to trace the influence of the stars upon human life. In short, when men failed, to check authority against experience, when they compounded error by deducing erroneous conclusions from erroneous or imperfectly understood premises, learning drifted away from truth.

In the Middle Ages, as we have previously noted, it was widely believed that all essential knowledge had already been discovered and that to learn it one had only to refer to past authorities. Nevertheless, a few men continued to make their own efforts at research, though it was literally dangerous to challenge the accepted authorities. Men like Roger Bacon in the thirteenth century were popularly suspected of dealing in black magic and had to conduct their researches in secret. Copernicus, as late as the sixteenth century, suffered persecution at the hands of the ecclesiastical authorities and had to renounce his theories publicly after he had substituted a heliocentric for a geocentric explanation of the planets' movements.

The great march of modern research, especially in the field of the natural sciences, can be only adumbrated here. It really began with Galileo's experimental work in physics at the dawn of the seventeenth century. This was a wonderful century, made glorious by such achievements as the invention of logarithms by Napier in 1614, the researches of Harvey on the circulation of the blood, the use of decimal notation by Briggs (1617), the publication of Francis Bacon's momentus theories in his *Novum Organum* (1620), Boyle's emergence as the "father of modern chemistry," and Newton's mathematical concepts of the laws of gravity (1679).

In the eighteenth century geology and biology rose as new fields for study. Later, in the nineteenth century, the work of such men as Lyell and Darwin in these areas transformed our entire picture of the physical world. The study of archaeology (beginning with the excavations at the site of Troy by Schliemann) and of psychology (growing out of the pseudo-sciences of physiognomy and phrenology) began in the nineteenth century. Such developments as the use of biochemistry and bacteriology in the conquest of medical problems and the use of new concepts in physics to accomplish the breaking-down of the atom have taken place largely during the twentieth century.

In the meantime, research has begun in such relatively new fields as social relations, economics, education, and similar areas. This means that we have now applied in these fields and in the humanities the methods of study previously used only in the field of science. We are nearing (though we have not yet achieved it) the perfection of the scientific method as a tool of research for all fields of human study. The remarkable growth of our technology and of all other elements in our present civilization may be attributed very largely to our use of research. To see its results, we have only to look around us.

The Scientific Method as a Means of Arriving at Truth

No one can confidently claim that the scientific method is the only means of arriving at truth. It is admittedly only a tool geared to the exploration of objective reality. Thus, scientific research may establish the date of a Shakespearean sonnet, but it cannot communicate the aesthetic experience of reading that sonnet — an experience that may be as much a part of the whole "truth" about that sonnet as the date. Scientific research can tell us what various people *have believed* or how they *have behaved* on certain social issues, but not what we *should believe* or how we *ought to behave*. What we can hope to do in extending the scientific method into hitherto nonscientific fields is to establish truth insofar as it is objectively demonstrable, and in so doing to widen the basis for rational agreement among men and to give our values more validity by anchoring them more firmly in what we can prove to be so.

The truth discovered by research does not necessarily constitute the whole or final truth about life and the universe. As we discover new facts and formulate new conclusions, our knowledge constantly has to be revised. Research appears preferable to other methods of adding to man's knowledge merely because it has proved more productive and more accurate than the others. We cannot yet say that it gives promise of solving all human problems.

Summary

Beginning with his natural curiosity about anything he could not understand, man has gradually developed ways of thinking and of investigating his problems which today are producing astonishing results. No longer does man ascribe natural phenomena to supernatural influences, and no longer does he rely blindly upon accepted authority. He has developed an orderly system of searching for truth which, by basing conclusions upon factual evidence, and by using logic as a means of showing relationships between related ideas, has given him better and more accurate answers to his many questions. This orderly system is what we call research.

2

THE GRADUATE STUDENT

AND HIS OPPORTUNITIES

The typical American graduate student seems to think of the graduate school as the unavoidable barrier which he must hurdle in his race for a higher degree. The degree itself, and not the education which he is receiving, too often is regarded as the main prize. The degree may be necessary to insure the student's advancement in his profession; it is a tangible badge of achievement for all to see and admire. The student is tempted, therefore, to think of all the many requirements which block the way between himself and the degree — the classwork, the comprehensive examinations, the thesis or dissertation, and so on — as annoying and arbitrary obstacles placed in his path by the graduate faculty.

Generally it requires maturity and several years of experience to understand and fully appreciate the opportunities presented in graduate study. The great libraries, the carefully selected faculty, the special facilities for individual research — these tremendous advantages, placed at the disposal of the student in the modern graduate school, have been brought together only as the result of long years of effort and considerable expenditure of money by university administrations. The student will derive the maximum benefit from his graduate career if he avoids the temptation to seek short cuts to his degree and concentrates his attention upon the proper use of the educational opportunities which the graduate school so richly provides.

Traditionally the student chooses his graduate school because he wants to work under the great scholars who are assembled on its faculty. In actual practice, however, many other factors also influence the student's choice. The location of the school, the reputation of certain of its academic departments, the cost of tuition, convenience, and even chance affect this vital decision. Furthermore, so many students are today crowding into our universities that a person may be forced by the competition of better qualified applicants to select some other school than the one he considers most desirable. At mid-century, approximately 200,000 students were reported to be enrolled in the graduate schools of the United States, and the number seems to be increasing each year. Unfortunately, all these factors have tended to destroy the close personal relationships between professor and student which are among the greatest of the joys and benefits of graduate study.

How Graduate Study Differs from Undergraduate Study

Is graduate work really different in kind from undergraduate work, or does it consist merely of additional courses and slightly more advanced instruction? Is there something distinctive and special about the courses with higher numbers in the college catalogue which in many cases are marked "open only to graduate students"? To many young people the answers to these questions remain a mystery until after several months of graduate study have been completed.

Actually there are profound and fundamental differences between the graduate program and the undergraduate program. While the line between them cannot always be clearly drawn, the aims of graduate education in American universities are not the same as those to which the student has become accustomed in his undergraduate experience.

Generally speaking, the first four years of college — especially in the standard college of liberal arts — are aimed at broadness and rich diversification of educational growth in the individual. President A. Whitney Griswold of Yale University once compared the ideal collegiate atmosphere to "Madison and Jefferson talking to each other about everything under the sun," and though not every educator would subscribe to Griswold's emphasis upon discussion and the mutual exchange of ideas as the elemental educating force in college, nearly all would agree upon the need for wide contacts with at least the major fields of human knowledge. As a matter of fact, our colleges almost without exception, even including those whose purposes are chiefly professional (that is, vocational), stress the so-called "liberalizing" function of the undergraduate program.

Former Dean McConnell of the University of Minnesota described the objectives of the typical undergraduate program in these terms:

> The purpose of the liberal college is to provide a well-rounded education that will fit men and women to utilize their abilities to the fullest extent in understanding the broad cultural foundations, the significant accomplishments, and the unfinished business of their society; in participating intelligently in community life and public affairs, in enjoying literature and the arts; in building a set of values that will constitute a "design for living"; in developing and maintaining sound physical and mental health; and in taking a socially responsible part in the world of work.[1]

Similarly, a great many modern educators have insisted that the aim of the American college must be not to prepare narrowly trained specialists, but to turn out men and women of broad cultural background.[2]

The ideal of developing liberally educated men and women is, of course, not new. Indeed, recent comments on the subject (like those of Griswold and McConnell, above) sound very much like the famous remarks of John Henry Newman, English clergyman and scholar of the nineteenth century. Newman described the ideally educated gentleman as one who

> is at home in any society, . . . has common ground with every class; he knows when to speak and when to be silent; he is able to converse, he is able to listen; he can ask a question pertinently, and gain a lesson seasonably, when he has nothing to impart himself; he is ever ready, yet never in the way; he is a pleasant companion, and a comrade you can depend upon; he knows when to be serious and when to

[1] T. R. McConnell, "Liberal Education and Specialization," in *The American College*, ed. P. F. Valentine (New York: Philosophical Library, 1949), p. 82.
[2] See, for example, the report of the Harvard committee, *General Education in a Free Society* (Cambridge: Harvard University Press, 1945).

trifle; and he has a sure tact which enables him to trifle with graceful-
ness and to be serious with effect. He has the repose of a mind which
lives in itself, while it lives in the world, and which has resources for
its happiness at home when it cannot go abroad. He has a gift which
serves him in public, and supports him in retirement, without which
good fortune is but vulgar, and with which failures and disappointment have a charm.[3]

It is essential to understand that these aims of a liberal education
— the development of the kind of person both Newman and McConnell so attractively describe, though speaking for different areas —
are not the aims of graduate education at all. The graduate school
assumes that its entering students have already been broadly educated. The ultimate purpose of the graduate school is to train
specialists. This is the first of the fundamental differences between
graduate and undergraduate programs.

In the kind of collegiate program offered in the undergraduate
years, it is easy to see that the student could successfully complete
his courses, receive a baccalaureate degree, and become what one
would recognize as a thoroughly cultured person without ever having
been, in the strict sense of the word, a scholar. The scholar is not
simply an educated person or one with high academic ability, though
the term is sometimes used loosely to indicate any person who is
attending school. By definition, the scholar is a *learned* person, one
with special competence in a particular branch of the world's knowledge. The graduate student is an apprentice in scholarship. By
entering the graduate school he has committed himself to the joys
as well as the tribulations of the scholar's life. What this really
means is that a new and challenging kind of existence is opening
before him.

Graduate Work Introduces Intensive Study of a Special Field.
An important aspect of graduate education, then, is concentration
upon one special field of study. Instead of the goal of broad cultural
development, the student now sets as his goal an expert and thorough
acquaintance with one subject. It is obvious that no one in our
modern world can be expert on every subject; therefore we have

[3] John Henry Newman, *The Idea of a University*, ed. Charles Frederick Har-
rold (New York and London: Longmans, Green and Co., 1947), pp. 157–158.

specialists. By narrowing the area to be studied, the student can dig deeper and acquire a greater understanding of details.

Some people fear over-specialization. If the graduate student has had the advantage of a broad, liberal education before beginning his concentration on a particular field, however, there would seem to be little point to such fears. Furthermore, the person who delves into one subject with real thoroughness quickly finds that it leads him into numerous other subjects. Literature, for example, cannot be studied intensively without a fairly good knowledge of history, philosophy, and linguistics. Investigations in the field of education require a thorough grounding in psychology and the social sciences. The deeper one goes into any subject, the more he is impressed by the essential unity of all areas of human learning. It is only the superficial scholar who becomes over-specialized. The true scholar broadens his knowledge at the same time that he carries forward his particular study of a narrow field.

Graduate Study Characteristically Involves Research. Undergraduate work ordinarily consists in reviewing facts and ideas that are already known. The graduate student, on the other hand, attempts to discover new truth. This is the second major difference between these two levels of educational experience.

In learning the vocation of the scholar, the graduate student must become familiar with the methods used in conducting sound research. The scholar's real reason for being is to acquire knowledge, not for himself but for mankind, by pushing back the boundaries of human ignorance. Scholarship means the search for new truth, even though the contributions of any one person can rarely be spectacular and can be arrived at only through painstaking labor. The individual scholar adds his bit to the world's discoveries, and by the slow accumulation of the small truths in many fields our civilization moves ahead. The systematic and efficient pursuit of this objective, by methods which are learned in graduate school, is what we mean by scholarly research.

Requiring, as it does, intellectual effort of the most demanding kind, the scholarly life rarely is anything but an arduous one. Yet it is one of the most challenging of human activities. Our knowledge of our universe and of our place in it remains extremely limited.

Vast areas for investigation and speculation lie unexplored. The search for new truth requires, of course, that the scholar shall have a firm knowledge of the discoveries already made; and this means endless acquisition and careful digestion of all the known facts and ideas in the student's field. Sometimes the long process of acquiring and organizing the materials that his predecessors have discovered may prove discouraging. Yet no scholar can hope to make new contributions to his field unless he is familiar with the existing body of knowledge.

As he gathers understanding of his field, the student soon learns that the world — and even the scholarly world — fairly swarms with half-truths and downright untruths. Thus the continued practice of the scholarly role tends to develop an attitude of skepticism toward accepted ideas. This need not prove a weak or unhealthy development. At its best, this attitude prevents the scholar from succumbing to false evidence and from reaching conclusions not based upon a critical examination of the facts. The critical attitude, in short, helps to eliminate error.

Most graduate students, once they have begun to familiarize themselves with the entire topography of one field of knowledge and have explored a little in the unknown region beyond its borders, feel that research is both valuable and intensely exciting, even though it may not have immediate "practical" bearing. There is, for example, no evidence that research makes better teachers — and the work of the scholar frequently includes teaching. On the other hand, many eminent scholars have been successful both in teaching and in research. The important thing for the graduate student to recognize, however, is that his graduate school experience will include both concentration upon the known materials in his own particular field of study (sometimes called the "major") and preparation for the more significant and serious duty of searching for new truth to add to that field. In other words, he must not only learn what others in his field have thought, but he must begin to do some original thinking of his own. These are the principal obligations of the scholar.

The Graduate Student as Apprentice in Scholarship

In one sense, the graduate student may be regarded as an apprentice. Just as craftsmen learn their skills by working under the direction of masters in the craft, so the young scholar may become acquainted with the spirit and methods of research by serving a kind of apprenticeship under one or more of the active research men on the faculty of the graduate school. Perhaps no more effective way of learning this type of activity could be devised. Besides providing a means of observing an expert in action, it also gives the beginner ideal conditions under which to learn through actual doing. Frequent consultations between professor and student — or master and apprentice — help to correct the learner's errors as well as to delineate the various techniques of research which will be most fruitful in his particular field. The expert will also be familiar with, and consequently will draw the student's attention to, the important men and the outstanding research already accomplished in that field.

On the other hand, the graduate student is expected — indeed, required — to attain the art of working independently. Although graduate study constitutes a period of training, during which the student continues to do his work under direction, even the first-year graduate student should be mature enough to exercise initiative in developing his own plan of study and research. He should not expect a blueprint of his program to be provided by his professors but should be able to acquire much of the necessary information through reading and observation. Research projects are not ordinarily assigned by the faculty, although occasionally they may be. It is more customary for a professor to act in the capacity of the student's adviser, approving, disapproving, or suggesting revisions of the student's plans.

Recently there has developed a new approach to some types of scholarly investigation in the form of what has been called "cooperative research." Instead of working individually upon a project, a group of research people interested in a major study will join forces and become a research team. This method is widely used in scientific laboratories, in social science surveys, and in the field of education. Work on the project is planned in such a way that various aspects of the study are allocated among the different members of the team. This has the advantage of bringing to bear upon a single project the varied judgments and special skills of the several workers who make up the group. The method can prove particularly effective when the project attacked is of considerable magnitude — the study, for example, of an entire school system or of the economic structure of a large city.

Other Aspects of Graduate Study

While training in research usually forms a part of graduate education, the work of the graduate school need not be aimed exclusively — or even primarily — at the production of trained investigators. In many colleges today students are admitted into graduate classes who have no intention of devoting their lives to research or even of acquiring advanced academic degrees. This has come about because colleges have acknowledged that persons preparing for certain careers may profit from graduate courses of their own choosing and that higher training in various combinations of subjects may sometimes be more useful and desirable, especially for teachers, than specialization in any one subject.

Yale University, following this line of reasoning, established in the thirties a division of general studies as a part of its graduate school. The student who enters this program is permitted to study advanced subjects in several related fields. At the time of its innovation, this departure from the traditional concentration upon one area seemed heretical to many educators. Numerous other institutions — for example, the University of California, the Colorado State College of Education, and several more in the western part of the United States — have abolished in some departments or for certain classes of student the customary requirement of a formal thesis in preparation for the Master of Arts degree. These changes probably indicate a trend away from exclusive concern with specialization and research in our graduate schools.

Nevertheless, the graduate student is wise if he keeps in mind the necessity of learning thoroughly the techniques and language of research. It is this aspect of his graduate education which is most likely to make the experience profitable and meaningful to him. If nothing else, the training will help him to read intelligently the reports of research in his field, without the knowledge of which he cannot hope to keep abreast of its most significant and interesting developments.

Recently some educators have been advising those who guide the destinies of the graduate schools to place more emphasis in the curriculum upon training for teaching. In all but a few fields, they argue, the majority of our graduate students will go on to earn their livings as professors in colleges, where the principal part of the job will be teaching and not research work.

No doubt it is true that, while the aim of advancing knowledge by training young investigators in the universities and research institutes has been pretty generally accepted as the traditional function of the graduate school, the teacher-training function has been neglected. It would seem logical, if a graduate student expects to become a teacher, to provide him with specific training for that goal. There are two opposing schools of thought on this question. Some educators insist that attention to such matters as teaching methods and educational theory will rob the student of time that he should be devoting to the study of his particular subject, and that teacher-training, in any case, is not the proper function of the graduate school. Others hold that the graduate school which is interested primarily in the advancement of knowledge cannot produce effective teachers.

While no attempt can be made here to settle the argument, it should be clear that not all graduate schools have the same purpose in mind. In fact, some graduate schools aim at more than one objective. Generally speaking, the most common purposes may be summarized as follows: (1) to advance human knowledge, (2) to train scholars for research work, (3) to prepare students for a profession, such as teaching, and (4) to offer one or more years of advanced instruction along the lines of the students' interests or special needs.

Regardless of the student's purpose in attending the graduate school, however, the study and practice of research can be definitely advantageous. As Professor Tufts has declared, personal contact with productive research workers can make the experience of graduate study in a university truly liberalizing. The great universities number on their faculties representatives of every major field of human knowledge. They are searching for truth on every front. There is a contagious enthusiasm in such a situation. Perhaps no teachers are more interesting and inspiring than those who are themselves contributing to new discovery through creative scholarship. Furthermore, when the student undertakes and carries through a piece of research, when he finds a new problem for study and applies to the solution his own original thought and his own analysis of the evidence relating to it, something of tremendous importance happens to him. He will never again be quite the same person.[4]

Different Methods of Instruction

The relatively greater maturity of graduate students as compared with undergraduate students, and their more extensive preparation in the subject matter, make it possible for graduate schools to use methods of instruction which may not be completely effective at the lower levels. One of these is the seminar. In the typical seminar class, a small group of students, having selected or been assigned certain problems for individual investigation, meet with a professor to talk about what they have discovered. Such meetings allow for a good deal of discussion and argument. New ideas or interpretations may be presented and challenged, and the student learns to defend the conclusions to which his investigations have led him. Frequently, in the seminar, the discussion follows the reading of a formal report upon some investigation by one of the students. At other times the professor or the students themselves may propose topics to be discussed by the entire group or by a panel of its members.

The seminar method, of course, is not confined exclusively to graduate classes, nor are all classes on the graduate level conducted in this way. The lecture method is rather commonly used, and in some fields there may be a considerable amount of laboratory work. Through the seminar, however, it has been found that open and free discussion among groups of graduate students, with one or more professors to guide and advise, is one of the most fruitful sources of original ideas and one of the best ways to inculcate the habit of critical thinking.

[4] See James H. Tufts, "The Graduate School," in *Higher Education in America*, ed. Raymond A. Kent (Boston: Ginn and Company, 1930), pp. 350–366.

Attitudes and Habits to Be Developed

It may be well to point out here some of the attitudes and habits which the student should develop or intensify in order to make the most of his graduate school experience.

The graduate student must be observant. He must notice details and be accurate in observing and interpreting them. Details are the raw materials of truth. If observation is careless or interpretation faulty, the generalizations or major conclusions based upon them will be unsound. For many centuries it was believed that small animals and insects were generated spontaneously from the rags, grains, and other refuse that collected in corners and from the mud and slime at the edges of pools. Observers who saw mice and insects emerging from piles of rubbish or rats struggling out of shallow water and mud banks interpreted these phenomena as examples of spontaneous generation. Even after the more complete and accurate observations of William Harvey (whose *Omnis ex Ovo* appeared in 1651) tended to show that all forms of life descended from older living things, the belief in spontaneous generation persisted as a legacy of inaccurate observation and interpretation.

There is an allied danger in reaching conclusions based upon insufficient observation. Until the invention of the microscope, for example, men had no way of knowing that certain minute forms of life existed. The microscope, in making possible more complete and accurate observation, overthrew many long-accepted theories about the nature of our world.

The graduate student must maintain an attitude of objectivity toward the pursuit of knowledge. Prejudices and premature decisions have no place in scholarship. The scholar does not make up his mind about a problem until he has gathered all the evidence and weighed every fact carefully and justly. Although it is not always easy to give up a pet theory or a comfortable belief, the scholar must be willing, like the judge and jury in a court of law, to let the weight of evidence decide the question.

The graduate student must be willing to study all the available evidence on any subject under consideration. In the first place, he must be familiar enough with his field to be able to find the evidence.

For example, he should never be satisfied that he has familiarized himself thoroughly with a subject until he has read everything, published or unpublished, which has been written about it. There are times when it will be necessary to travel considerable distances or to purchase photostatic copies of documents, and this involves both time and expense. Research foundations are sometimes called upon, though not as a rule by graduate students, to supply funds for such expense when a scholar is not able to bear the full cost himself. By whatever means he may proceed, however, the student should recognize the fact that he cannot fully understand a subject or arrive at sound conclusions about it unless he can get at the evidence.

Furthermore, he must never ignore adverse evidence. It is tempting, in the development of a new idea, to skirt around facts and arguments that are contrary to the proposition which the scholar is trying to prove. A good scholar — and an honest one — does not hide contrary evidence but either explains it and refutes it or changes his theories to fit the facts. If there are facts which defy explanation or which cannot be reconciled with the pattern of the scholar's theory, they must at least be admitted. To use an example from recent scholarship, the discoveries in the field of extra-sensory perception which have been made by Rhine and his associates at Duke University cannot be reconciled with our present knowledge of the physical world. Although the experiments have been carried on in accordance with accepted practices in psychology, very few scholars are inclined to accept the conclusions which have been reached. It seems obvious that either the methods and conclusions are fallacious or some of our current conceptions of the world need to be revised. In any case, the Rhine experiments cannot be ignored entirely.

The graduate student must be able to recognize relationships of cause and effect. He must be logical in his approach to knowledge. That is, he must exercise caution in attributing to any phenomenon the power to cause another phenomenon until he has eliminated all other possibilities. This whole question will be discussed at some length later in this book. It is enough here to say that the student's ideas in any study that he makes must be developed logically and consistently.

The graduate student must be original in his thinking. Too many beginners in scholarship seem to believe that research consists merely of searching for and cataloguing the statements of other people on the subject being studied. It is not uncommon for a student in a graduate class to hand in a paper which is nothing more than a long series of quotations or paraphrases of published materials. Simply to know what others have discovered about a subject is not enough. The one essential ingredient of research is original thought. The ability of the student to use his own mind in formulating fresh and unhackneyed ideas will determine more accurately than anything else the measure of his success in graduate work.

Applying the Scientific Attitude

All these habits and attitudes of the scholar, of course, imply that the true scholar bases his conclusions not upon fancy but upon facts and that he discovers and analyzes these facts in an orderly way. This process we sometimes call the scientific method and this point of view the scientific attitude. It means basing generalizations not upon the authority of others or upon abstract logic or upon one's own opinions but chiefly upon carefully observed facts.

The scientific attitude is characteristic of the leading thinking of our time. Not only in the natural sciences and in scholarship generally, but in all phases of our civilized life, its influence may be discerned. Alfred P. Sloan, Jr., former head of the General Motors Corporation, emphasizes its importance in the development of American industry and business:

> The great difference in managerial technique between the industry of today as compared with that of yesterday is what might be referred to as the necessity of the scientific approach, the elimination of operation by hunches; this affects men, tools and methods. Many associate the word scientific with physics. But it means much more than that. Scientific management means a constant search for the facts, the true actualities, and their intelligent, unprejudiced analysis. Thus, and in no other way, policies and their administration are determined. I keep saying to the General Motors organization that we are prepared to spend any proper amount of money to get the facts. Only by increased knowledge can we progress, perhaps I had better say survive. That is really research, but few realize that research can and should be just as effectively used in all functional branches of industry as in physics.[5]

[5] Alfred P. Sloan, Jr., and Boyden Sparkes, *Adventures of a White-Collar Man* (New York: Doubleday, Doran and Co., 1941), pp. 140–141.

It should not be assumed, however, that all research must have a practical, utilitarian object. When the structure of the atom was first investigated, it is doubtful if any scientist working at the problem had in mind the ultimate construction of an atomic bomb. The incentive which really impels the scholar is *the desire to know*. Men seek the truth because that is the character of the human mind. The curiosity inherent in us is apparent even among small children in the explanations they demand as they become aware of life's phenomena. The scholar searches more diligently for his facts than does the average person, but his motive remains the same. He simply wishes to know.

While the importance of research in the development of our modern civilization has been discussed in the preceding chapter, it must be clearly understood that no research activity need be justified by its probable contribution to comfort, convenience, or profit. Adding his bit — however lacking in practical usefulness it may seem at the time — to the sum total of the world's knowledge amply suffices as a reason for the scholar's existence. Sooner or later his discoveries may have a practical use, as when the knowledge possessed by scholars in the field of linguistics helped to break enemy codes during World War II. But immediately applicable or not, the quest for new truth can be justified by man's natural interest in breaking down the barriers of the unknown.

From the scholarly point of view, the study of ancient archaeological ruins for the purpose of learning the characteristics of an early culture in an obscure corner of the earth is as important as the application of newly discovered physical principles to the manufacture of an industrial machine. Truth, in other words, is worth discovering for its own sake. The scholar selects that area of study in which he as an individual has developed the greatest personal interest and seeks to expand mankind's knowledge of that field.

Reporting the Results of Scholarly Investigations

In addition to learning acceptable techniques of research — that is, techniques likely to assist him in locating and analyzing his data and in arriving at sound conclusions about them — in addition to this and to building in himself the attitudes and habits which mark the true scholar, the graduate student must also learn how to present his discoveries to the world in effective form. The ultimate goal of research is publication of its results.

The first step in this respect for the graduate student will be to distinguish clearly between the research report and the essay. As an undergraduate, he probably wrote a number of essays, and these consisted very largely of expressions of his own opinion or summaries of his reading. Any originality in these essays no doubt came from the uniqueness of the student's impressions, from new ways of putting together the information presented, or from the manner of writing. The essays were judged as to accuracy and completeness of subject matter, clarity of style, general organization, interest, and so on; but the student was not held to such rigid standards of form and content as is the writer of a research report.

It should be remembered that the research report is written for informed scholars in one's own field. This does not mean that it needs to be uninteresting or stuffy. Scholars, like other people, appreciate clear and well-organized writing. Nevertheless, the research report seldom has a popular appeal, because only a small number of persons are sufficiently oriented to the scholar's field to read reports of research with full understanding. The report, then, is necessarily addressed to a limited and very critical audience.

Preparing the report of a scholarly study is in many ways like the preparation of a legal brief. Certain kinds of material are barred. For example, just as hearsay evidence is not admitted in a court of law, in a research report ideas based upon conjecture or derived from uncertain or questionable sources must usually be ruled out as invalid. The scholar must carefully describe the problem he has studied, the methods by which he has gathered and analyzed his data, and the significant conclusions he has reached.

Four kinds of statement may be admitted in the research report. These are: (1) a basic assumption, (2) a statement of fact, (3) the writer's opinion, and (4) the opinion of an authority in the field. A *basic assumption* is any presumed fact so commonly known and accepted that it needs no proof. No study can be made without assuming certain things as true. These things need not be supported by examples or documentation, but they should be named in such a way that the reader will readily recognize them as basic assumptions which the scholar believes to be commonly accepted as true. For every *statement of fact* the scholar should indicate the source. That is, he should explain exactly how he knows it to be a fact. Usually this is accomplished either by using a footnote which gives full details as to where the information may be found or by describing the writer's first-hand observation of some phenomenon. The *writer's opinion* should always be labeled as opinion and not presented as fact. In general, it is better to avoid statements of opinion, even though there may be instances in which they are justified. When presenting the *opinion of a recognized authority* as evidence for any contention, the student should be careful to evaluate the worth of such opinion as well as to distinguish clearly between this type of evidence and that which is derived from direct observation or demonstrable fact. These matters will be discussed later in much more detail. They are mentioned here principally to show that a real difference exists between the research report and the ordinary collegiate essay.

It goes without saying that the written report prepared by a student should be perfect as to mechanical details. That is, the student should use acceptable grammar and should not expect his professors to correct errors in English usage. The physical form in which a report can be presented — the nature of the title page, the style used in footnotes, and similar considerations — usually is prescribed by the university and fully described in one of its publications or in a style book which it recommends. Needless to say, the student should become thoroughly acquainted with such requirements before putting his report into its final form.

Most institutions regard the thesis or dissertation as evidence that the student has developed the capacity to pursue the study of a worthwhile problem independently and successfully and that he knows how to present the results of such a study in acceptable form.

The Objective of the Graduate School

"*Connaitre — c'est chercher*," said Pascal. Graduate schools, for the most part, are committed to the philosophy that every student must learn the truth for himself through independent inquiry. For this purpose great libraries and other facilities are placed at the disposal of the student. He is trained in tried and sound methods for the pursuit of truth. He is expected not only to become familiar in detail with all the present knowledge of his field but also to discover on his own initiative previously unrecorded facts and ideas.

The late President Nicholas Murray Butler of Columbia University called the fully trained scholar "a broad man sharpened to a point." Graduate work should provide the necessary sharpening of the student already broadly educated. His energies and abilities will then be directed at effective and satisfying activity in one field. This ideal — the cultured and well-informed man trained as a specialist in one segment of human knowledge and able to exercise leadership in the intellectual life of the nation and the world — is the ultimate objective of the typical American graduate school.

Summary

Graduate education differs from undergraduate education chiefly in its concentration on a single area of subject matter, in its attention to research, and, to some degree, in the methods of instruction used. The graduate student may be described as an apprentice in scholarship. His task is to develop in himself the scientific attitude — that is, accurate observation, objectivity, willingness to study all forms of evidence before arriving at conclusions, ability to recognize causal relationships, and originality and independence in thinking. By training himself in this attitude and by applying the appropriate techniques of the scientific method to the solution of his chosen problem, the graduate student moves toward the scholar's goal of contributing to the sum total of human knowledge.

3

HOW THE GRADUATE

SCHOOL CAME INTO BEING

Even less than a century ago, an American student seriously interested in graduate study would have been unable to pursue it in his own country. Hundreds of our young men went abroad to advance their education in the universities of Europe, and especially those of Germany. Although at least one of our institutions of higher learning, the University of Virginia, had been founded (in 1822) upon Jeffersonian principles that included complete freedom of inquiry, and although Harvard, Yale, Columbia, and others had begun to offer occasional courses beyond the level of the baccalaureate degree, for one reason or another (e.g., the dearth of qualified students, the lack of adequately trained professors, and financial stringencies) no true graduate school appeared in the United States until near the end of the nineteenth century.[1]

In Germany, on the other hand, modern universities had evolved years before out of the tremendous flowering of interest in science and research. Universities there had freed themselves from the domination of church dogma and had become state agencies for the advancement of secular learning. Professors could claim freedom to study any problem and to follow boldly any line of inquiry, freedom to teach the knowledge discovered through these efforts, and free-

---

[1] At such American universities as Harvard and Yale a graduate obtained the master's degree a year or two after the baccalaureate simply by paying a fee and providing testimony of good character (i.e., "keeping out of jail").

36

dom to publish to the entire world the results of their studies. Students, for their part, had the right of relatively free selection among the course programs offered. Such freedom in teaching and in learning (*Lehrfreiheit* and *Lernfreiheit*) was enviously regarded by some scholars in our own colleges, which aped the worn traditions of the English institutions, notably Oxford and Cambridge, and in many of which it still was customary for members of the faculty to subscribe to certain religious beliefs in qualifying for their positions. (The English model copied by our colleges provided a program intended primarily to prepare young men for the Christian ministry. Even though such a program had clearly grown out of date by 1636, when Harvard was founded, our early colleges kept it in force in this country for another two hundred years.)

The agitation of leading American educators to establish in the United States institutions for advanced learning and research modeled after those of Germany began shortly before the middle of the nineteenth century. In 1851, Henry Tappan, soon to become the first president of the University of Michigan, proposed a thoroughgoing reform of higher education. He praised the German universities as progressive examples for Americans to follow and suggested that our freshman and sophomore years be eliminated immediately from the university system. This change, he declared, would permit our universities to accomplish greater things by concentrating their efforts upon more advanced studies and research.[2] Unfortunately, Tappan later lost his position at Michigan because of charges that he was attempting to "Prussianize" American education. Because of dissatisfaction with our outmoded curriculum and the salutary influence which university research in Germany obviously exerted upon the expanding economy of that nation, however, most thoughtful American educators no doubt shared Tappan's new views and hoped for a change in our educational system.

Even earlier, in 1849, President Francis Wayland of Brown University had submitted his resignation to his trustees on the grounds of his disgust with what he termed the backwardness and decaying conservatism of the collegiate curriculum. Invited by the trustees

[2] Henry P. Tappan, *University Education* (New York: George P. Putnam, 1851).

to describe his own ideas of an effective university program, Wayland urged, among other things, the abandonment of the prescribed course of study (which then consisted almost entirely of Greek, Latin, and mathematics) and the substitution of a plan under which new courses in science and other contemporaneous knowledge would be available and every student would be free to select the subjects he preferred.[3]

A slow movement in the direction of advanced courses and the encouragement of scholarship took shape during the period between 1825 and 1875, but the National Teachers' Association could complain with justice at its meeting in Trenton, New Jersey, in 1869: "We have as yet no near approach to a real university in America." [4]

What this association of teachers meant (and what Tappan had meant) by a "real university" must be understood, of course, as the German type of higher institution, in which the major work was research. This must be distinguished both from the traditional undergraduate college, which for the most part has concerned itself with the transmission of general knowledge to students (that is, with teaching), and from the professional school, which exists to prepare students for particular professions (law, medicine, architecture, education, and the like). In such a university, primary attention is given to the search for new knowledge and secondary attention to the training of young scholars in the techniques of the search. The ideal of this "real university" has been adopted in America not in the precise form which it had in Germany but in a rather different form as that institution which we Americans call the graduate school.

The First American Graduate School

No university on the German pattern existed among the American institutions of higher learning when, in 1867, a wealthy Quaker merchant of Baltimore set aside in trust the sum of $3,500,000 for aid to education. This merchant, Mr. Johns Hopkins, gave the full

3 See Francis Wayland and H. L. Wayland, A *Memoir of the Life and Labors of Francis Wayland*, 2 v. (New York: Sheldon & Co., 1867), II, 82–92.
4 See *Report of the Commissioner of Education Made to the Secretary of the Interior for the Year 1870* (Washington: U.S. Govt. Printing Office, 1870), pp. 418–421.

management of his bequest into the hands of a board of trustees, with instructions that the capital funds were not to be expended for buildings but with practically no other restrictions on their use. To the trustees he left the vital decision as to the precise type of institution which ought to be established.

The trustees, a somewhat remarkable and certainly able group of men, began their work by seriously attempting to inform themselves with regard to the status of higher education in America and Europe and by searching carefully for an outstanding educational leader to take charge of the proposed institution. They read and studied a large number of the contemporaneous books about collegiate programs and problems, and they traveled in various sections of the country to visit other universities and interview their presidents. They were clearly disposed to create an institution in which the highest academic standards would be maintained and in which the developing needs of scholarship would be met.[5]

On the advice of President Eliot of Harvard, President Angell of Michigan, and President White of Cornell, the trustees in 1874 elected to the first presidency of the Johns Hopkins University Daniel Coit Gilman, then head of the University of California. Gilman, a graduate of Yale, had a broad experience of travel, teaching, public school work, and university administration. He spent the first year of his appointment gathering information in Europe regarding university programs there and professors who might be attracted to this side of the Atlantic. Gilman's advice to his trustees was to the effect that the new institution should be not just another college, of which there were already a sufficient number in and near Baltimore, but a full-fledged university. The first real graduate school in the United States opened its doors in 1876, though it was five years more before graduate work as such was actually under way there.

A Graduate Program. For his first faculty Gilman selected men already known for their scholarship, and he recruited them both from Europe and from this country. Fortunately, he was able to pay them salaries which, for that period, were unusually high. While teaching ability came into consideration, probably more importance

[5] See Daniel Coit Gilman, *The Launching of a University* (New York: Dodd, Mead and Co., 1906).

was attached to success in research. In the curriculum there were some offerings in classical studies, but Gilman felt that the chief emphasis should be placed upon science, including the relatively new subject of biology. Thomas Henry Huxley, the famous English biologist, gave the principal address at the formal opening of the institution — a fact that symbolized, in effect, the university's interest in scientific studies. Huxley's appearance was not without its dangers to the new institution, for some people considered him an atheist.

The program itself consisted of regular lectures in courses conducted by members of the faculty, supplemented by laboratory demonstrations in some subjects and a system of visiting lecturers. This latter system proved a significant innovation. Hopkins could hardly afford to bring together on its permanent faculty all the eminent scholars of the world, however desirable such an achievement might be, but it could invite many of them from time to time to visit the campus as lecturers. They might remain for a term or a year and thus bring to the campus the best thinking and the newest ideas in their various fields and, as Gilman phrased it, prevent the instruction of the university from falling into a rut. "A company of non-resident professors and lecturers," remaining at Johns Hopkins for brief periods of time and then returning to their own institutions, maintained excellent contacts for both students and faculty with the entire modern world of scholarship. Among the earliest lecturers under this plan were such famous men as James Bryce, Alexander Graham Bell, Francis J. Child, Charles W. Eliot, William James, Sidney Lanier, James Russell Lowell, Charles S. Peirce, and Woodrow Wilson.

The ultimate aim of the Johns Hopkins program was to develop trained leaders in the various fields of scholarship and to aid in the general advancement of human learning. Gilman hoped that, like the German universities, Hopkins would offer advanced work only, which meant eliminating the subject matter customarily given on the freshman and sophomore level. For various reasons, however, this part of his plan proved impracticable, and the traditional undergraduate program of four years was maintained here as at other colleges. In this respect the institution never became a true university in the sense in which Gilman understood the term.

Students, nevertheless, were selected very carefully, and twenty annual fellowships were awarded to young men who seemed to show special aptitude for scholarly achievement. The seminar method of instruction was adopted with marked success in several courses. Freedom of thinking and freedom of teaching were insisted upon, including the right of every student to pursue studies in that field of knowledge in which he had a special interest. The responsibilities of scholarship also were stressed. Students entering advanced studies were expected to be well grounded in fundamental knowledge. Before a student was ready to accept the privilege of advanced work in the field of his own choice, Gilman believed, he must be fully mature and well prepared in the general areas of collegiate study.

No grades or prizes of any kind were awarded, and, unlike other colleges, Hopkins made no periodic announcements of the relative standings of students. Such incentives were deemed unnecessary for mature persons. Because of the small numbers enrolled in the early days of the institution's history, an informal atmosphere, with close attention to the qualifications and progress of every student, proved possible.

Other Features of the Plan. The essential difference between Johns Hopkins and the other American universities of the time lay in the encouragement given to original research by members of the faculty. This took the form not only of allowing the necessary time for investigative work in a professor's weekly schedule but also of establishing a number of scholarly journals in which the results of the investigations could be recorded. To print scholarly books and reports, a university press was set up.

The scholarly periodical has become recognized as a vital service to modern scholarship. The products of research must be published to the world, and particularly to other scholars in the several fields. This idea was already well established in Europe when Johns Hopkins was founded, but the existing journals in the United States at the time were chiefly for general circulation and not for specialized scholars.

Gilman constantly stressed his belief that professors must unselfishly devote themselves to the search for truth and must renounce all financial rewards for their discoveries. Since they had been granted the privilege of almost complete freedom in the conduct of research, with reasonable salaries and limited teaching duties, the faculty were willing to agree that any remuneration which might come as the result of their scientific or other discoveries ought to be used exclusively for further research. This ethical principle still is believed in by many, if not most, of those who have dedicated their lives to scholarship, though in some few instances we have seen the encroachment of more mundane ideas.

Hopkins carefully kept its program free of domination by any sectarian religious groups, a major stumbling block in the path of change at many other institutions. Not that Gilman opposed religion. As a matter of fact, he took an active hand in church work. But he feared the influence of sectarian dogma on the development of the curriculum, especially in science, and he wished the pursuit of truth to be free of all preconceived convictions or prejudices. Religious control might be altogether suitable for the American undergraduate college, but it had no place, he believed, in the organization of the true university.

Once the pattern of graduate education, based on the example of Germany, had been firmly introduced at Johns Hopkins University, similar developments at other large institutions took place.

Clark University

In 1886 Mr. Jonas Gilman Clark, a highly successful business man of Worcester, Massachusetts, invited a group of prominent local citizens to serve with him as trustees of a new university which he proposed to endow with money and his name. Clark was a self-educated man who had acquired a huge fortune in various enterprises throughout the country. The kind of institution he seems to have planned was a charity college for poor boys, with a curriculum devoted to practical rather than theoretical subject matter and not necessarily of the best quality.

Clark's notion of the first important step in the furthering of his enterprise was the construction of one or more buildings. He himself proposed plans for the campus and the main building even before the nature of the program had been thoroughly worked out. In 1887 the project was chartered by the state legislature as Clark University.

The trustees, after seeking advice from several sources, decided upon G. Stanley Hall, then a professor of psychology and pedagogy at Johns Hopkins, as the best candidate for the presidency. Hall, incidentally, had previously been considered very favorably by the Hopkins trustees before their selection of Gilman. A graduate of Williams College and a student at Union Theological Seminary and at universities in Bonn and Berlin, Hall had been an outstanding teacher at Antioch College and at Harvard University (where he received his doctoral degree). He had studied theology, philosophy, and psychology before deciding upon pedagogy and experimental psychology as his specialties. On his second visit to Germany he had become acquainted with some of the psychological laboratories just being developed there. After lecturing with great success on pedagogy at Harvard (immediately following this second excursion in Germany), he had been persuaded by Gilman to join the Hopkins faculty and to establish there a psychological laboratory, the first in America. He had also founded the *American Journal of Psychology.*

Hall reluctantly left his post at Hopkins in 1888 and assumed control of the new institution, apparently without any clear ideas as to the kind of program he was expected to initiate. The trustees, in fact, left this matter almost entirely to his judgment. He secured a year's leave of absence to travel in Europe, where he visited universities, inspected laboratories and libraries, collected books and pamphlets, purchased equipment, and interviewed professors. He came back imbued with zeal for the establishment of a great center for advanced learning more nearly like the German pattern even than Johns Hopkins — a project apparently far different from the original intentions of Mr. Clark.

An Auspicious Beginning. With a small group of selected advanced students and a superb faculty of research men, Clark University inaugurated its program in the fall of 1889. In addition to land and buildings, Mr. Clark presented the institution during its first year with $600,000 as an endowment, plus $100,000 for the support of the library. It was understood that he would continue his benefactions from year to year and leave a final substantial gift in his will.

Many educators have stated that Clark University during its early years could claim one of the best faculties ever assembled for purposes of graduate education. The seminar method of instruction, in which the students had excellent opportunities to exchange ideas with one another and with their professors, was extensively used. For at least two years the work of the new university impressed educational leaders throughout America as markedly successful and as a prime example for others to follow. In the third year, however, serious troubles began, centering largely on the financial situation.

Obviously the university that Hall created was not what Mr. Clark originally had conceived. Evidences of the founder's dissatisfaction began to appear. He refused to indicate clearly the extent to which his further financial support could be relied on. Furthermore, he insisted on having a hand in details which must have been beyond the scope of his experience or competency — for example, the fitting up of the laboratories. He is said to have treated Hall and the professors much as he would have treated the hired help in a business concern. A division of opinion between Hall on the one hand and the institution's principal benefactor on the other could not fail to have bad results.

The faculty felt the strain of this difference of opinion and the growing uncertainty of the university's future course. Morale sank low, and many of the faculty began to speak of resigning. Hall hoped that he might win Mr. Clark's eventual approval of the university program in which he himself so deeply believed; Clark seems to have set his heart on the establishment of the more familiar undergraduate college. In the end the founder became so skeptical of the program's worth and of Hall's ideas that he entirely withdrew his monetary aid, leaving the whole project in a precarious condition.

The discontent of the faculty finally culminated in a mass resignation of about half of the professors, partly for financial reasons and partly because of strained relations with the president. Several of the faculty turned, at William Rainey Harper's invitation, to positions at the University of Chicago, which was being reorganized by Harper as a true university. A few remained at Clark to await better times or to resign later.

When Mr. Clark died in 1900, he left provision in his will for the establishment of a separate college for undergraduates. This was to have a president other than Hall at its head and, though it would use the same library and buildings, was to be in most respects a separate institution. Some funds were also left for an addition to the Clark University endowment, an art gallery, and the improvement of the library.

During its first three years Clark University made a brilliant contribution to American graduate education. It came actually nearer to the ideal of the true university than did Johns Hopkins, and its achievements in research work set a standard seldom surpassed. The brilliance of its first years, however, was never afterward recaptured. Nevertheless, it furnished a goal in graduate studies which others could strive to reach.[6]

The new spirit of research that President Hall made possible at Clark University was eloquently described by him in his admirable address given at the Clark decennial celebration in 1899:

Have we duly considered, even the best of us, what a real university is and means, how widely it differs from a college, and what a wealth of vast, new, and in themselves most educative problems it opens? A college is for general, the university for special, culture. The former develops a wide basis of training and information, while the latter brings to a definite apex. One makes broad men, the other sharpens them to a point. The college digests and impresses second-hand knowledge as highly vitalized as good pedagogy can make it, while the university, as one of its choicest functions, creates new knowledge by research and discovery. The well furnished bachelor of arts, on turning from the receptivity of knowing to creative research, is at first helpless as a new-born babe, and needs abundant and personal direction and encouragement before he can walk alone; but when the new powers are once acquired they are veritable regeneration. He scorns the mere luxury of knowing, and wishes to achieve, to become an authority and not an echo. His ambition is to know how it looks near and beyond the frontier of knowledge, and to wrest if possible a new inch of territory from the nescient realm of chaos and old night, and this becomes a new and consuming passion which makes him feel a certain kinship with the great creative minds of all ages, and having contributed ever so little, he realizes for the first time what true

[6] See especially G. Stanley Hall, *Life and Confessions of a Psychologist* (New York: D. Appleton and Co., 1927), and Edmund C. Sanford, "A Sketch of the History of Clark University," *Publications of the Clark University Library*, VII, 1–10 (January, 1923).

intellectual freedom is, and attains intellectual manhood and maturity. This thrill of discovery, once felt, is the royal accolade of science, which says to the novice, stand erect, look about you, that henceforth you may light your own way with independent knowledge.[7]

The University of Chicago

The greatest beneficiary of the troubles at Clark University was the University of Chicago. This institution, first begun in 1859 as a Baptist academy and college, had closed in 1886 after severe financial reverses and two disastrous fires. Through the influence of Baptist groups and a gift of $600,000 from John D. Rockefeller, it was revived in 1890 under the leadership of President William Rainey Harper.

Harper was a Biblical specialist; yet what he desired for Chicago was not a denominational college but a real university for advanced and professional studies. He felt that the establishment of any other kind of institution would be a bitter mistake and would entirely fail to meet the vital educational needs of the time. A long process of negotiation and friendly argument among those involved in launching the enterprise became necessary before the matter could be settled. Though he agreed without enthusiasm to an undergraduate program (along with a preparatory academy) within the new institution, at least as a temporary expedient, Harper firmly held to his insistence upon a secular university, in which there would be advanced scholarship, research, and unhampered freedom of inquiry. He expressed at first some doubts as to whether he would be regarded by denominational leaders as sufficiently orthodox in his religious views to serve as the head of a Baptist institution. The founding group, however, placed great pressure upon Harper to accept the presidency, and their eagerness to secure him for the position was probably not at all abated by Yale's reluctance to lose him from its faculty. As a matter of fact, the administration at Yale had just raised, with much difficulty, a fund for the permanent endowment of his professorship there.

Severing his ties with Yale, Harper entered upon his duties as president of the University of Chicago in 1891. Students began to

[7] *Clark University, 1889–1899: Decennial Celebration* (Worcester: Clark University Press, 1899), pp. 53–54.

be admitted into its reorganized program during the following year. Besides the graduate school in which Harper's chief interest apparently lay, there were also an academy, an undergraduate college, an extension program, and a divinity school — all going into operation during the first four years of his administration. Rockefeller was prevailed upon to add another million dollars to the endowment for the express purpose of graduate education.

The Program. Harper himself seems to have considered the new university to be in part experimental — that is, a new tack in higher education for the United States, different from either Johns Hopkins or the traditional American college. He organized three divisions of the program: (1) the University Proper (the academy, a college of liberal arts, a college of science, a college of literature, a college of practical arts, the graduate schools, and various professional schools); (2) the University Extension Work (lectures, evening courses, correspondence work, and the like); and (3) the University Publication Work (partly consisting of a program for publishing the research studies of the faculty).

A distinction was made between the so-called "academic college" (freshman and sophomore years) and the "university college" (junior and senior years). Later the two divisions became known as the "junior college" (probably the first use of this term in America) and the "senior college." A summer quarter also was introduced as a part of the plan, and the upper levels of the program were coeducational. To some extent, these were new ideas in our system of higher education; like correspondence courses, they met with little approval among our more conservative educators. A relatively light load of teaching for the faculty (about eight to ten hours per week) was designed to allow ample time for independent research and study. Some educators criticized Harper's program because no provision had been made in it for ascertaining the religious orthodoxy of the professors. He overrode, however, all objections and predictions of failure.

Unlike Johns Hopkins, the University of Chicago retained the custom of giving students regular grades in their courses and ranking them according to their academic standing. In the curriculum itself considerable emphasis was placed upon science, although the other

fields were not neglected. A gift of over half a million dollars from
the estate of William B. Ogden, a former trustee of the first University of Chicago, made possible the establishment of the Ogden
Graduate School of Science.

While both Johns Hopkins and Clark University for a long time
remained fairly small institutions, the growth at Chicago proved
remarkable. Its fame and promise quickly spread, and students
flocked hopefully to its doors. Within four years it had already out-
stripped both Yale and Harvard in enrollment, and it continued to
enlarge its numbers rapidly. Part of this growth resulted undoubtedly
from the magic effect upon the popular imagination of Rockefeller's
backing, but a large part also came from the powerful personality of
William Rainey Harper and his uncanny ability to arouse public
enthusiasm.

The Faculty. Harper desired at the start a faculty of experienced
and capable scholars, men already prominent in their several fields.
Bringing together such a group of specialists proved anything but an
easy task. Most of the noted scholars of the day showed reluctance
to leave secure positions in order to join the faculty of a budding
university which might, after all, end in failure. They saw no reason
to exchange a certainty for a promise.

Not until the differences of opinion at Clark University caused
rumblings of discontent at that institution did Harper succeed in
attracting the first portion of his faculty to Chicago. The professors
at Clark were all admirably trained and had been working together
successfully under President Hall. They knew exactly the kind of
institution that Harper hoped to establish and made precisely the
sort of material that he had been seeking. He visited Worcester
briefly in 1892, at a moment when faculty morale there was at a low
ebb, and at a single stroke acquired the nucleus of his faculty for
Chicago. While the blow could not fail to be a severe one for
Clark, it provided Chicago with a ready-made faculty of the kind
Harper had been vainly trying for several months to gather together.
To this nucleus he gradually added a distinguished body of scholars
from other great universities of the world. As a departure from tradition, women scholars as well as men were welcomed to places on the
new faculty.

Harper knew that the University of Chicago would become widely known chiefly through the achievements of its faculty, and he spent immeasurable time and energy in selecting the right persons. Strangely enough, the institution had maintained even in its pre-Harper days the rule that "no religious test or particular religious profession [should] ever be held as requisite for admission to any department of the University, or for election to any professorship or other place of honor or emolument in it, but the same [should] be open alike to persons of any religious faith or profession." [8] Harper continued and even strengthened this policy under the reorganization and promised his professors independence in teaching and learning. While he was willing to accede a place in higher education to colleges in which a special belief was taught or a particular kind of instruction was prescribed, he carefully distinguished between these and the true university.

Among Harper's faculty were many whose opinions and teachings on various matters stood in direct opposition to the idea of other professors on that same faculty, yet freedom of expression was given to all, and academic harmony reigned. All who visited the institution seemed struck by the spirit of real unity. While Harper constantly remarked upon the evils of one-sided partisanship and urged his faculty not to abuse their liberty by promulgating untested opinions as truth, he believed that even the abuse of free expression was preferable to restrictions on research. Perhaps much of the harmony and expansive energy noticeable in the early history of the new University of Chicago may be attributed to the significant fact that Harper and his faculty regarded their work as a pioneering venture.

Other Developments in Graduate Study

Johns Hopkins, Clark, and Chicago broke forcibly with the decadent English tradition in our system of higher education and established a different pattern soon to be copied by many other universities. All three were founded upon the conviction that the American educational needs of the late nineteenth century were not being adequately served by the American college. Adopting (with some revisions) the German plan of the university, they placed the greatest emphasis upon the advancement of knowledge through

---

[8] See Thomas W. Goodspeed, A History of the University of Chicago: The First Quarter Century (Chicago: University of Chicago Press, 1916), p. 372.

single-handed achievement by the individual scholar, as well as upon the enforcement of rigid standards of objectivity in the search for truth. As the basic philosophy on which their activities were based, they accepted the doctrine that the true university exists not only to transmit all the best learning of the past but also to produce new learning of high quality and significance.

Students who entered the advanced courses of these institutions (not including, of course, the undergraduate program) took the role of the apprentice scholar. Out of this role grew an atmosphere of hard work, informality, friendly guidance, and even affection in the relationship developed between student and master. All areas of human learning were open to investigation. While the most careful tests of an objective nature had to be applied to the discoveries and new ideas which arose out of research, the quest for truth was kept unhampered, insofar as this is possible, by preconceived beliefs and prejudices. The very air of these new institutions, at least by contrast with the typical situation in the older colleges, must have breathed freedom and stimulation for the student.

The advantages of this type of program appealed strongly to the American student, and it quickly spread into many other institutions. The number of students enrolled in graduate work rose rapidly as more opportunities became available. A former specialist in higher education on the staff of the United States Office of Education has recorded that the enrollment of graduate students in the United States increased from slightly more than 400 in the year 1880 to 2,382 (of whom 409 were women) a decade later.[9] By 1900 there were 5,831 (1,179 women); by 1910, 9,370 (2,866 women); by 1920, 15,612 (5,775 women); and by 1930, 47,255(18,185 women). The number of master's degrees awarded by American institutions grew from about 70 in 1890 to 14,495 in 1930; and the number of Ph.D. degrees, from 44 in 1876 to 2,024 in 1930. At the present time there are probably well over 250,000 students in our graduate and professional schools.[10]

[9] Walton C. John, *Graduate Study in Universities and Colleges in the United States*, Bulletin of the U.S. Office of Education, 1934, No. 20 (Washington: U.S. Government Printing Office, 1935). See especially pp. 12–19.

[10] The *Biennial Survey of Education in the United States*, compiled by the U.S. Office of Education, reported 233,327 post-baccalaureate students enrolled in the academic year 1951–52. Of these, 118,015 were in professional schools and the rest in graduate schools of arts and sciences.

It should be kept in mind that the new graduate schools which have been developing during the past three-quarters of a century have inherited not only the tradition of advanced study in course work, which had been present in many of our colleges almost from the beginning (Harvard offered a program for the master's degree as early as 1642, and Yale awarded the first American Ph.D. degree in 1861), but also the more modern emphasis on research for the scientific advancement of knowledge (John Hopkins was the earliest American university specifically to adopt this as its major purpose).

Teacher Training

Since the nineteen-thirties especially, increasing attention has been paid to the question of using graduate programs to improve the training of teachers. Many state laws for the certification of public school teachers now require at least a full year of graduate study in addition to undergraduate preparation. For several years the majority of candidates for the doctorate have been students interested in becoming college instructors. It has been argued with some justice that if the graduate student is to earn his living by teaching, he should become familiar with at least the rudiments of his profession. The trained research worker, some say, is not likely to prove entirely successful in dealing with teaching problems. A number of graduate schools throughout the country seem to have adopted this point of view, and as a result they have become somewhat less concerned with the aim of advancing human knowledge and correspondingly more interested in that of providing for the acquisition of instructional skills.

A graduate school, many now believe, may claim as its fundamental aim the advancement of learning and the training of research scholars, or it may place its principal stress upon the task of preparing students to become effective teachers. It may even offer post-baccalaureate courses without having in view either of the aforementioned objectives. On the other hand, some graduate schools accept a variety of aims as legitimate and try to achieve each one as fully as it is possible to do so, depending upon the varying desires and needs of the students.

The ideal envisioned by such early leaders in graduate education as Daniel Coit Gilman, G. Stanley Hall, and William Rainey Harper, however, still remains the most potent force in most of our graduate programs. It was reaffirmed only a few years ago in a statement by Professor George Boas of the Johns Hopkins University, who, in describing some new plans devised by the faculty of that precedent-breaking institution, thus epitomized the essential purpose of its program:

The Johns Hopkins University has chosen as its own goal one of the many legitimate ends of higher education: the training of scientists and scholars, people who engage in research which, it is hoped, will be disinterested. Such people must above all things be acutely aware of problems when they arise, and consequently their training must orient them towards spotting the unusual event, the event which is an exception to the rule. It is admitted that no one knows how to train the creative imagination, but we do know more or less what impedes its functioning. We know, for instance, that a Charles Darwin, a Freud, an Einstein, a Willard Gibbs simply could not arise in a society governed by the principles of authority and tradition. I do not say that in some societies, like the monastery and the army, tradition and obedience to it are not essential to the common good. But I do say that in the society of scholars the original mind, the recalcitrant individual, the man who looks for himself and stubbornly refuses to accept the word of authority merely because it is that of an authority, is the man who contributes something to the sum total of knowledge.

If that is so, then the problem of the educator in such a university is first of all to admit to his society only such people as have shown a genuine interest in discovery. He must surround himself, in the second place, with scholars who have already achieved — or show promise of achieving — a position of eminence as creative scholars. The professor who gives standard courses out of textbooks may do a good job of teaching in certain kinds of colleges; but he has no place here. In the third place, the student must be regarded not as an empty mind into which the teacher is to pour his accumulated wisdom, but as an associate with his teachers in the acquiring of knowledge. In the fourth place, every effort must be made by the teacher to adjust the program of study to the student's needs, rather than to force the student to take a standardized course of study after which he will be given a standardized degree. And in the fifth place, it must be assumed that some problems have already been solved and become obsolete as problems, that new problems are always arising and are calling for solution, and that finally the teacher in association with his students will stand on the frontiers of knowledge and attempt their solution.[11]

Summary

The modern American graduate school had its beginnings at the Johns Hopkins University, Clark University, and the University of Chicago. Here the traditional but now decadent English pattern of higher education which American colleges had copied for generations was cast aside in favor of the German idea of a true university. Under the new system, later adopted by others, graduate work meant not merely the addition of more courses to the program but concentration within the program upon a systematic search for truth, to the end that the present boundaries of learning might be extended. This ideal since has come to be accepted as the major objective of the graduate school.

The older collegiate plan, however, did not go entirely into the discard. Even at Hopkins the undergraduate program was retained. In spite of long efforts to reform the basic organization of American higher education by relegating the freshman and sophmore years of study to the secondary school or the junior college, thus permitting the work of the university to consist exclusively of advanced or specialized studies, nearly all American universities have held onto the collegiate structure, merely superimposing a graduate school upon it. Since 1880 the growth of graduate programs throughout the nation has been rapid. Of recent years some educators have become increasingly concerned over the problem of teacher-training on the graduate level.

While the aims of graduate study may vary among the different institutions, the influence of the pioneering efforts made at Hopkins, Clark, and Chicago has been a profound one. The important core around which most graduate programs today are built is objective research — or, to state it more broadly, the free and unhampered inquiry after truth.

[11] George Boas, "New Plans at Hopkins," *The Johns Hopkins Magazine*, III, 3 (February, 1952). Quoted by the kind permission of Professor Boas.

PART TWO

The Ways of Scholarship

4
THE SCHOLAR AS
DETECTIVE: THE RULES
OF EVIDENCE

The work of adding new truth to the present store of the world's knowledge cannot be regarded as a simple or easy thing. While the average person accepts many ideas as true merely because they seem plausible or prove temporarily workable, the scholar searches with comprehensive thoroughness for all the available trustworthy evidence, both pro and con, and weighs it carefully before coming to a decision as to its accuracy and value.

The successful scholar must be just as painstaking in his investigations and just as precise in his methods as a detective engaged in the search for clues leading to the solution of a crime or a district attorney engaged in prosecuting a criminal in the courts. What the scholar seeks — as the detective or the attorney does — is evidence of every kind that can be shown logically to be linked in a cause-and-effect relationship with the problem or question under consideration. While the scholar may deal with somewhat less spectacular events than the detective or the attorney, the methods he employs are essentially the same, and the same care is used in fitting clues together and in demonstrating where the weight of the evidence lies. Occasionally in scholarship, as in police work, a problem cannot be solved because the evidence is insufficient or because it does not hold together when tested by logic or reason.

To illustrate the analogy between legal procedures and scholarship, let us examine some of the facts relating to an actual crime. Our attention should be focused on the procedures used in bringing the alleged criminal to justice and in avoiding errors which would place him in undue jeopardy. It should be noted that legal procedures are aimed at the same objective as all research — that is, the determination of the truth.

An Analogy from Criminal Procedure

Two police officers, driving one day in a police cruiser through a suburban area in Maryland were shocked by the sudden spectacle of an automobile careening at high speed and apparently out of control down a slanting street. After striking obstacles on both sides of the street, the automobile ran up over one of the curbings and overturned. When the two police officers approached the wrecked vehicle, they found its motor still running and its wheels rapidly spinning. Inside was the dead body of a woman with several deep gashes in her forehead.

To the ordinary observer, this event had every appearance of that common occurrence in America, a traffic accident, although a rather unusual one. It would be reasonable in the light of everyday experience to suppose that the driver, descending the hill at far too high a rate of speed, had lost control or had fainted and that she had been killed by striking her head against some sharp object inside the automobile when it overturned. The police officers, on the other hand, being specially trained observers, noticed several facts that others might have overlooked.

The continued running of the motor at high speed after the apparent accident they regarded as unusual. They attempted to ascertain the cause and soon discovered that a small pebble was wedged under the accelerator pedal — another unusual circumstance. Was it likely that such an object could have lodged itself there accidentally? Experience would argue to the contrary. Yet this evidence could not be considered as conclusive; it merely raised serious doubts. Indications that blood from the dead woman's body on the floor and upholstery had flowed in a direction opposite from that which might normally be expected as the result of the automobile's position also aroused some suspicions. Liquids do not flow uphill. Furthermore, no trace of the woman's purse (or her eyeglasses, it was later learned) could be found. The observed facts, then, indicated a certain unreasonableness in the situation. Some of the evidence did not fit the logical pattern of a traffic accident.

Medical examination by a skilled physician revealed later that the skull fractures and the wounds on the forehead could not conceivably have been caused by any object found within the automobile. Besides, the absence of injuries or contusions on other parts of the body, which normally should have been present if death had been caused by the impact of the body against portions of the car, tended to show that the woman had been dead before the events witnessed by the two police officers had occurred. Thus the first hypothesis about the incident — the belief that the woman's death was accidental — which the police officers had formulated almost automatically while watching the incident happen, had to be rejected. Reasoning from the facts established by an observation of details and by known principles of science, the authorities turned from the hypothesis of accidental death to the hypothesis of murder.

Note that the police officers and the physician, because of their training in observation and their previous knowledge and experience, were able to detect certain things which an ordinary person might not have noticed, or the significance of which he might have missed. Note also that the pattern of reasoning used in reaching the hypothesis that a murder had been committed consisted in the piecing together of bits of pertinent evidence to reach a conclusion by which all the unusual facts of the case could be accounted for.

The problem now was to bring the criminal to justice. Having decided that a murder had been committed, the authorities began their search for the guilty person by trying to formulate and then test out various hypotheses as to possible motives for the crime — that is, they sought its cause. One hypothesis developed from the failure to find any trace of the woman's purse. This fact suggested the possibility of robbery as a motive. If the woman had been robbed and beaten (the beating resulting in her death), the robber, to conceal his crime, could have contrived the events witnessed by police officers. To test this hypothesis, the authorities made an investigation to determine whether any known criminals could be shown to have been anywhere near the scene of the crime at the time it was committed. The search proved unfruitful, however, and this hypothesis had to be laid aside; no strong evidence was uncovered which tended to substantiate it.

Meanwhile, efforts were being made to learn as much as possible about the victim's life, her family, her friends, and her daily habits. The investigation centered upon this question: Who might have had a reasonable (or plausible) motive to murder her? The police obviously believed (a basic assumption derived from extensive experience) that murders are seldom committed without impelling motives.

When the police learned, by sifting and cross-checking all the facts and opinions which they could unearth in a study of the victim's life, that her husband appeared to be in love with another woman, a strong motive for the crime suggested itself. When the husband seemed also to have been the last person to see the victim alive — and this not long before her death, the police were convinced of his guilt. He was indicted, brought to trial for murder, and convicted.

Presenting the Evidence

The data presented above, of course, do not in themselves establish the fact of the criminal's guilt. While the police may have been satisfied that these facts adequately demonstrated the guilt of the accused, the man himself was entitled by law to defend his innocence, to provide some other explanation for the facts disclosed, and to require the presentation of conclusive evidence of his guilt before a jury.

The prosecuting attorney, in order to prevent error, demonstrate the truth, and establish justice in the case, was given the problem of analyzing and classifying all the evidence found, of presenting it in a logical order to the jury, of explaining any contradictory or unclear pieces of evidence, of showing how the evidence pointed to the guilt of the accused, and of generally demonstrating a clear-cut conclusion of guilt based on logic, known probabilities, and established facts.

In presenting a case before a judge or jury, an attorney is bound by certain rules of procedure devised for the purpose of eliminating error. Particularly is this true in the presentation of evidence. In the judicial sense, evidence means any demonstrable fact, presumed fact, or expert opinion which has a bearing on the question in dispute and from which inferences regarding the main question may be drawn. (To illustrate what is meant here by a presumed fact, we may point out that it is not necessary for anyone to dip his finger into a steaming cup of coffee in order to determine whether the coffee is hot. Past experience leads to the presumption that the presence of steam indicates heat in the coffee.) Certain types of evidence, however, cannot be offered at all, either because they have no direct bearing on the case in question or because they are obviously unreliable or (in some instances) because they are likely to appeal merely to prejudice or emotion.

The laws of the United States provide that no person can be presumed guilty until definite evidence of his guilt can be demonstrated; that is, he must be accorded a fair trial. Thus the burden of proof rests not with the accused to prove himself innocent, but with the prosecuting attorney to prove him guilty. In a murder case, such as that described above, the prosecuting attorney is required by legal rules to prove, beyond any reasonable doubt, certain facts, which may be classified briefly as follows:

1. *Proof of death* (*corpus delicti*). He must bring evidence to court (for example, the signed statement of a medical examiner or the oral testimony of a qualified witness) fixing the identity of the victim and proving that the victim is actually dead. Had the wife in the Maryland case merely disappeared without a trace, her murder could not have been presumed without some very strong evidence pointing to the fact that her death really had occurred.

2. *Cause of death.* The circumstances of the death must be such as to give cause for the presumption of murder. In the case above, the observations of the police officers and the report of the medical examiner were such as to establish the presumption of murder, though not necessarily to prove it.

3. *The connection of the defendant with the murder.* It must be shown that the defendant had the opportunity of committing the crime. Had the husband in this case been able to prove that he was

in another city at the time of the murder, he could not have been
convicted. He was unable, however, to supply a sufficiently strong
"alibi" of this kind.

4. *Intention to commit murder.* Since it is a basic assumption in
law that no murder can be committed without a definite intention,
it is necessary to give some evidence of malice and forethought on
the part of the defendant. This usually means finding the defendant's
motive. In this case, the husband's proved passion for another
woman — described by her in oral testimony before the court —
established a plausible motive.

Some Principles Underlying Presentation of Evidence

What principles may be derived from the legal proceedings briefly
summarized here, and how do these apply to scholarship?

In the first place, it should be noted that a murder trial (or any
other case in court) and scholarly research have essentially the same
purpose. This is to solve a problem honestly and fairly, to establish
truth based on sound evidence. Occasionally justice may go astray
and scholarship fall into error. Elaborate safeguards, however, have
been set up to prevent such occurrences so far as possible.

In the second place, the burden of proof in law is upon the person
who brings the case into court. Unless he can present sufficient evidence to substantiate his claims, he loses his case. In a similar way,
the burden of proving a case in scholarship rests with the scholar who
believes he has made a new discovery in his field. His belief in the
proposition he supports is not sufficient; he must have good evidence
to back up his claims. To be sure, facts and ideas which are already
generally known and accepted may be stated without any special sup-
porting evidence. Such basic assumptions as the fact that water flows
downhill, that a live coal will burn the hand, that the purpose of
schools is to educate children, and the like, need not be argued.
Other facts used by the lawyer and the scholar in proving their
cases, however, must be supported by clear evidence.

In the third place, the evidence offered must be relevant (that is,
related clearly to the problem which is being solved); it must be
material (that is, of sufficient importance to carry some weight in
proving the case); and it must be competent (that is, derived from
sources that can be relied upon as qualified and truthful). The

scholar, like the lawyer, should ask himself, when dealing with any type of evidence: Does this fact have real bearing on the question at hand? Does this fact actually have significance and importance in the solution of the problem? Is this fact learned from a trustworthy source? Some of these aspects of evidence will be examined more fully in a later chapter; at this point the essential thing is to realize the great necessity for inspecting evidence carefully before using it in the solution of a problem.

In the fourth place, a line must be drawn between factual evidence and the kind of evidence which is mere opinion. Generally speaking, both in law and in scholarship, evidence ought to consist of facts, and from these facts opinions (or generalizations) may be drawn by those judging the case. In the strict sense, of course, everything which we regard as a fact really amounts to an opinion derived from our sensory impressions. Thus, as a practical rule of procedure, we accept as a fact any evidence based upon direct sensory knowledge of the events in question. For example, if a witness in a court of law positively identifies a suspected person as someone with whom he has long been familar, we are likely to accept his inference (based upon the senses of sight and hearing) as factual. In the same way, the chemist who mixes two colorless liquids together and sees the mixture turn green can report the incident as a fact. He has inferred the change in color from seeing it happen — that is, from direct sensory knowledge.

Opinion cannot have the weight of factual evidence in proving any case. On the other hand, there are times when opinion may be the best evidence available. In such cases, care is exercised to make sure that the opinion offered is qualified and authoritative. Ordinarily, this means the opinion of one who is an expert with regard to the matter under consideration. To determine and provide evidence on the cause of a person's death, a medical examiner may be asked to perform an autopsy on the body and then testify as to what, in his opinion, was the cause of death. Expert opinion of this kind has almost the weight of factual evidence, though even experts will sometimes disagree. But though *expert opinion* may have its uses when factual evidence proves insufficient or inconclusive, *opinion in general* has little weight and is not admissible as evidence.

In the fifth place, evidence derived at second-hand usually is considered of small value. With some exceptions, hearsay evidence cannot be used in courts of law. It is too unreliable and it usually cannot be substantiated. Furthermore, since memory is faulty, errors are easy to make in reporting anything learned from someone else. Sometimes, of course, hearsay evidence may represent the truth, but how is one to be sure? For a century and a half a rumor or legend persisted in Denmark to the effect that Giertrud Birgitte Bodenhoff, a wealthy young widow of the eighteenth century, had been buried alive and that grave-robbers, digging up her coffin to steal the jewels which had been interred with her body, had killed her with a spade. There was no evidence to support the gruesome story — a story based on hearsay — until 1953, when the body of Giertrud was exhumed. A skull found in the grave not only lay face down but had a distinct and sharp dent in the brow. The skeleton was discovered to be in a curiously twisted position. With such evidence of a factual nature to support the hearsay, the old legend would seem to be vindicated.

Finally, the evidence used in solving a problem — assuming that it is relevant, material, and competent — must fit together into a logical pattern, and this pattern must point conclusively to a definite solution of the problem. In law, that solution may be the guilt or innocence of an accused person or the establishment of liability; in scholarship, it is the correct answer to the question which the scholar has chosen to study.

Steps in Pursuing an Investigation

How does the scholar ordinarily proceed in the study of a problem in his field? The usual steps in pursuing a scholarly investigation may be clearly distinguished. It will be seen how closely they parallel the main steps followed in solving the crime described earlier in this chapter.

The Problem. First, there must be a problem to solve. It may be stated as a general rule that all scholarly studies are undertaken to solve specific problems. Just as the police investigator examines the circumstances of someone's death in order to discover what caused it, so the scholar has in mind some definite thing that he wishes to learn from his study. That thing is the solution to a specific problem.

The Data. Once the problem has been defined, the next step is to begin a thorough examination of the data — the facts of the case. And it is vital to have all the relevant facts. If, as frequently happens, some pertinent information is overlooked by the person who is insufficiently trained, the investigation will go astray. The police officers in the Maryland case might have overlooked some of the circumstances which led them to suspect murder. They might not have noticed, for example, that the woman's purse was missing, or they might simply have shut off the ignition switch without wondering why the motor continued to run after the car had overturned. But these facts were necessary as evidence in substantiating the idea of murder.

The Hypothesis. After a preliminary examination of the data, sooner or later some possible solution to the problem suggests itself to the investigator. This tentative solution may easily be the wrong one. It will be recalled that the police in the Maryland case at first assumed that the woman's death was accidentally caused. Then, even after they were quite convinced of the probability of murder, they searched for the criminal in the wrong direction because they argued that robbery must have been the motive. It is natural and useful, however, to make reasonable guesses as to the possible solution of a problem even at the very beginning of an investigation. Such a guess we call a hypothesis. It may prove to be correct and in agreement with all the facts, or it may be wrong and have to be discarded.

Testing the Hypothesis. The formulation of a reasonable guess, or hypothesis, as to the solution of a problem helps in determining where to look for evidence. Thus, even when the hypothesis turns out to be the wrong one, it aids the study. After the hypothesis has been decided upon, there begins the work of collecting evidence from as many sources as possible to test it. Through discovering new facts and applying accepted principles of knowledge and logic, it will be determined whether the hypothesis adequately accounts for the facts in the case. This careful search for data, guided by the tentative hypothesis, constitutes the chief labor of all research, just as of criminal investigation.

The Conclusion. After testing the hypothesis by gathering as much information as possible and fitting it into a logical pattern, the investigator either discards the hypothesis as unproved or decides that it is correct. If correct, it forms his major conclusion in the study. In other words, the study must continue until the investigator is convinced of the truth of his hypothesis *and is able to convince others by the weight of the evidence.* In the same way that a prosecuting attorney must present a case that will stand up in court, the scholar must report his findings in such a way that his conclusions will be acceptable to informed people in his field.

The Scholar as Thinker

It should be kept firmly in mind that the essential thing about any study is not merely the gathering of data, the accumulation of facts, but the scholar's interpretation of what the facts mean and how they fit together into a logical, usable pattern. In other words, research requires thought.

The particular kind of thinking which goes into research has been variously referred to as *scientific thinking* or *critical thinking;* as *reflective thinking* or simply *reflection;* and as *ratiocination* (by Edgar Allan Poe and others), a word which really means *careful reasoning.* Whatever the term we employ, it is obvious that scholarly work requires a much more complex type of thinking than that to which we are accustomed in our daily experience.

Most of our thinking in everyday life seems undirected. We simply react with the least effort necessary to the experiences we meet. We are likely to generalize about our experiences without thinking very hard about them and without gathering all the facts essential to a wise decision. After a time we learn by this undirected thinking how to act so that the results are pleasant rather than unpleasant. But random thinking of this kind, because of its limited extent and because of the inaccuracy of many of our casual observations, can lead us into error.

In contrast with the usual random flow of our thought, reflection is defined by John Dewey as an "active, persistent, and careful consideration of any belief or supposed form of knowledge in the light of the grounds that support it and the further conclusions to which it tends." [1] Furthermore, this type of thinking centers on a problem

[1] John Dewey, *How We Think* (Boston: D. C. Heath and Co., 1933), p. 9.

or question and seeks to solve or answer it with the greatest possible degree of accuracy.

As we have noted in a previous chapter, mankind has for many centuries attempted by various methods to explain the phenomena which are observed in this life. Man's method has been sometimes to explain the unknown as magic; sometimes to depend for his explanations upon the dictums of authorities; and sometimes to seek explanations through syllogistic reasoning. Reflection as defined by Dewey is the latest step in man's development of his power to think and thus to solve his problems. It is our chief weapon in the advancement of human knowledge when used by an observant and thoughtful person, thoroughly familiar with the general field in which he is working, who applies both deductive and inductive reasoning to the collection and analysis of the facts relating to a problem and who fits all the relevant, material, and competent evidence available into a logical pattern and thus into a satisfactory solution.

Dangers to Straight Thinking

In following the procedures of investigation recommended above, whether one is attempting to solve a crime or a scholarly problem, the investigator will avoid serious error only if he is wary of several pitfalls. Among these we may number premature conclusions, the tendency to ignore adverse evidence, the habit of thinking within fixed limits (lack of originality or perspective), inability to obtain all the related facts, inaccuracy of observation, the mistaking of coincidence for cause-and-effect, and personal prejudice (lack of objectivity). Any of these can destroy the value of a study.

Premature Conclusions. Many a scholar, carried away by his own enthusiasm, has clung fast to a pleasing or attention-getting theory even while realizing that the evidence to support it was flimsy indeed. A little patience, a little more time spent in hunting down the facts, might have saved him from error. The careful investigator does not make up his mind until all the evidence is in and has been painstakingly checked. This is a safeguard against wrong conclusions in the same way that legal procedures are a safeguard against injustice. During the early history of the western United States, before law and order were well established, men are known to have been accused falsely of certain crimes (as a typical example, horse stealing) and condemned by informal courts under mob or lynch law on the merest suspicion of guilt. Frequently the circumstance that a man was a stranger turned this kind of court against him. Thus, through lack of knowledge of legal safeguards, well-intentioned citizens often hanged innocent men. Scholars can be similarly mistaken in their work when they jump to firm conclusions without a sufficient search for evidence.

Ignoring Adverse Evidence. A scholar may even grow so enthusiastic about his hypothesis that he glosses over or ignores important adverse evidence. Perhaps this kind of thing may be condoned in a political debate, in which the object is to win the argument at all costs. But scholarly studies and reports are not made to win arguments; their purpose is to discover truth. Adverse evidence must be given the same weight as confirming evidence, even though it may mean changing the hypothesis.

Thinking Within Fixed Limits. Nothing is more deadening to productive scholarship than the habits we form throughout the years of thinking within fixed limits. More and more, as we grow older, we seem to react in much the same way to similar kinds of experience. Thus, in thinking about a problem, our thoughts tend to follow a certain course; and each time we think about the same problem, the same course of thinking is followed. Psychologists have observed that, even in such a simple thing as adding up a column of figures, an error once made has a tendency to be repeated. The scholar must make efforts to avoid rigid patterns in his thinking. He must encourage his own habits of originality. New situations or unexpected results arising from a study should find him ready to adapt himself and willing to recognize the unforeseen.

Numerous vital discoveries have actually been made because of mistakes or accidents occurring during a study, provided the investigator was willing to notice their possible implications and adopt a new line of investigation. Röntgen, while studying the rays of light produced by electrical discharges within a vacuum tube, happened one day to leave a screen coated with barium platinocyanide on his work bench near one of these tubes. The screen was cut off from any visible rays of light by black paper which Röntgen had placed around the tube; yet Röntgen, to his amazement, noticed that it had begun to glow. Further study of this phenomenon (the X ray) brought him to the conclusion that certain rays of light will penetrate opaque objects. While accident obviously played a part in this discovery, it was the scientist's alertness to the unexpected which enabled him to capitalize upon the incident. Although imagination and originality are sometimes mistakenly thought of as handicaps to straight thinking about scholarly problems, all the great research men of history appear to have been liberally endowed with these qualities.

Inability to Obtain All the Relevant Facts. In undertaking some studies, scholars may encounter considerable difficulty in securing sufficient evidence to form valid conclusions. The inability to obtain all the pertinent facts must be recognized in these cases. For example, when Ptolemy studied the movements of the stars, the telescope had not yet been invented. To him the stars were merely points of light in the sky, and he had no means of determining their characteristics except by the naked eye and some primitive tools for measuring angles. Again, to cite a modern example, we may arrive at certain conjectures about the activities of the Norsemen or the early Irishmen in pre-Columbian America, but so little evidence clearly connected with their life here has been found that, until more definite information is unearthed, our knowledge must remain fragmentary and inconclusive. Important errors have been made by scholars drawing broad conclusions from scanty evidence.

Inaccuracy of Observation. Inaccuracy of observation presents another danger. When men imagined that certain forms of life were spontaneously generated and actually believed they saw small animals being formed out of the mud and ooze at the edges of pools, they were simply not observing accurately. Experiments often must be repeated several times to make sure that all the elements have been properly observed. In any kind of research, it is surprisingly easy to overlook some factors or to see only what one is prepared to see. Not long ago the discovery of chemical Element 87 was announced. The method used was X-ray analysis. X rays emanating from a substance supposedly containing Element 87 were reflected from a crystal of calcite. The spectral lines formed in the reflection made a pattern like that which had been predicted for the previously undiscovered element. But scientists who repeated the experiment reported that these spectral lines were caused by the surface irregularities of the crystal; they could even be made to vanish when the crystal was moved.

Mistaking Coincidence for Cause-and-Effect. Another danger is that of mistaking coincidence for a cause-and-effect relationship. A few years ago a New York City newspaperman pointed out, in fun, that the years during which the New York Giants had won baseball championships had been years of economic prosperity everywhere in the country. His delighted conclusion: To achieve prosperity, allow the Giants to win the pennant! Unfortunately, serious conclusions are sometimes drawn by poorly trained scholars from situations no less far-fetched than this one.

Lack of Objectivity. The final danger to be mentioned here is lack of objectivity. The scholar should have no ax to grind. He should be seeking for truth. Studies undertaken merely to support some belief or ideology to which the scholar previously has committed himself serve a doubtful purpose. In the Soviet Union biological scientists (particularly the geneticists) have been expected by the authorities to subscribe to the so-called Lysenko theory relating to the inheritance of acquired characteristics. According to this theory, the nature of any organism can be changed by artificial means, and this change can be transmitted to the offspring. This belief conforms to the minor Marxist doctrine that the nature of man is determined by his social environment. Discredited by progressive biologists in other countries, this restricted belief has no doubt been secretly rejected by many Russian scientists, but even pretended adherence to it would hinder free research.

To be sure, some problems cannot be treated with complete objectivity. They may, for instance, involve human emotions or tastes. Who can describe, except subjectively, the taste of whale's milk? A color that seems attractive to one person may seem unattractive to another. Perfect objectivity in research, therefore, must be regarded as impossible. Nor is the kind of subjective judgment mentioned here necessarily to be avoided, especially when several investigators agree on their reactions to sensory stimuli and describe their observations in much the same way. If everyone tasting sugar agrees that it is sweet, then the fact is established.

The kind of subjectivity which needs to be avoided is prejudice, failure to keep an open mind. Twisting or selecting the data simply on the basis of their agreement with accepted dogma or the investigator's own general beliefs is anathema to good research.

Summary

Scholarship may be compared to police work and courtroom procedure. As the detective and the lawyer face the problems of putting clues together into a logical pattern and presenting sound evidence before the court in an orderly way as the means of solving a crime and bringing the criminal to justice through the discovery of truth, so the scholar faces problems and procedural rules of a similar nature in attacking problems of scholarship. Conclusions must be based upon clear evidence (data), and such evidence must be relevant, material, and drawn from competent and credible sources.

Scholarship requires a particular kind of thinking, involving both deductive and inductive reasoning, and the formulation of a logical pattern of evidence in support of the scholar's conclusions. Dangers to effective thinking in relation to scholarly (as well as other) problems include forming premature conclusions, ignoring adverse evidence, thinking within fixed limits, failing to observe all related facts, being inaccurate in observation, mistaking coincidence for cause-and-effect relationships, and allowing oneself to be influenced by subjectivity or prejudice.[2]

[2] For helpful advice on principles of legal procedure discussed in this chapter, the author is deeply grateful to Judge John Joseph Dooley, Weld County, Colorado.

5 THE SCHOLAR AS

DETECTIVE: THE SEARCH

FOR CLUES

The quality in a well-written detective story that gives it intellectual as well as emotional appeal is the cleverness and skill with which the detective-hero searches out the clues in solving a crime. His almost superhuman powers of observation and the deductions he draws from these observations — as in the stories of Sherlock Holmes — fascinate the reader. Sometimes we hear speculations regarding a "perfect crime," by which term we mean a crime that leaves no clues to betray the criminal. Detectives of long experience maintain that a crime without clues is so rare as to be practically unheard of.

Suppose that a boy riding his bicycle on a city street has been struck down and injured by an automobile. The operator of the automobile, instead of stopping to assist the victim and to report the accident to the police, as he should, rapidly drives away; he is, in short, a hit-and-run driver. How can he be apprehended?

The police undoubtedly will begin their search for the culprit by first observing and recording as many *facts* about the incident (clues) as they can. How did the accident occur? They make photographs of the scene, look for tire marks on the street, measure the distance of the bicycle and of the boy's body from the probable point of impact. This may tell something about the speed and direction the automobile traveled. What were the make and model of the automobile? The police may find pieces of glass from a broken headlight or flakes of paint scraped from the surface of the car. They examine the marks left on the bicycle. They may even analyze in the police laboratory the dirt or dust shaken from underneath the automobile's fenders at the scene. They search for eye-witnesses who may have seen the accident or caught a glimpse of the car as it sped away. What was its color, its make, its model? Could the license number be read? Was the witness able to see the driver's face? Was the driver a man or a woman?

From any pertinent facts or opinions obtained in this fashion, the police will draw such preliminary conclusions as may be warranted. But suppose no witnesses at all can be found. Then perhaps a little may be learned by examining the small traces of paint which have been found adhering to some parts of the bicycle — paint presumably scraped from the automobile during the collision. Such paint can be inspected under the microscope and analyzed with chemicals, — a process that may lead to an identification of both the color and the type of paint used. The records of automobile manufacturers may then reveal the make of car for which this type of paint was made. Pieces of glass from the headlight may also provide a clue to the make and model. Furthermore, by deductions based on calculations regarding the speed at which the vehicle was traveling, it may be inferred that a fender was damaged and will need to be repaired. The police may visit garagemen in the community and ask them to be on the lookout for an automobile of a certain color and make which has a dented fender. By such methods the erring driver may often be located.

Clues in Scholarship

Problem-solving in scholarship involves just such methods as are here demonstrated. The chief principle underlying the hypothetical illustration used above is simply that problems can be solved by those who know how and where to look for the pertinent clues. Ordinarily only the trained person can do this. The untrained person would not be likely to know where the necessary information could be found, and still less would he understand how to classify and analyze the information when it was found.

How does this principle apply to the scholar? It means, first of all, that he must be familiar with all the important sources of information in his own field. It means also that he must be able to use the tools of research which are available to him. Most of these tools he will find in the library or the laboratory.

Just as the detective should have experience and special training in order to know where best to exert his efforts in an investigation (that is, where he is most likely to find the clues), so too the scholar, for much the same purpose, must be thoroughly familiar with all the basic discoveries made in his field; he must be, in other words, an expert within that field. His first step in solving a problem within his academic field, then, is usually to review carefully the present state of knowledge with regard to that problem. This essential step has two purposes: It refreshes his mind on what previous investigators have contributed toward the solution of the problem, thus preventing unnecessary duplication of work already done by others; and it may suggest methods of research which he can use in attacking the problem.

In a practical sense, this means that the scholar must carefully read, or re-read, all the published and unpublished materials that have any relation to the question being studied. Often a bibliography on the subject will lead him to several books or articles which deal with it in some degree; these books and articles in turn may suggest further sources of information. He should also ascertain whether doctoral dissertations or master's theses have been written on the topic or have touched on it in any way; if these are available, he should consult them. Lists of research projects in progress may tell him of other scholars who are already working on the same or similar subjects. He may very well correspond with these fellow-workers to exchange information and also to avoid encroachment upon areas of study which they have previously claimed. A scholar does not knowingly undertake the solution of a problem which another scholar is already studying. But the point is to know exactly what has been done and is being done. Once the scholar has a firm understanding of the facts and opinions revealed through this painstaking "review of related literature" (as it is frequently called), he can then proceed with an orderly search for clues which others may have overlooked or with the application of new methods of analyzing data already available.

Knowing Where to Look

The chief source of the preliminary information used in any scholarly study is, of course, the library. The better and more complete the collection of materials on a given subject in the library, the more likely is the scholar to be successful in his search for clues. For this reason universities and other institutions annually spend huge amounts of money to collect published and unpublished writings of many sorts. Without great libraries the task of the scholar would be difficult indeed. Even the experimental scientist consults the library before planning a project in the laboratory.

But even within a good library some sources of information will prove better than others. In the order of their probable usefulness to research, the principal materials to be found in the library include (1) official documents and original manuscripts having a direct bearing on the problem being studied, (2) other scholarly studies of the problem or of one related closely to it, (3) books and articles expressing opinions on the subject by persons having special competence or experience in dealing with it, and (4) other miscellaneous writings on the problem or any aspect of it. To these might also be added the bibliographies, reviews of research, catalogues, and other tools useful in helping the scholar to locate the materials mentioned above.

For the young scholar, to whom the search for clues may be a new experience, a word of caution regarding the relative importance of these different kinds of material may be beneficial. Some periodicals in almost every field publish direct reports of scholarly studies, and these are by all odds the most useful periodicals for the scholar. They provide in very exact language a record of recent and essential discoveries by investigators in the field. Other periodicals merely comment upon these discoveries. To be sure, essays by competent authorities, giving expert opinion, often may be of considerable value; they do not normally, however, prove as sound a basis for scholarly evidence as do the reports of actual research. A third class of periodical may seek to interpret scholarly discoveries to the general public, and these the scholar will find of extremely limited value for his purposes. Often their intention is to entertain the reader instead of accurately informing him.

If a young scholar wishes to determine whether a particular periodical is of one type or another, he may find it helpful to glance at the title page and consider three questions:

1. *Who publishes the periodical?* If it is published by a scholarly organization, a university press, or perhaps a governmental agency, one may ordinarily assume that it enforces fairly high standards of scholarship in its articles.

2. *Who are its editors?* If there is a board of editors consisting of reputable scholars and leaders in the field, the articles no doubt have been carefully read and sifted by these experts to insure their accuracy and their value to scholars.

3. *Are the articles, whether essays or reports of studies, clearly documented?* That is, do they have footnotes or some other device for citing evidence in support of the statements made, so that the reader can, if he wishes, go to the sources and inspect the evidence for himself?

A little experience and inquiry will soon reveal which are the standard and the reliable scholarly periodicals in any field, and the young scholar should make himself thoroughly acquainted with these.

Primary and Secondary Sources

A graduate student recently turned in to his professor the report of a study in which he used certain information relating to a court case involving school taxes. His facts about the case were derived entirely from newspaper accounts and from articles appearing in such popular magazines as *Time* and *Newsweek*. After examining the report, the professor asked the student this question: "Why did you not inspect the actual court records in this case?" The student replied that this possibility had simply not occurred to him.

If scholarly investigations are to be accurate, they must make use not of second-hand information, which can be very inexact or incomplete, but of primary source materials. In the instance mentioned above, the student should of course have consulted the court records.

In general, school and college textbooks, encyclopedias, almanacs, digests, and other summaries of information for popular consumption may be regarded as secondary sources. They are seldom used in research except as the means of tracking down other materials and references; in the student's footnotes and bibliography they are not usually mentioned. The reason ought to be obvious: the information contained in them is derived from other sources and is given in summarized form. To find the full details about a subject and to be sure of exact information, it is necessary to go beyond the encyclopedias and the textbooks and search out the primary sources. Furthermore, the presentation of material in a secondary source almost invariably includes an interpretation or a selection of the facts or a judgment by the author or compiler. The careful scholar will not be satisfied with second-hand opinions and judgments; he will wish to arrive at his own conclusions from his own examination of the source materials. Every time a fact or an idea is transmitted from a primary source to a secondary source, there is the chance of error, omission, or wrong interpretation.

Experience in research and familiarity with his field will help the young investigator more than anything else in determining which are primary sources of data for his purposes and which are secondary. If he is making a biographical study — say, for example, the life of Abraham Lincoln or some phase of it — the standard biographies of Lincoln will provide him with a general framework and the broad sequence of events which he must record; but these are not enough. To find the facts he must go to primary sources — to letters, diaries, old newspapers, official governmental records, and the like. Merely to repeat, recombine, or put into new words the facts which others have previously collected and published is not scholarship. The essential thing is to seek for clues which have hitherto been overlooked and thus to learn and bring to light something new in one's field. This, of course, can be done properly only by direct observation of the evidence at its original source.

Note, moreover, that it is the relation of the material to the problem, rather than the nature of the material itself, that determines whether it is to be classed as a primary or a secondary source. For example, if a study entailing a comparison of school textbooks is being made, then the textbooks themselves become primary sources. Again, if the editorial policies and practices of *Time* or *Newsweek* are being studied, the student must examine copies of the magazine to obtain the facts he will need in forming his conclusions, and in such a case these materials become primary sources.

Many inexperienced young scholars appear to think that, once they have made a review of all the related literature, the study has been completed. On the contrary, such a summary of the studies and opinions of others is merely the first step in any research project. It clears the way for the investigator's advance into the unknown. If he is able to use the foundations already laid by earlier studies and achieve one further step in the advancement of the knowledge of his field, he will have embarked upon real research and may soon experience the joys of scholarly discovery.

The Library: Storehouse of Learning

The library constitutes a storehouse of learning written down and arranged in some usable order. Successful research often depends upon the extent and quality of the library facilities which are available. Of course, in these days of scholarly cooperation libraries often borrow materials from each other; if a particular library does not have the book or document needed for a certain study, some other library may be willing to lend it. If not, the student is faced with the necessity of traveling to the library which has the material he needs. Much, however, is being done to assist the scholar in his constant search for evidence. Photostatic reproductions of rare items may be made and supplied to him under some circumstances at a nominal cost. Microfilming adds a method of increasing a library's holdings and conserving space.

Manuscripts, it is true, cannot ordinarily be sent from one library to another; there is too much danger of loss or damage. Rare and fragile books, as well as other scarce or irreplaceable items, must be guarded against damage, loss, or theft. One cannot, for example, expect the Harvard University Library to place its rare Shakespeare folios at the mercy of the mails or even of a possibly careless scholar. But the serious and honest scholar who is reasonable in his requests will find libraries and librarians only too happy to help him locate the things he needs. Without their help, he would in most cases be unable to accomplish his work.

No library can store or acquire everything that is needed for every research project. Some books and manuscripts, for example, remain in private hands and are sometimes inaccessible. Until quite recently the relatives of Emily Dickinson, the American poet, withheld most of the original copies of her poems from scrutiny by anyone outside the family; as long as these materials remained out of reach, it was not possible for scholars to determine whether the published versions of these poems were in the form in which she wrote them. Libraries cannot find or afford to purchase complete files of all newspapers or all magazines or all books that have been published. The larger the library, however, the better are the scholar's chances of locating the materials he requires for his research. This accounts for much of the concentration of graduate study in the larger and older universities, which have been able to build up immense collections of manuscripts, books, and periodicals for the use of their students. Because of the tremendous cost and effort involved in assembling a comprehensive collection, most modern university libraries have tended to specialize in a few fields. One library may be pre-eminent in the field of economics, another in seventeenth-century English literature, another in American education, another in medieval European history, and so on. The scholar should learn as early as possible where the best collections of the materials in his own field are to be found.

The Use of the Library

It goes without saying that skill in the correct use of the library is highly essential in a scholarly investigation. By the time the student has achieved graduate-school status, he should have become familiar with the general principles and practices of library usage. As a scholar with a problem to solve, however, his relation to the library will in many ways be different, at least in degree, from what it was when he was an undergraduate. Instead of depending on course reading lists, for instance, he must now compile his own lists of reference materials. The more he knows about the systems and practices of libraries in general, and of his college or university library in particular, the more effective can he be in tapping library resources. It may prove helpful briefly to review some of the fundamentals of library usage in the light of the research scholar's special needs and purposes.

Systems of Classification. Every library has its own arrangement and system of shelving and cataloguing. Usually there is a logical and recognizable classification of the materials by subject. Books and periodicals are numbered and placed on the shelves in some understandable order. The scholar must expect to spend some time studying and exploring each library he uses so that its particular system will become familiar to him. If he is permitted by the library rules to study and browse among the shelves, or stacks, he will find this privilege a most profitable and welcome one. Searching the shelves often results in the discovery of books which might not have come to his attention in any other way. On the other hand, if the library does not allow the scholar access to the shelves, he must realize that this restriction exists for the purpose of protecting the library's treasures. Unfortunately, vital materials in libraries, unless carefully safeguarded, have an exasperating way of disappearing.

Even though libraries differ from one another both in methods and in details of arrangement and classification, there are two systems of classification which every scholar should know by heart; for most American libraries (though not all) now employ one or the other. These are the Dewey Decimal system and the Library of Congress system.

The Dewey Decimal system, invented by Melvil Dewey, a noted American librarian, arranges all published materials in a library under ten principal headings, as follows:

000	General Works	500	Natural Science
100	Philosophy	600	Useful Arts
200	Religion	700	Fine Arts
300	Sociology	800	Literature
400	Philology	900	History

The Library of Congress arrangement has the advantage of greater diversification. Instead of ten major divisions, it has twenty, and consequently it is much more likely to be useful to a very large library. The headings are:

A	General Works	M	Music
B	Philosophy and Religion	N	Fine Arts
C	General History	P	Language and Literature
D	Foreign History	Q	Science
E	and F American History	R	Medicine
G	Geography and Anthro-	S	Agriculture
	pology	T	Technology
H	Social Sciences	U	Military Science
J	Political Science	V	Naval Science
K	Law	Z	Library Science and Bibli-
L	Education		ography

Besides its general classification by subject area, each book in a library is classified somewhat more specifically according to its exact subject and is then given a class number. Thus, under the Dewey Decimal system, a book on music goes in the general classification of 700 (Fine Arts), but within that classification it would fall somewhere between the numbers 780 and 789, which are especially reserved for the field of music. In one library of the author's acquaintance, the book entitled Our Musical Heritage, by Curt Sachs, (picked at random) has the class number 780.9, and in the same class are found all other books on musical history and criticism. But the book also has an author number (S121o) and can be located on the shelves of the library by finding first the class number and then, within the class, the author number under an alphabetical arrangement. No two books in a library will have the same complete number; thus each one, if properly shelved, can be found in its own particular location.

The essential thing to remember is that every library needs to be studied and its particular system of classification thoroughly understood. This knowledge can save many frustrating hours of hunting for elusive source material when conducting a scholarly study.

The Card Catalogue. To aid the scholar in learning what items may be found among the library's holdings, there is normally a card catalogue in which are filed (usually in alphabetical order) one or more cards for each book on the shelves. For most items, at least three cards are filed: on one of these the title of the book is mentioned first, on another the author's name, and on a third the subject matter of the book. The card catalogue is an ever-present friend of the scholar, for it tells him whether the library has the item he wants and also tells him under what classification number it can be found. If the book deals with several subjects or can be classified in more than one way, there will probably be several subject cards in the file to help him find it. Its location on the library shelves, as we have already noted, is indicated by a code number which appears on the catalogue card and usually on the book itself.

Periodicals. Periodicals in most libraries are kept in a separate room or section. Articles within periodicals ordinarily are not catalogued on individual cards but must be searched for by consulting an index or a bibliography. Most periodicals supply their own annual indexes, either within a certain issue or in loose-leaf form to be used when the library binds the individual issues in annual, semi-annual, or quarterly volumes. Even more useful are the annual bibliographies published by scholars in various fields, which try to record all the books and articles published within a given field during the year. Such general indexes as *Poole's Index to Periodical Literature* (1802–1906), the *Reader's Guide to Periodical Literature* (1900–   ), and the *International Index to Periodical Literature* (1907–   ) are useful in several fields of study. They do not, however, list articles appearing in the more technical and specialized periodicals, and for such information the scholar must look elsewhere.

Compiling a Working Bibliography

The scholar's review of the related literature — that is, his search for all books and articles which have been published on the subject he has undertaken to study, as well as for all work completed or in progress but still remaining unpublished — ordinarily begins with the compilation of a "working bibliography," a list of the items he needs for his own study. First he writes down the titles and authors of all works on the subject which he has read or has heard about. Next he may consult the library's card catalogue to see what other books on the subject the library may have. After this he may go to the periodical section of the library and make a careful check through the indexes and bibliographies kept there. Finally he will look through all the library's list or indexes of unpublished materials, such as *Doctoral Dissertations Accepted by American Universities* (an annual publication of the H. W. Wilson Company). By this time his list of works to consult should be a fairly long one, and as he reads these the various references in them will lead him to still other items. He may also correspond with bibliographers or other scholars in his field and ask them whether they know of any other relevant studies or of any materials not generally accessible. Each book, article, or unpublished work read by the scholar should be combed minutely for clues leading to further sources of information. It goes without saying that no study can be thorough and complete unless the scholar makes every reasonable effort to obtain and read each work listed in his working bibliography. He cannot be sure that he is not overlooking important data if he fails to consult even one of the known sources.

Taking Notes

While reading the materials he has collected in his search for clues which will help him solve his problem, the investigator must be sure to compile careful and adequate notes of all the statements, facts, and other points he is likely to use. Since he cannot always tell in advance which clues may prove most fruitful and which will have to be discarded, he will do better to err in the direction of too much note-taking rather than too little. If the notes are full and exact, all necessary materials will be at hand when the study is brought into final shape.

Notes may be recorded in any way that is most convenient and useful for the scholar. Many students find that reasonably small file cards or slips of paper (4 by 6 inches, or thereabouts) offer the advantage of easy handling and filing. Others prefer somewhat larger cards or loose-leaf notebook paper. Notes taken on cards or slips of uniform size are more easy to handle and to organize than notes taken in some less consistent fashion. The important thing is to have in orderly notes everything essential to the study, so that the investigator does not have to dig back through volumes he has already read for information he neglected to write down systematically during the first reading.

It is best to make a separate bibliographical card or page for each book or article on which notes are taken. The first item written down ought to be the full name of the author as given on the title page, then the full title of the work, the date of publication, the place of publication, and all other pertinent facts about the source — in a word, the complete bibliographical reference. Care must be exercised to avoid small errors. Not only will this procedure help in finding the item again if it should ever be needed, but all the detailed facts will be at hand for use in footnotes or in the final bibliography.

Having carefully recorded the bibliographical reference on a card by itself, the scholar may next abstract or copy materials that will be of use to him, indicating the source by a short title or a code reference to the bibliographical card, and giving the exact page number on which each item is found. The experienced scholar never takes notes indiscriminately, but tries to anticipate how he will use them. Since part of his task in note-taking is to assimilate the materials he reads, making an abstract or a summary in his own words will often serve his purpose better than a verbatim extract from the source. Anything that is directly quoted from any book or article read should be placed within quotation marks to avert possible future errors or plagiarisms caused by faulty memory. When excerpts are copied, moreover, they should be copied exactly, with no changes of any kind. In his final report, of course, the investigator may wish to make certain changes in the quoted material. He may, for example, wish to leave out a few unnecessary words here and there or to correct some obvious typographical error or misspelling in the original. This is permissible, especially if it will help the reader understand the quoted passage; but any changes (including both omissions and emendations) must be indicated with appropriate punctuation, the details of which can be found in any good handbook on style and usage.[1]

[1] See, for example, William Giles Campbell, *Form and Style in Thesis Writing* (Boston: Houghton Mifflin Co., 1954).

The Importance of Reading Skills

The most successful scholars develop the ability to read rapidly. For some studies hundreds or even thousands of books and articles must be consulted; unless one has the reading skill to go through these quickly and pick out unerringly the useful materials for the study, the process may consume a vast amount of time. One of the things a scholar learns to do is to *skim* the books and articles he reads. This means looking at each page of the work and picking out the important paragraphs, then finding the important sentence or two in each important paragraph. Much of the material in many of the books or articles one reads is likely to prove of no significance for the particular study being made; to waste time on unessential reading would be pointless. When the important paragraphs and sentences in the work are found, however, they should be read through very carefully and the notes taken.

Some students complain that they cannot skim but must read very slowly in order to be sure they do not miss any essential information. Rapid reading is a skill that can be mastered, however, and the time saved will sometimes prove amazing. At first the effort required in skimming may seem considerable, but a little practice will gradually improve the habit. Skill in reading is of the highest importance to the scholar.

When materials essential to the study can be found only in books or periodicals written in foreign languages, it goes without saying that the scholar must either know these languages or have access to competent translations. It is generally assumed that most scholars will have a reading knowledge of German and French. A knowledge of Latin may be helpful in some fields. Other languages are less frequently used, except in certain areas of study. In general, some acquaintance with foreign languages is almost indispensable to thorough scholarship, though in some fields — education, for example — it seems less important than in others.

Summary

Problems of scholarship, like other problems, are solved by those who know how and where to look for clues. An important part of the value of graduate study lies in the training it provides in searching out, classifying, and analyzing clues. The scholar's first task must be to cover the ground thoroughly — that is, to make himself familiar with all the sources of information bearing on his particular problem. Most commonly the search begins in the library, as a review of the present state of knowledge on the chosen problem, and the wise scholar will therefore master early and thoroughly such bibliographical techniques as making effective use of the library's resources, tracking down information in books and periodicals, and evaluating sources. An indispensable skill in the process of running down clues is the ability to pick out quickly, from masses of reading matter, those items which are relevant and useful to the purpose at hand, and to make full and adequate notes on them. Although it is the lesser of two evils to err on the side of too much than of too little, the well-equipped scholar will have learned how to strike a golden mean both in his reading and in his note-taking.

6

THE THREE TYPES

OF RESEARCH

It is customary to label all activities of the scholar as research, but a brief glance at the published scholarly articles in any field will reveal many fundamental differences among them. Some articles describe scientific experiments and their results. Others report on surveys of opinion. Some announce broad generalizations based upon evidence. Others merely convey, in essay form, the impressions a scholar has gained from uncontrolled contacts with a subject and from reasoning about it. The activities of scholarship are many. They include experimentation, scientific surveys, analysis of documents, historical studies, interpretation of ideas, editing, and many other things.

In general, however, scholarly activities may be classified into three types. The first is *fact-finding*; the second is *critical interpretation;* and the third we may call, for want of a better term, *complete research.* It may be helpful to examine these three types of activity one by one.

Fact-Finding

A medical scientist in a laboratory decides to test the effectiveness of a new drug in killing different species of germs. He proceeds by bringing the drug into contact with one type of disease germ after another, carefully recording whether the drug kills the germ and, if so, how long a time is required, what potency of solution is most effective, and so on. What can the scientist learn from this procedure? He learns *facts* about the experimental drug with relation to certain disease germs under laboratory conditions. There are many other steps to be taken, of course, before the drug actually can be used in treating a disease, but that is beside the point for our present purposes. The main thing to note here is that the above procedure is one of *fact-finding* and little else. This does not, of course, mean that it is unimportant.

Suppose a scholar is investigating the history of a certain college. He collects old records, catalogues, newspaper accounts, letters, diaries, and so on to establish the facts of the institution's growth and development. He is trying to discover and write down an accurate statement of the facts about the college he has chosen to study. Unless he is seeking to prove some generalization about the college, his task essentially consists of fact-finding.

The same would ordinarily be true for a scholar attempting to write the biography of some notable person in his field. Unless the study goes into such matters as an evaluation of the person's character, an assessment of the benefits derived from his contributions to the field, or judgments of a similar nature, the work involved in the study amounts almost entirely to fact-finding.

A scholar who compiles a bibliography of all books and articles published on a certain topic, or a dictionary of some language, or a statistical examination of school enrollments in a given place during a given period — or, indeed, any one of a vast number of activities in scholarship which involve making a record of the facts relating to a situation which is being investigated — such a scholar is conducting research on the fact-finding level. Not long ago scientists at the California Institute of Technology examined the structure of human hair and found that it is made up of long, coiled chains of protein molecules. Seven of these chains, one in the middle and six others coiled around it, form a spiraled cable; and each human hair consists of huge numbers of such complicated cables twisted together. Now, complex as this study was, it still did not go beyond fact-finding.

When, however, a professor of geography at Johns Hopkins University found some chipped rocks and some partially shaped (or "worked") smaller stones in an ancient stream bed near San Diego,

California, he concluded from the estimated age of the stream bed that man must have occupied the area some 300,000 to 400,000 years ago and may have reached here from Asia between the third and fourth Ice Ages. He was thus going beyond fact-finding to generalizations derived from these facts. This distinction is important to keep in mind.

Critical Interpretation

In certain fields — philosophy and literature, for example — one may be dealing with ideas a great deal more than with facts. Research may then consist largely of a *critical interpretation* of these ideas. What, for instance, did Herman Melville *mean* in the story of *Moby-Dick?* Did he write merely a fictional tale of sea-going adventure, or did he use the narrative to convey his philosophical ideas about the world? Such questions cannot always be answered by reliance upon facts. By knowing something about Melville's life, by comparing *Moby-Dick* with his other works, and by examining the thoughts expressed in his letters and elsewhere, it is possible to arrive at a reasonable and supportable thesis as to Melville's underlying meaning. Since the facts of the matter — in the form of a definite statement by Melville saying just what he meant — probably cannot be ascertained, we are left with the alternative of *reasoning out* the answer from the evidence available. This involves critical interpretation.

The chief devices used in this kind of research are perspicacity, experience, and logic. Suppose one were to attempt a study of what the functions of an American graduate school should be. After carefully reading all the books and articles which have been written on the subject, inspecting the publications of all the graduate schools, and questioning the deans and faculties of as many graduate schools as possible, the scholar would still find himself dealing pretty largely with a vast body of *opinion*. While the scholar could perhaps determine the facts as to what functions graduate schools *do* perform, it would be another matter to decide what functions they *should* perform. Probably the only method of approach to the question would be an analysis and classification of the opinions expressed and a critical interpretation of them, showing in a logical way the strength and weakness, the reasonableness or unreasonableness, of each opinion found and of any further ideas on the matter which the scholar himself might have. Then, having reasoned out in his own mind a logical and acceptable answer to the question, the scholar might state this answer as his own considered opinion. This often results in an essay rather than in a research report.

While it may be possible to determine the salient facts of a man's life, agreement as to what his ideas were and how valuable they have proved to be rests largely upon human judgment. As an example, let us take Horace Mann — usually regarded as the foremost American educator. The fact-finding process will tell us the outward acts and incidents of his life. It will not, however, tell us much about what went on inside Horace Mann's mind. This we can only infer, through critical interpretation, from his writings and speeches, from some of his actions, and from the comments of those who knew him. Furthermore, how is one to determine whether Mann actually *was* the leading American educator? After all, such an evaluation rests mainly on opinion, though a sound scholar should be able to advance logical reasons for holding such an opinion. Wherever conclusions rest mainly upon logic and reasoned opinion, we are dealing not with fact-finding but with *critical interpretation*.

This process in scholarship has undeniable values. Without it, we might find it impossible to arrive at workable conclusions on matters about which definable facts are scarce. While it is true that research has been accumulating for us more and more facts about man and his universe, there still remains a vast part of human experience, artistic production, and thought which is not approachable by the factual method. Our only approach is through critical interpretation. Much of the research now being conducted in that academic area designated as the humanities is of this nature.

Three particular characteristics must be present in critical interpretation. First, the argument must be based upon, or at least agree with, known facts and principles in the field in which the study is being carried on. Some years ago a German literary scholar tried ingeniously to prove that John Milton, the great English poet, had borrowed some of his ideas and language from an earlier writer. He attempted this by showing that certain identical words could be found in paragraphs chosen from the works of the two authors, and he proposed the principle of comparing "word clusters" in the writings of two different literary men to discover whether one had borrowed from the other. This principle, however, has been rejected by modern scholars because it conflicts with a known fact in literature; namely, that two authors writing about the same subject are very likely to employ many of the same words in describing it. Thus, critical interpretation with conclusions based upon the rejected principle of "word clusters" would today be regarded as fallacious and unacceptable.

Second, the arguments advanced in critical interpretation must be clear and reasonable — that is, they must follow logic. Generalizations and conclusions arrived at in this type of research should be derived logically from the known facts and from the principles applied by the scholar in dealing with his material. Furthermore, the steps in reasoning which have led the scholar to his conclusion must be clearly demonstrable. The basic procedure in critical interpretation is reasoning, but this reasoning should be so impeccably honest and so thoroughly complete that the reader will be able to follow the argument without any difficulty and be impelled by it to accept the scholar's conclusions.

Third, critical interpretation is expected to result in some generalization or conclusion which follows from the reasoning which the scholar has done. The argument, in other words, must have an outcome. This outcome usually amounts to the reasoned opinion of the scholar with respect to the problem in hand. But, most important, this opinion is based upon accepted facts and principles in the scholar's field and is fully supported by both logic and the available evidence. The chief danger to be avoided in this process is that of stating a conclusion which relies upon the scholar's intuitive or general impressions rather than upon specific and reasoned argument.

Complete Research

What we may call, for want of a better term, *complete research* makes use of both *fact-finding* and *reasoning*. Yet it is also something more. To regard any study as complete research, we must be able to find in it several definite factors. The first of these is a problem to be solved. The second is evidence, consisting usually of provable facts and occasionally of expert opinion. The third is a careful analysis and classification of the evidence, by means of which the evidence is arranged in a logical pattern and tested with regard to its application to the problem. The fourth is the use of reason and logic to arrange the evidence into arguments or factual supports leading to a solution of the problem. The fifth is a definite solution, an answer to the question which the scholar's problem poses.

Note that *fact-finding* alone does not necessarily solve any problems. Note also that *critical interpretation*, while usually aimed at solving a problem and based upon the method of logical reasoning, cannot always build its case on factual evidence but must often rely to a great extent on mere speculation. *Complete research*, on the other hand, is expected to base its conclusions chiefly upon facts. Thus, after the problem has been defined, the first step toward a solution involves an attempt at answering the question, "What are the *facts* in the case?" In addition to gathering the facts, the scholar may also ask, "What has expert opinion to say on this problem?" Opinion, however, no matter how expert, can never carry the weight of solid fact and is useful chiefly for corroborative purposes. Having ascertained the facts, the scholar then raises the next question, "What do these facts suggest as to the solution of the problem?"

After deciding what he thinks is the correct solution, the scholar is in duty bound to test and challenge his conclusion in every way possible in order to be certain he is right. Does the solution agree with all the known facts? Are the facts clear enough and numerous enough to support the conclusion? Are the facts honestly used? Is the line of argument a logical one?

It should be obvious that *complete research* goes considerably beyond *fact-finding* but that it makes far greater use of factual evidence than does *critical interpretation*.

Scientists have long speculated about how the planets and their satellites were formed. What evidence other than pure reasoning is there, for example, to support the theory that the moon is an offshoot of the earth? Actually some interesting and rather convincing factual evidence has been turned up. One observable fact is what appears to be a definite scar in the surface of the earth itself.

Of course, if the moon had been thrown off by its parent body during the earth's molten stage (assuming that such a stage once existed), there would probably be no evidence of the event which could be observed in the earth's present surface. On the other hand, if the moon was formed after the earth had acquired a solid crust, there should remain some distinct indications of the exact spot at which this gigantic rupture took place. An examination of the earth's crust reveals a discernible scar in the area occupied by the Pacific Ocean. This area, comprising approximately a third of the earth's entire surface, resembles, first of all, an immense basin or hole such as one would expect if a roughly circular mass had been removed at that spot. Surrounding the Pacific Ocean is a ring of high and actively volcanic mountains — the so-called "ring of fire" — which makes a kind of ridge encircling the hollowed-out area. Furthermore, although every other part of the earth is covered with a layer of granite resting on a bed of basalt, the floor of the Pacific is made up entirely of basalt, with not a trace of granite. Since these conditions, when tested by known physical laws, resemble exactly what we should expect to find if the moon's mass had broken away from the earth at this point, they provide evidence for an acceptable explanation of the moon's origin. (There is, in addition, further evidence not mentioned above.) We have thus a speculative conclusion, or hypothesis, in agreement with observable facts and accepted physical principles — a conclusion logically arrived at through demonstrable evidence (only the bare essentials of which we have touched on here): The moon was formed at a time when the earth was covered with a crust, and it broke away from that part of the globe now occupied by the Pacific Ocean.

This illustration, though presented crudely and without any details, is intended to show how facts, once discovered, can be put together in a logical pattern (by the use of reason) to reach a generalization. It is possible that evidence discovered at a later time could prove the present hypothesis untrue and perhaps provide a better answer to the question. For the moment, however, the weight of evidence appears in favor of the conclusion that has been stated here. We *think* this is probably how the moon came to be.

Complete research nearly always involves a long and painstaking

search for factual evidence (including the results of previous investigations by other scholars), whereas *critical interpretation* may often
proceed upon only a slight factual basis, most of the process consisting of sound reasoning. On the other hand, complete research
always goes beyond mere *fact-finding* to the solution of some scholarly problem and the statement of a generalization based on the
available evidence.

What Is Not Research?

The beginning scholar sometimes imagines that, when he has
recorded the opinions of a great many experts upon some subject
and then announced his own opinion, he has done research. This is
not the case. To know the opinions of others may be helpful, but
it solves no problems. Problem-solving can be accomplished scientifically only through gathering and weighing the factual evidence.

Furthermore, the beginning scholar is likely to think that, because
he has invented a plausible theory to explain the phenomenon he is
investigating, his work has been completed. The theory still remains
to be tested and proved — that is, the scholar must marshal his
evidence in support of his idea. Too many scholars fall in love with
hypotheses which have no support except their inventors' faith.

Summary

Three types of scholarly research activity may be distinguished:
(1) *fact-finding,* which consists of a search for facts without any
attempt to generalize or to use these facts to solve a problem; (2)
critical interpretation, which makes use largely of the method of
logical reasoning to arrive at the solutions of problems, and is
applied usually when ideas rather than facts are to be dealt with;
and (3) the process we have termed *complete research,* which aims
at solving problems and stating generalizations after a thorough
search for the pertinent facts, an analysis and logical classification of
all the evidence found, and the development of a reasonable pattern
of support for the conclusions reached. Anything other than one of
these three processes, while not necessarily wasted effort in terms of
scholarship, is nevertheless not research.

7

SELECTING THE PROBLEM

FOR INVESTIGATION

There is never any lack of problems that require investigation in any field of study. New areas for exploration open every day, and the discoveries already made merely suggest the limitless possibilities for further research. Though Columbus discovered a whole New World, he probably died completely unaware of the vastness of the great continent lying to the west of the islands on which he landed. Compared with the body of knowledge that still remains to be discovered, the present achievement of human learning is about at the Columbian stage; that is, we have yet before us the task of exploring and mastering a huge continent of new information about the universe and about ourselves.

Why, then, do beginners in research often find it so difficult to select suitable problems for investigation? The chief answer lies usually in the lack of complete familiarity with one's field.

Knowing the Field

A thorough understanding of the known facts and accepted ideas in the department or area in which the scholar's work is being pursued constitutes the first and most important step in selecting a problem for study. If the scholar is familiar with his field and knows what research has already been completed in it, he will also know something of the many problems that remain. Gaps exist in every field of human knowledge; these gaps must be filled in at some time or other, and they stand as challenges to the ingenuity of the young scholar.

Not only will the scholar himself notice a number of unsolved problems and unexplored areas during the course of his general study in his field, but he can frequently lay his hands on summaries and reviews of research that point these gaps out. Periodicals published for the scholarly reader often contain long lists of topics upon which additional research is needed. Also, from published articles and reports of research one can glean ideas and suggestions for subjects requiring further study. These aids can sometimes be of real help to the young scholar when he is casting about for a suitable problem to attack. In many cases, however, a broad knowledge of subject matter will be enough to reveal the multitude of problems that cry for solution.

The annual bibliographies which appear in most fields of study will help to keep the scholar informed about the research going on in his field. They may also suggest to him possible new topics for his own researches. Thus, even though the scholar probably cannot read every article listed in the annual bibliography, he can at least gather a fairly accurate picture of what his contemporaries in the field have been doing, and this in turn should give him ideas for subjects to study for himself.

The Goad of Curiosity

In general, a natural curiosity is the best guide in selecting a problem. The scholar usually decides to investigate a problem because it interests him, because he wants to know the solution. Furthermore, he is likely to do a better job of research with a topic that he selects because of the interest it holds for him than with one that is arbitrarily imposed. When the scholar has become convinced of the need for solving a particular problem or when he feels an overpowering interest in finding the answer to some puzzling question in his field, he not only appears to do his best work but also derives the greatest pleasure out of the investigation.

Satisfaction of personal curiosity — the "felt need" or natural interest in a problem — would seem, then, to be the most desirable incentive in the selection of a topic for study. This comes ordinarily, as we have already remarked, from having a thorough knowledge of one's field and of the gaps that exist in it.

Some young scholars, however, try to select research topics too soon — that is, before they have really achieved familiarity with a special field of study. It is the rare graduate student, for example, who conducts research and writes his thesis upon the topic which interested him at the time he entered graduate school. Experience teaches him that there are problems of greater interest and deeper concern than those which he considered when he had only a smattering of knowledge in his field. Again, young scholars may make the mistake of selecting a problem which already has been adequately studied by someone else or of choosing one which is far too broad in scope. They look for subjects of earth-shaking importance, which unfortunately prove to be far beyond their power to handle. In most cases it would be better to stake out a small plot of ground and study it well. The amount of research necessary to solve even an apparently insignificant problem can prove surprising.

The scholar should not expect another person to choose his topic for him. Sometimes, it is true, a colleague or fellow-student or professor may make excellent suggestions that open the scholar's eyes to some new possibility which had not previously occurred to him, but in the last analysis every scholar should select for himself the problem he wishes to investigate. Certainly the young scholar should never proceed in the manner described so humorously but so aptly in the following article.

THE EDITOR TURNS PROFESSOR [1]

The nine o'clock chimes have scarcely ended their morning salute when the peace of the editorial sanctum is invaded by the clerk from the outer office. "Mr. Blank to see you by appointment," says she. The editor, whose editorial position is considerably subordinate to his professorial duties, recalls that this is his office hour — a period set apart expressly for the conversationally minded students. Evidently this is an interview which cannot be evaded.

Enter Mr. Blank. "Good morning, Mr. — uh, Mr. — " What was it Miss Graham said his name was? Mr. Blank obliges, and the editor

[1] [B. R. Buckingham], "The Editor Turns Professor," *Educational Research Bulletin*, VI, 252–253 (September 14, 1927). Quoted by permission.

takes time out to jot down the name where he can see it and make apparently spontaneous use of it during the subsequent interview. "You have an appointment with me this morning, Mr. Blank?" Mr. Blank confirms the fact, already sufficiently attested, that he has; and without undue delay gets down to business.

"I've got to write a Master's thesis," says he, "and I'd like to talk to you about a topic." The statement ends with a slight upward inflection as if, in spite of its grammatical form, a sort of question were implied. After an awkward pause Mr. Blank repeats that he would like to talk about a thesis topic. Whereupon the editor suggests that he go ahead and do so.

It transpires, however, that the editor-professor has misconceived Mr. Blank's meaning. He has no topic to talk about. In fact, instead of coming with a topic, he has come to get one. He looks so expectant, too; purely, as one might say, in a receptive mood.

No, he has no problems to suggest. He gives one the impression of having just learned about this thesis business, and of being entirely open-minded on the subject. At least, one gathers he has no bias toward any particular topic and certainly no preconceived notions.

A conversation ensues. The editor — playing for the nonce his professorial role — asks in what department Mr. Blank is majoring, what courses he has taken, what positions he has held, and for what type of educational service he is fitting himself. At one stage of the resulting exchange of ideas Mr. Blank brightens. With some modesty, yet with the undeniable air of a discoverer, he suggests that he might correlate intelligence and achievement in the high school. He could give some tests in the school with which he is connected; and his friend, the principal of the X school, would probably let him give some tests there; and maybe he could get one or two more schools if he stopped to think about the matter. And, O yes! how many schools does the professor think would be needed to get results that you could depend on? On being told that intelligence and achievement — so far as either is now measurable — have already been correlated by hundreds of people, Mr. Blank helplessly withdraws within himself, a discouraged seeker after truth in a world where all the problems have been solved.

Mr. Blank is a type. There are others. There is the student who has a topic, or at least has thought about one, but whose topic is trivial. Here the professor is on dangerous ground. No problem, if it is truly a problem, is valueless; and if a student has a real desire to work on a relatively unimportant problem, he should be allowed to do so — provided, of course, it is feasible and has not already been solved. Ordinarily, however, students have no strong convictions as to the problem upon which they wish to turn the light of investigation.

Moreover, it is not to be denied that in their bearing upon the real work of education some problems are far less vital than others. One may hazard the opinion that "The Legal Status of the School Board Member" is a less significant topic even for the administrator than "Teachers' Meetings as Means of In-Service Training" or "Classroom Visiting."

Then there is the student whose topic is so broad that no penetrating treatment of it is possible. Probably both of the subjects just suggested would be still better if they were more sharply delimited. McCall tells of a person — he calls him an "experimenter," but it is suspected that he was a graduate student — who formulated this problem: "What Is the Effect of Various Factors upon Learning?" After a little urging, says McCall, he departed and returned later with this formulation: "What Are the Effects of Distribution of Time upon Learning?" At a later stage the problem became: "Will a Typical Fourth-Grade Class in Silent Reading, Spending Three Thirty-Minute Periods per Week, Accomplish More or Less than an Equivalent Class Spending Five Periods of Eighteen Minutes Each per Week?"

There are still other types of students who impinge upon the editor in his office hours as professor — the student whose sole idea of the means of getting data is the questionnaire, the student whose topic is real but incapable of solution with the means at his disposal, the student who, without a sense of values or meanings, has only his industry to commend him. This last type will labor without ceasing; he will cover hundreds of data sheets and filing cards, and, if you set him at computing, he will figure long and furiously; but his labor is vain, because his data sheets, his cards, and his figures are without meaning to him.

And then there is the student who may or may not come with a problem, but who in any event has benefited by his experience and thought as he studied. He has a sense of values. He is a worker, but he glorifies drudgery by his enthusiasm. The editor-professor knows no keener delight than working with him. He gives him a push here, and a prod there; but mostly he just watches him grow. This student is the compensation for all the ills that professorial life is heir to. When he turns in his thesis, one tries to look severely critical and can't manage to do so. When he steps up to the President on Commencement Day to receive his degree one feels a glow of pride, and later a sense of loneliness. Something has gone from one's life. Will there be another to take his place?

In selecting his problem for study, the scholar has as much opportunity for the exercise of originality and initiative as he has in devising the means of solving it. Unless he chooses wisely, however, he cannot hope to find true satisfaction in his work.

Other Ways of Selecting Problems

Often it happens that a scholar will read an article with which he violently disagrees. This immediately suggests the possibility of his investigating for himself the problem discussed in the article and perhaps of presenting his own point of view. Many a beginning scholar has made an excellent start in research merely by trying to prove someone else wrong. Out of such disagreements important new discoveries are sometimes born.

Actual and pressing problems may also arise out of the scholar's everyday experience. If he is a teacher, for instance, he may meet some instructional difficulty which can be overcome only by a scientific study of all its aspects. He may — let us say — wish to see whether a particular method of teaching or a special type of examination can be shown to be superior to those commonly in use. This will require careful investigation by scholarly processes. In business and industry, when serious problems arise, the solution is often found as the result of research. Thus actual experience can suggest many topics that need study.

A special type of scholarly work consists in the task of devising and constructing necessary tools of research, that is, aids that may be used by other scholars. Before an automobile can be manufactured in the form in which we purchase it, a large number of machine tools must be made which are essential in its construction. Someone must provide the carpenter's tools before the carpenter can build a house. In the same way, tools of research have to be developed to make the work of research easier for others.

At the University of California, as a means of studying the movements of people's eyes while reading, a special motion picture camera was designed and constructed so that research men could photograph the eye movements. This piece of equipment was planned by persons well trained in scholarly methods; it is a tool of scholarly research which helps to obtain data that might not otherwise be accessible. The chemist in his laboratory plans and constructs flasks and test tubes of unusual shapes which give him better control over his experiments. Other common tools of research include such things as bibliographies of books and articles on various topics, official statistical summaries of special information (such as the census reports), guides to research which others have conducted (for instance, encyclopedias and yearbooks in certain fields), dictionaries, and so on. These tools must be devised and constructed by trained scholars for the use of others in their fields, and they comprise a fairly large area for scholarly activity. The young scholar may profitably look into the need for tools of research in his own field; the inspection may suggest an interesting and highly useful subject of investigation to him.

Questions to Ask about the Problem

When considering a problem which he may undertake to study, the scholar should ask himself a number of questions about it. These will help him to decide whether the problem under consideration is really one which he ought to adopt. The most important of these questions are the following: (1) Is the problem interesting? (2) Is it new? (3) Will it add to knowledge? (4) Is it feasible? (5) Has anyone else a prior claim to it?

1. *Is the problem interesting?* Since this aspect of the matter already has been discussed, we need only say that the investigation of a problem in which the scholar has little or no interest can prove the most irksome kind of drudgery. When real curiosity has been aroused, however, it almost invariably leads to the formulation of a worth-while problem. To the young scholar, the best advice in most instances appears to be: Follow your interests.

2. *Is it new?* Obviously there would be no purpose in studying a topic which had already been adequately investigated by others. Besides, there are so many unsolved problems in the world that no scholar needs to repeat another person's research except with the intention of checking upon its accuracy. The young scholar, however, may unwittingly duplicate someone else's work simply because he is not aware of everything that has been done in his field. In ignorance he may conduct a research project which is not at all new. In such a case his disappointment will be keen, indeed, when he discovers his error. To avoid such duplication and the chagrin

which results from learning too late that one has wasted his time by repeating work already adequately done by others, it is necessary to examine very carefully the record of research completed in one's field. No problem should be selected — we are deliberately excepting, of course, those investigations which are consciously repeated in order to test their accuracy — until a thorough search has established the fact that it really is a new problem, one which has never before been investigated successfully.

3. *Will it add to knowledge?* Not every problem is of equal importance, and a trivial one may produce results of little value in the scholar's field. For this reason, any topic which is being considered should be scrutinized for its possible significance in making a worthwhile contribution to knowledge. To be sure, one cannot always be certain of what a given piece of research may produce in the way of results. Occasionally vital discoveries have been made quite by accident. Yet it seems only sensible for the scholar to think over what he hopes to accomplish in a particular study. What is his *purpose* in undertaking to solve the particular problem he has chosen? In other words, what new knowledge does he hope to add to the sum-total of what is known? And what value is this new knowledge likely to have? If the solution of his problem seems likely to add nothing of real importance to the scholar's field, that problem should in most instances be discarded as too trivial.

4. *Is it feasible?* There are numerous and weighty problems which would be excellent choices for the scholar if only some way could be devised for solving them. Unfortunately, in our present state of learning, not every problem is capable of solution. While it may be possible in working with certain problems to review all the facts and opinions relating to them, unless these facts and opinions can be brought into a pattern which points to a clear and logical solution, the study cannot really be completed. Can one prove that living creatures occupy the planet Mars? Is it possible to know whether the continent of Atlantis ever existed as a great center of civilization? As yet our methods of study have not approached near enough to perfection and our sources of information have been too meager to provide more than a guess on matters of this kind. Whenever an acceptable method of solving a problem is not known to be available and cannot be devised by the scholar, the problem has to be

set aside for the moment as not feasible. Such problems are still numerous in every field. Inaccessibility of the sources of information, even when these are known to exist, also may rule out a problem as non-feasible.

5. *Has anyone else a prior claim?* The ethics of scholarship require that any scholar who has undertaken to solve a given problem shall have the first claim upon it and that other scholars will avoid working on it, except with his full knowledge and permission. In selecting a topic, the young scholar would be well advised to take advantage of the various means at his disposal for determining whether anyone else is already at work on it. He can, for example, inspect the latest reports of research in progress which are available at regular intervals in most fields. If his project is a doctoral study or some similar major effort, he will do well to announce in one of the periodicals of his field his intention of undertaking the work. Sometimes two scholars find themselves engaged in studying the same subject and arrange to pool their efforts or to divide the subject between them. The old and senseless habit of acquisitive competition among scholars to see who can be first in solving a problem and thus in receiving personal credit for the feat is no longer held in high regard. Since the work of scholars constitutes a gratuitous contribution to the world's knowledge, and since there are in any case plenty of topics to go around, modern scholarship expects ethical conduct from its practitioners in this as in other respects. It may be emphasized here again, too, that any fact or idea taken from the work of another scholar should invariably be acknowledged. Fortunately, little need be said on matters of this kind, since it is well understood in the world of scholarship that to be a scholar is also to be a gentleman.

Stating the Problem

The scholar must, of course, be certain that he knows exactly what his problem is before he begins work on it, and this matter does not always turn out to be as simple as it sounds. A common error is to hit upon some large and vague topic without consciously formulating a specific problem out of it. This can result in the accumulation of a formless mass of information, in a considerable vagueness about what actually has been discovered, or even in com-

plete frustration for the investigator. Suppose a literary scholar were
to choose the topic: "Factors Influencing the Thinking of Walt
Whitman." This topic is so general, and the probable factors which
can influence anyone's thinking are so numerous and so hard to
pin down accurately, that years of study would be necessary to reach
any satisfactory and comprehensive conclusion. A better problem,
because more limited and specific, would be: "The Influence of
Scientific Literature upon Walt Whitman's Writings."

Before beginning work on his topic, the scholar will find it helpful
to pause and ask himself: Exactly what am I hoping to discover? Precisely what problem am I seeking to solve? Sometimes the answer
will be much more complex than it would appear at first glance, and
this very complexity may suggest the wisdom of limiting or sharpening one's approach. Narrowing down the topic to workable size is
extremely important at the very start.

One excellent way of making a problem clear and concise is to
turn the statement of it into a question. If one states the problem
in question form, it obviously requires a specific answer, and this
answer then becomes the objective of the study. Suppose we were
to become interested in examining the requirements of American
graduate schools for the master's degree. What could we hope to
learn from such a study? In the first place, we might succeed better
by being somewhat more specific in the statement of our problem.
Do we simply wish to discover what the customary requirements are,
or do we wish to go deeper and aim at learning what the reasons
for them are and how they may be justified? If the latter is our intention, then we are launched upon a fairly extensive study. Some
pruning of the problem may very well be in order.

We might prune the above problem by examining only one requirement for the master's degree instead of all requirements. In
other words, we can limit the problem somewhat. For example,
suppose we limit it by confining ourselves to a study of the thesis
requirement only. Suppose we further limit ourselves to the thesis
requirement in relation to the master's degree in only one field —
say, education. The question then arises: Exactly what do we wish
to learn about this requirement? Presumably we might wish to
learn whether such a requirement is useful and sound, whether it
has validity. The whole matter might be clarified by turning the

problem into a specific question, such as: "Should the Thesis Be Required for the Master's Degree in Education?" We now have a reasonably workable problem, the answer to which can be positive (yes), negative (no), or conditional (yes, in certain circumstances; no, in others). The study would probably give us one of these answers and show the reasons for it.

By deciding in advance upon the limits of his problem, the scholar can also save himself much useless work. The problem we have just been considering has been limited, for example, to the thesis requirement for the master's degree in the field of education only; other departments and their requirements will not be taken into consideration at all. Such limitations as this must be clear to the scholar very early in the course of his attack upon the problem. Furthermore, as we shall see later, all the limitations which apply to a problem ought to be pointed out clearly when the final report of the study is written. At the moment we are interested primarily in getting an accurate idea of the problem to be studied before any work is done to solve it. Knowing what we are searching for is often half the battle.

In other words, the steps described above are means of easing the burdens of research by a clear and precise definition of the problem. At every subsequent step, the elimination of as many sources of misunderstanding as possible and the avoidance of all vagueness, either in the problem or in the data which are gathered in order to solve it, must be scrupulously attempted. The firmer and clearer the picture which the scholar has in his own mind of the problem he is to solve, the better are his chances of successfully solving it.

The following rules will be found helpful in setting down on paper the final definition of a problem:

1. Be sure that the topic chosen is neither too vague nor too broad in scope.

2. To make the problem clearer and more understandable, state it as a question which requires a definite answer.

3. Carefully state the limits of the problem, eliminating all aspects and factors which will not be considered in the study.

4. Define any special terms that must be used in the statement of your problem.

Defining Special Terms. Definitions of terms used in a study are not necessary unless these terms might be interpreted in more than one way or have particular meanings in the study itself. When such is the case, however, the terms will need to be carefully defined, not only for the sake of readers of the final research report, but also for the scholar's own benefit, so that he will not make the mistake of using a term in two different ways at two different times.

The word *curriculum* — to take a common example — is frequently interpreted by writers on education to mean the entire program of a school, including both classwork and other activities as well. But some writers use the term to mean classwork only. Thus, in the description of any problem having to do with a school curriculum, the meaning of *curriculum* for that particular study has to be determined in advance. Otherwise there is a good chance for confusion to develop within the study. The scholar should be clear as to which meaning he has in mind, and he should be consistent in his use of the term.

Another source of potential difficulty stemming from carelessness in the use of terms is the frequent confusion between the *purpose* of a study and the *problem* to be studied. The purpose of a study is generally understood as the reason *why* the study has been undertaken; whereas the problem is *what* the scholar specifically hopes to solve. If the purpose of a research project is considered, it should be regarded as an explanation of the possible uses to which the results of the study may be put. It should concern the probable value of the study. In brief, it should explain why the study was undertaken and not what the subject is. The purpose concerns the *why*, and the problem concerns the *what* of the study.

How Good Is the Problem?

To determine just how good the chosen topic is, the recommended procedure is to make a preliminary investigation of the more obvious evidence. Many a problem is chosen but later dropped, often because there are not enough data available to provide a solution. Whatever the reason may be, there is no disgrace in dropping a problem that gives no promise of resolution. Trial-and-error is often the only method by which we can learn whether an investigation is likely to prove at all fruitful. If every scholar would make a preliminary investigation of the most accessible data before deciding finally on the choice of a problem, there would be fewer failures in research.

Summary

Countless unsolved problems exist in every scholarly field, and familiarity with the field cannot fail to reveal many of them to the young scholar. In addition, he can find problems for study through such means as disagreeing with results of previous research, studying lists and summaries of both completed and needed projects, and meeting and recognizing problems in his own daily experience. The problem the scholar chooses should be of genuine interest to him, should be new, of real value in his field of specialization, feasible, and not claimed by someone else. He must take pains to state it carefully and clearly in order to eliminate vagueness and any possible confusion which might hinder his search for a solution. The problem should be sufficiently narrowed down to give promise of a fruitful conclusion, its limits should be clearly set, and the terms used in its formulation should be specific and understandable. In selecting his problem, the scholar will often find that a preliminary investigation of the more obvious data is a helpful test of feasibility.

8 THE HYPOTHESIS:

WHAT IS IT?

In an earlier chapter we drew certain parallels between the investigation of a scholarly problem and the work a detective does in solving a crime. We should remember that a detective's usual aim is to build up from his clues a plausible theory as to how and why and by whom the crime was committed. It must be a theory in full agreement with all the facts in the case and one which provides a logical explanation that will hold together and prove convincing when it is brought under careful scrutiny in a court of law. The scholar similarly labors to produce a sound *theory* (or *generalization* or *conclusion*) from the data which he gathers. In fact, the ultimate aim of any complete scholarly study should be the presentation of a new and better *explanation* regarding the subject studied than any which has previously been advanced.

The Better Theory

When we speak of a "better" theory, we mean one which provides a more natural and logical explanation for the observable facts. It was once common to account for shells and other remnants of marine life discovered on the slopes of mountains as a kind of *lusus naturae*, as a miraculous production of the earth itself. Hardly anyone, however, now subscribes to that theory. Today we believe that such remains were deposited centuries ago when the area in which they are found was covered by the sea.

During the eighteenth century Lamarck proposed the theory of "the inheritance of acquired characteristics" to explain how new species may be formed in biological evolution. He contended that an organism which has been changed by its environment may transmit the change to its offspring. According to this belief, it should be possible to produce a race of short-tailed dogs by cutting off the tails of one generation of the species. The theory, widely accepted in its day, was challenged in 1883 by Weismann and is no longer credited by modern biologists anywhere except in the Soviet Union.

In the nineteenth century Charles Darwin proposed another theory, that of "the survival of the fittest." Since every organism competes against others in the "struggle for existence," Darwin said, those organisms which prove most adaptable and have the best characteristics for the environment in which they are found seem the most likely to survive and to pass these characteristics along to succeeding generations. This process he called "natural selection." Although widely accepted among biologists, the theory fails to explain how changes in organisms actually occur.

At the beginning of the twentieth century De Vries advanced the "mutation theory" to account for the changes which occur from time to time in various species. He contended that such changes are taking place constantly in the world of nature through a kind of spontaneous mutation. If the change proves advantageous to the individual organism, it helps the organism to survive and is passed along to the offspring. If disadvantageous, it is likely to disappear through the process of natural selection. According to the De Vries theory, a change of this type takes place within the organism and is not caused by outside factors, as Lamarck supposed.

All these theories, it must be admitted, were based upon very careful observations of the known facts of biological evolution, and in each case the theory was consistent with all that was known by the best-informed biologists of the time. Yet Lamarck's ideas now generally have been discarded, and those of De Vries require much more evidence before scientists of the present day will consider them as firmly established. Modern biologists are continuing to study the many problems concerned with biological evolution and may produce theories which will eventually supplant those we now hold. Thus all principles of human knowledge, however well founded, should be thought of not as fixed and final statements of truth but as reasonable theories, supported by the best evidence mankind has thus far been able to adduce. The best we can say for any of them is that they *seem* to be true and that they may actually work.

The essential thing to keep in mind here is that what we aim at in research is a sound theory — and we cannot regard any solution as any more than a theory — that satisfactorily explains the facts. We may call this theory a solution or a conclusion or a generalization; these terms all mean much the same thing when used in this connection — they mean whatever learning of importance results from the study itself.

The Provisional Theory

Before we reach the final *theory* or *conclusion* in a scholarly study, however, it usually happens that one or two possible solutions to the problem are suggested to the scholar by his data. These provisional or temporary theories — held only until all the evidence has been collected and one of the possible solutions has been decided upon as the correct one — we call *hypotheses*. They consist, if we describe them simply, of theoretical explanations of the data which may be right or wrong, or of all the possible answers which the scholar may find for the question under study. Each hypothesis must be tested carefully to find out what evidence supports it and thus, by testing, to decide upon its truth or falsity. As soon as the scholar has examined enough of the facts to formulate a hypothesis, or temporary theory of explanation, this hypothesis will guide the direction of his further study of the subject.

In the past, candidates for college degrees were expected to defend some *thesis* (or theory) by public argument. A thesis, roughly speaking, means a proposition to be defended or proved. At Harvard College during the eighteenth century candidates for the Master of Arts degree defended such theses as the following:

> That civil government has its origins in a contract.
> That private profit ought not to be the chief end of moral actions.
> That the dissolution of solids in corrosive liquids is performed through the means of attraction.
> That the Christian religion ought not be spread by force of arms.

Each of these constituted a belief or theory which had to be defended by the student through the marshaling of all the available evidence and particularly through the use of logic. We still say to a student who is writing a paper for a graduate class: "What is your thesis?" What we mean by the question is: "What *conclusion* or *theory* are you defending?"

Etymologically speaking, the *hypothesis* consists of something "less than" (*hypo*) or "less certain than" a thesis. It may be described as a reasonable guess or supposition based upon the evidence available at the time the guess is made. A scholar may develop several hypotheses during the course of a study until he at last finds one which fits the case best or which most satisfactorily explains all the data. This *final hypothesis*, then, becomes the chief *conclusion* drawn from the study.[1]

It is not uncommon for a scholar, in investigating a problem, to make up his mind fairly early as to the solution which he thinks most probable. Further study, however, may cause him to change his mind. What he must remember is the necessity of testing his hypothesis objectively by carefully observing and examining all the related facts of the case. If his hypothesis is not supported by his evidence, the scholar will certainly discard it and search for another one.

A few years ago a well-known literary scholar advanced the hypothesis in a biographical study that the rather disagreeable and proud hero of Hawthorne's tale, "Ethan Brand," was intended as a portrait of Hawthorne's friend and neighbor, Herman Melville. The scholar based this hypothesis upon his analysis of Melville's person-

---

[1] The terms *hypothesis, theory, law, generalization,* and *conclusion* all mean much the same thing in relation to a study. They refer to the *solution* which investigation has revealed for the problem studied. From the research scholar's point of view, the hypothesis may be conveniently considered as a tentative or working assumption, and the theory as the surviving or final hypothesis which is most defensibly supported by all the evidence. But since knowledge arrived at through the scientific method is subject to revision in the light of new data, a theory is in only one sense always only a working assumption, so that the conventional distinction between *hypothesis* and *theory* (on the basis of increasing adequacy of evidence and hence of greater certainty) is a relative one. For all practical purposes, the duality of the term *hypothesis* need not concern the research scholar except to serve as a salutary reminder that no conclusion reached by the scientific method is necessarily a fixed and final truth.

ality and upon the fact that "Ethan Brand" was published not long after Hawthorne and Melville met. But other scholars quickly pointed out an essential bit of evidence which the hypothesis had overlooked. In Hawthorne's notebooks there appeared a plan for the tale of "Ethan Brand" which had been written down long before Hawthorne knew Melville, and thus the author of *Moby-Dick* hardly could have served as the model for its chief character. This hypothesis clearly was proved wrong.

In considering the general nature of the hypothesis in a scholarly study, we must keep the following ideas in mind: (1) The hypothesis represents a possible solution of the problem under investigation; (2) after preliminary examination of the data (or evidence), two or three hypotheses (possible solutions) may suggest themselves to the investigator; (3) each hypothesis which appears as if it might be the correct solution of the problem should be taken up separately and considered in the light of all evidence available; and (4) the hypothesis which best meets this test and fits all the evidence may then be decided upon as the proper solution of the problem, and it becomes the *conclusion* reached in the study.

A Theory Supplanted: Ptolemy vs. Copernicus

A plausible hypothesis — one which explains all the observable data — may be accepted as a correct and authoritative theory for years, even for centuries, before new methods of research and new discoveries prove it wrong or a better hypothesis can be developed. In order to understand how this can happen, we may look at the history of the Ptolemaic and Copernican theories (or hypotheses) in astronomy.

Ptolemy of Alexandria was a brilliant scholar who lived in the second century after Christ. The achievement for which he is best remembered is his mathematical system for calculating the movements of the planets. This great system, in which Ptolemy accumulated and coordinated the teachings of all his predecessors in the field of astronomy, he described in a book which Arabian astronomers later called the *Almagest*.

It should be kept in mind that in Ptolemy's time the telescope had not yet been invented, and that he also lacked other instruments of precise measurement which have since been developed. Furthermore, the prevailing authorities of his day believed that the movements of all heavenly bodies were directly attributable to the agency of supernatural beings; that the stars and planets moved more or less at the whim of certain gods. Ptolemy deliberately ignored this possibility and looked for natural explanations instead. He dealt only with such facts and principles as he found verifiable by actual observation. In doing this he took a long step toward the modern scientific method.

What observers in Ptolemy's time saw when they looked at the night sky was virtually the same thing we see today with the unaided eye — thousands of tiny points of light. Most of these, like the sun and the moon, seem to rotate in fixed positions around the earth every twenty four hours. A few (the planets), however, apparently wander about the sky in what seems a haphazard manner. They are seen in one position tonight, in another position two months from now. To account for these aimless and strange wanderings of the planets was what interested Ptolemy. His great accomplishment was his remarkable ability to take huge quantities of data and relate them all mathematically into a single harmonious theory.

In working out his theory Ptolemy of course had to make certain basic assumptions. He assumed, for example, that the earth must be the center of the entire universe, arguing that, if this were not so, one part of the heavens would be nearer to us than another and the stars in it consequently would appear larger than those in the farther part. He also recalled the fact that anything falling "from the sky" tends to fall toward the earth, and he thought this phenomenon to be evidence for the theory of an earth-centered universe. Like most other scholars of his time, he regarded the earth as an unmoving sphere, assuming that any motion of such a sphere would cause objects on its outer surface to fall away or at least lose their equilibrium.

Ptolemy's theory, when first announced, met strong opposition, especially from ecclesiastical authorities; but its practical value for astronomers at last became recognized, and for over a thousand years it remained the prevailing theory for all astronomical calculations and predictions. It was not seriously challenged until Copernicus (1473–1543), a Polish scientist of great genius, published his *De*

Revolutionibus Orbium Coelestium and argued for a heliocentric or sun-centered theory of the universe. Much as Ptolemy was attacked by other scholars for heretical teaching in his day, so too Copernicus had to bear the label of heretic for seeming to dispute the accepted authorities. In the end, however, the new ideas were generally adopted because they proved more useful than the old and were apparently in greater accord with the observable facts. Acceptance of the heliocentric theory as proposed by Copernicus took about a century.

Ptolemy postulated a spherical earth entirely surrounded by a greater sphere in which the permanent stars are fixed. Thus as the outer sphere turns, the stars move slowly across the heavens at a regular rate of speed. The position of each of the fixed stars remains constant. The planets, Ptolemy observed, are not fixed in this outer circling sphere; each has an additional movement of its own which he described as an epicycle. Assuming the existence of such an epicycle (or smaller circle in which the planet moves, the center of which is on the surface of the outer sphere) explains what would otherwise appear to be irregular and erratic motion on the part of each of the planets. A separate epicycle must be assumed for every planet and its relative size determined by observation. The discovery of a new planet means the invention of a new epicycle to account for its movements. Copernicus, on the other hand, taught that, once the idea of a heliocentric rather than a geocentric universe is accepted, the motions of the planets can be calculated and accounted for without assuming the existence of epicycles and without having to invent new epicycles when a new planet is found. This amounts to a considerable simplification in theory.

Neither Ptolemy nor Copernicus conducted any experiments to test his hypothesis. Indeed, neither would have considered that any experimental work, when dealing with celestial bodies, was either necessary or possible. They both reasoned logically from the facts they observed. Thus we cannot say that Copernicus really had any *proof* to show his predecessor's theory false. He did so simply by supplying a less complicated and therefore more logical theory, that is, a "better" theory. In essence, what he did was to show that, if we are willing to assume a universe in which the earth moves around the sun (rather than one in which the sun moves around the earth), many facts can easily be explained which would otherwise need elaborate and complex explanations. In other words, the principal advantage of the Copernican theory, when compared with that of Ptolemy, lay in its relative simplicity — in its power to explain more of the facts with fewer modifications of the theory itself. Later it was also shown that the ideas of Copernicus were far more useful for predictive purposes. Early in the nineteenth century the planet Neptune was located largely as the result of conclusions based upon the Copernican theory. Such a discovery very likely would not have been made, except through accident, under the Ptolemaic system.

Nevertheless, it must be understood that the Ptolemaic theory did explain the movements of the planets (although not the reason for their movements) and was just as sound mathematically as the Copernican explanation of the same facts. Astronomers may be said to have had placed before them two rival theories of planetary motion, each of which competently accounted for the observable facts. If either theory would explain the facts, and if accurate calculations could be made according to either, why should astronomers have come to prefer one to the other? The answer is that one theory was much more simple and all-encompassing than the other; it explained more of the data with fewer complications in the theory itself. Later, of course, with the invention of better instruments it became possible to observe more and more facts which had been unknown to both Ptolemy and Copernicus and which gave further weight to the Copernican explanation.

The Marks of a Good Theory

The conclusion or theory resulting from any piece of thorough scholarly research can be judged and evaluated according to the success with which it meets the criteria of certain desirable characteristics. For instance, a satisfactory theory about anything must agree with and account for all the important observable facts in the case. To be sure, not every phenomenon can be satisfactorily explained, and then we sometimes merely make a guess, hoping that further study may reveal the proper explanation. Sometimes a theory will explain part of the evidence but fail to explain the rest of it, and such a theory must be regarded usually as incomplete. In general, no theory in any field of knowledge can be regarded as final and adequate unless it is able to explain all the data which have been observed.

Besides judging a theory on its ability to explain the facts, we may say also that the theory which has fewer complexities and assumptions — in a word, the simpler theory — is preferable to the more complicated one. As we have seen, greater simplicity was one of the advantages causing the acceptance of the Copernican theory. It requires no complicated system of epicycles to explain the planets' movements. As Isaac Newton so aptly phrased it, "Nature is pleased with simplicity." In different words, we may consider that theory best which explains the greatest number of observable facts without revisions of the theory. This idea has come to be known in scholarship as the Law of Parsimony.

Thus, a good theory ought to be capable of explaining all the known facts relating to any particular problem; and the more simply it can explain these facts, the better is the theory. Besides this, a theory may receive added weight if predictions based upon it actually turn out to be true. As a matter of fact, the success of a theory for predictive purposes constitutes one of the most useful criteria by which it may be judged. To elaborate on an instance already mentioned, the existence of the planet which later became known as Neptune could be predicted with certainty according to the principles of the Copernican theory (reinforced by Newton's ideas regarding gravitation) long before the planet itself was ever sighted through the telescope. Furthermore, astronomers for many years contended, without being able to secure exact measurements to test the idea, that if Copernicus was correct in arguing that the earth revolves around the sun, even a fixed star would have to appear in different positions if seen from two different points in the earth's orbit. That is to say, the revolution of the earth would cause changes in the actual distance between a star and any given point on the earth's surface. After a sufficiently powerful telescope had been developed, Bessel was able to verify this fact by observation in 1838 — a very difficult feat, indeed.

It should be said finally of the good theory in scholarship that it ought to be fruitful of new discoveries. It should suggest further areas of knowledge to be investigated. One of the great achievements of the Copernican theory consisted in opening the door to the Newtonian mechanics upon which much of our modern technological development has depended. Probably the better the theory, the more new doors of knowledge it will unlock.

The Hypothesis as a Temporary Guess

As we have seen, the hypothesis may be looked at in two different ways. On the one hand, it may be regarded as a *principle* or *generalization* which has resulted from the careful and thorough study of a given problem. In this sense, the term *theory* or even *law* is often used, meaning a hypothesis adequately substantiated by evidence. On the other hand, in any study (particularly during the early stages) there may be one or more tentative hypotheses which really are nothing more than *temporary guesses at possible solutions* which the scholar makes to guide him in searching for further data and thus in reaching his final, correct conclusion. A scholar may test and reject any number of hypotheses in the course of a single research project.

When we speak of the hypothesis as a temporary guess or tentative solution of a scholarly problem, we find that it is arrived at and used much as follows:

1. The investigator, after a preliminary gathering of data or evidence which he believes to be related to the problem he is studying, employs inductive reasoning to reach a preliminary conclusion (or probable solution). This constitutes merely the first or trial hypothesis.

2. Having adopted this hypothesis temporarily as the most probable answer to the question he is investigating, the scholar next makes use of deductive reasoning to decide what kind of data he should expect to find if the hypothesis is true. In other words, he determines what should logically follow from the principle or generalization he is testing.

3. Having decided through his reasoning and previous knowledge exactly what kind of data to look for, the investigator then proceeds to test his hypothesis by gathering all possible data and considering whether the actual evidence and his hypothesis are fully in agreement.

4. If the evidence found in this way fails to support his first hypothesis, the investigator must reject the hypothesis. He will then search further until he has hit upon a second hypothesis or possible solution, which he tests in turn by comparing it with the evidence already available and with any further evidence that can be found. If, however, his first hypothesis proves good enough to survive all tests, the investigator may make up his mind that it constitutes the correct solution of his problem, and he need go no further.

To prevent error, it may often be helpful to consider several hypotheses (or at least more than one) when dealing with a problem. When each of these is tested in turn, the best one usually will stand out clearly. To this procedure it is frequently objected that the testing of several hypotheses, especially when some of them seem very unlikely, will be a waste of the investigator's time. Unfortunately, too great a reliance upon what has appeared altogether obvious and the failure to test possible alternative hypotheses have occasionally led even experienced scholars into serious mistakes.

Perhaps the most important fact to be remembered about the hypothesis as a temporary guess is this: Its purpose is not that of supplying a ready-made answer to a scholarly question or of setting up an arbitrary generalization to be defended by the scholar's ingenuity in argument. Rather, it is chiefly useful in suggesting new lines of observation and experiment. It leads, in other words, to the evidence. Improperly handled, the hypothesis can degenerate into someone's "pet theory" and lose its value for scholarship. Handled with skill and care, it can prove a vital tool in the hands of the trained investigator.

Is the Hypothesis Always Necessary?

When fact-finding alone is the purpose of a study, there may sometimes be little use for a hypothesis. If the scholar is investigating the history of a city or nation, the life of a man, or the present status of teachers' salaries, his work will consist entirely of determining what the facts are. The same is true if he is attempting to compile a comprehensive bibliography, a concordance, or some other factual catalogue. When fact-finding alone is the aim of the study, a hypothesis may not be required.

Most major studies, however, involve not only fact-finding but interpretation of facts. If a scholar is tracing the history of a school district or of an industry or of a political party, the facts he gathers will prove useful only if he is able to draw conclusions from them — that is, generalize about what those facts can teach us. Ordinarily, no major study is made without the hypothesis or generalization. After the facts have been discovered, what do they mean? What conclusions can we draw from them? Probably no American graduate school would accept a doctoral dissertation which involved only fact-finding and no hypothesis.

We had better say, then, that although studies *can* be made without any hypothesis whatever, the hypothesis is expected in every major study. Not the facts alone, but the conclusions that we can draw from them, must be regarded as the chief objective of research.

Summary

The hypothesis has been described in this chapter as (1) the theory or generalization or conclusion ("final" hypothesis) which results from the study of any problem, and (2) the temporary guess or working assumption which the scholar makes early in his investigation to guide him in the search for further data. The temporary guess at a correct solution may prove wrong, and if so it must be rejected in favor of some other possibility.

In the absolute sense, the "final" hypothesis or theory arrived at in a scientifically conducted study cannot be regarded as final truth; it really represents only the best answer available with the present data. A better theory may supplant it later if it fails to meet the test of time and of new discoveries.

A hypothesis or theory finally selected by the scholar after thorough study, and one which he is prepared to defend, must meet the following tests if it is to be acceptable: First and most important, it must be capable of explaining all the data; second, it must conform to the so-called Law of Parsimony and explain the data more simply than do other theories; third, it must be so accurate that predictions based upon it will come true; and finally, it should be fruitful of new discoveries in its field.

While the hypothesis may not be necessary in a purely fact-finding study, it is generally considered indispensable to the completion of any major piece of scholarly research.

PART THREE

Investigative Techniques

9

SOME COMMON SENSE

ABOUT TECHNIQUES OF

RESEARCH

In the foregoing chapters we have been concerned with the underlying philosophy of research and the general mental approach that seems necessary in order to use research as a means of discovering new truth. We have seen that research in the various academic fields always entails the search for previously undiscovered knowledge. Invariably such knowledge takes the form of acceptable and provable hypotheses which, taken together, constitute all the principles and facts that we call human learning. We have seen that such knowledge is arrived at usually through a deliberate and often laborious attempt to solve a specific problem. We have learned that, once this problem has occurred to the mind of the investigator and has been carefully considered and accurately defined, the first step toward a solution must be an inspection of all the available facts, opinions, and known principles which may have any bearing upon the problem.

This inspection ordinarily leads the scholar to some tentative hypothesis, or possible solution, but not necessarily to his final conclusion. He next proceeds to test his hypothesis, in order to see whether it is correct, by gathering and analyzing further data — that is, by making sure that the hypothesis conforms with all the discoverable facts and accepted principles in the case and also that sufficient evidence exists to support the hypothesis effectively. Where to look for such evidence is frequently suggested by the hypothesis itself. If the hypothesis fails to stand up under this test, if the evidence proves too weak to support it, or if it is seen to be not in conformity with the facts discovered, the scholar discards it and begins over again with a new hypothesis, which he tests just as thoroughly as he did the first one.

Testing the Hypothesis

It is this testing of the hypothesis which concerns us next. This is what we mean when we speak of the *techniques* or *methods* of research.

The techniques used in solving a scholarly problem are of the utmost importance. Obviously, if wrong techniques are employed, a correct solution can hardly be reached, unless by accident. For this reason the investigator must learn as much as possible about the techniques which have proved fruitful in his field and must acquire skill in using them. No good means of acquiring that skill really exists, of course, except actual practice. In a general way, however, the techniques of research can be described and broadly classified, and this may help to make the process of learning the skills easier and faster.

The exact techniques which are decided upon in investigating any scholarly problem will depend upon the nature of the problem itself. Probably no two problems can ever be solved in quite the same way. Furthermore, the data which need to be observed in working toward the solutions of different problems will differ in important respects. Thus, before the proper method of attack can be chosen, each problem has to be considered in the light of its particular characteristics and of the type of data available.

Research techniques or methods, as we use the terms to describe ways of testing the hypothesis, include these two principal steps: first, finding the data necessary to serve as the basis for any solution, and second, analyzing and classifying these data in such a way that the preliminary hypothesis about the problem can be tested and shown to be either correct or incorrect.

While there may be countless ways of uncovering evidence and of analyzing and classifying it for purposes of research, they can all be described broadly under four headings: (1) documentary or historical research, (2) experiment, (3) descriptive research or the survey, and (4) the case study. In any given investigation, it may even be necessary (in fact, it is frequently desirable) to use two or more of these general types of research in combination. There is no reason, for instance, why one should not seek the solution of a problem by studying its history through an examination of documents (documentary research) and then determining its present status by some sort of survey (descriptive research). Thus, although it may be the more common practice to use one technique only in any one study, the different methods can also be applied effectively in combination. At any rate, the decision as to which method will be used always depends upon the kind of problem under attack and the nature of the available data. It goes without saying that no investigator selects a problem for study simply because it lends itself to a particular technique of investigation.

Any notion that these various techniques are mysterious or unusually complex ought to be dispelled at once. Basically they are simple and are founded upon common sense. Occasionally the discussions which are carried on about these techniques may seem a little strange and complicated because of the use of technical terms not commonly heard in the average person's vocabulary.

What we are speaking of here is the principle underlying research techniques — a principle which in itself need not be difficult to understand. We are not saying that the solution of problems is easy. Far from it. We are not saying that it is easy to find all the necessary data or to interpret such data correctly. What we are saying is that the methods employed in doing so entail the exercise of common sense and adherence to one basic principle. That principle is the belief that hypotheses are not tested and scholarly problems are not solved merely by flashes of intuition (however valuable they may be), by unconsidered experience, or by reason and logic alone. They require carefully planned methods of study that will eliminate errors of judgment as well as errors of fact and that will build a solid foundation of acceptable evidence for the conclusions reached.

The different methods or techniques which we shall consider in the following chapters, then, have been devised as tools to be wielded in the search for truth. Their purpose is to assist the scholar both in his quest for evidence with which to test his hypothesis and reach his final conclusions and also in his detailed examination of that evidence. While description can never serve as a satisfactory substitute for actual practice in scholarship, these chapters may help to explain how successful scholars find the data necessary to their investigations and how they analyze and classify these data as a means of reaching sound conclusions.

Words of Caution

A few words of caution should be given about methods of research. In the first place, there is no special merit in being able merely to *name* or *identify* a method used. What *is* important is being able to devise a technique of study which will accurately solve the problem. No method, however ingenious, can be called successful unless it leads to true conclusions. The technique or method, therefore, should not be regarded as an end in itself but rather as the means to an end.

Further, the investigator should fully and clearly understand the method he has hit upon for solving his problem. He ought to plan in advance, so far as he can, the steps he will take in progressing toward a solution. While changes and additions in his technique will no doubt result from the discovery of more and more evidence as he develops the study, his main plan should be carefully drawn up at the start. Moreover, the method he chooses to test his hypothesis and thus reach a final conclusion should be so firmly fixed in his mind and so definite and precise in its details that he will have no difficulty in describing to someone else exactly what his plan is. This ability to describe in detail the specific method being used, incidentally, constitutes a very good way of determining whether the method chosen has been worked out properly and is likely to prove effective. If the scholar cannot clearly describe his method, the chances are that it is too vague and general to yield him satisfactory results.

Finally, there are at least three major dangers to be watched for in the collection and analysis of data. The first of these concerns the adequacy of the data. The investigator must always ask himself, before finishing the study, whether the evidence discovered actually is sufficient to support the conclusions reached and also just how reliable it is. If evidence is either weak or insufficient, the results of the study cannot be regarded as convincing or conclusive.

The second danger involves the handling of the data. Evidence must always be carefully sifted and considered for its accuracy and authenticity. Errors in the set-up of an experiment (such as admitting chemical impurities or failing to account for all variables) or fallacies in the construction of a questionnaire (such as including leading questions) or the misreading of a document can be fatal to accurate work in the scholarly study. Besides making sure that he has uncovered the very best evidence and enough of it for his purpose, the investigator must be certain that he has handled the evidence properly.

Finally, there remains the danger of deriving wrong conclusions from the data — of thinking they mean something other than what they do mean. Does the evidence really mean what it seems to? This question invariably presents itself to the scholar who is sincerely striving for objectivity. He must resist the attractive temptation of seeing in the evidence meanings which he would like to see but which are not really there.

Summary

Four major techniques or methods of research may be distinguished: documentary (or historical) research; experiment; descriptive research (the survey); and the case study. These methods are tools to assist the scholar in testing his hypothesis through the collection and analysis of data, and he will regard them as tools, or means, not as ends in themselves. The choice of the appropriate method, or combination of methods, depends upon the nature of the problem and upon the kind of data the problem entails. If the scholar has selected his method carefully in relation to his problem, and clearly understands both the method and his reasons for using it, he should thereby be enabled to gather enough reliable data, and to handle and interpret it properly, to support a valid conclusion. By a "method" or "technique" of research, then, we mean a reasonable plan for attacking and solving the problem under investigation, making use not of intuition or chance experience or pure logic, but of scientific principles based upon objectivity and common sense.

10 DOCUMENTARY RESEARCH

Documentary research receives its name from the scholarly activities involved in learning new facts and principles through the study of documents and records. While this type of research can be and is used extensively in every academic field, it has been particularly important in the study of history, literature and linguistics, and the humanities in general. Historians use this method so constantly that it sometimes is called the "historical" method. Although useful in investigating the events of the past (in fact, really the only practicable method), it may also be applied profitably to the study of current matters. For example, the documentary method of research aided American cryptographers in solving enemy codes and thus translating military messages during World War II. Documentary research need not be thought of as limited exclusively to historical studies.

This method of collecting and analyzing data can probably be considered the oldest form of true research. The Greek historian Thucydides contributed one of the earliest examples of its use when he tried to establish certain principles of human behavior and government by examining closely the origins and conduct of the Peloponnesian War. Aristotle also applied the method of documentary research when he made his provocative studies of Greek drama and poetry. The method in modern times, however, has been greatly refined and thus made far more exact than it was when the ancient Greek historians and philosophers first began to develop it.

Basically, documentary research consists in putting together in a logical way the evidence derived from documents and records, and from that evidence forming conclusions which either establish facts hitherto unknown or offer sound generalizations with respect to past or present events, human motives, characterisics, and thoughts. The process, while applied more commonly in dealing with human documents, can also be effective in studying non-human records of several types. In geology, for example, the story of the earth's development may be pieced together by a study of rock strata, fossils, and the like. Here the "documents" examined are not written records or even relics of human activity. They are simply natural facts that constitute observable and more or less permanent records of events. The fossil itself tells us more about prehistoric life than we could learn from a written record, however complete and accurate it might be.

Before considering how documents are studied, we might first ask why we study them at all. The answer lies in man's desire to learn. Whether a knowledge of recorded human history or of prehistoric times has any practical value or not, most of us are interested in learning and speculating about past events. Our curiosity, therefore, would provide enough justification in any case for documentary study; but it seems likely also that by this means we can make generalizations from past events which may guide us in our present actions. Furthermore, current ideas, tastes, and attitudes seem better understood when we have determined their origins and the steps in their growth. Documents, then, do not have merely antiquarian value but can also give us increased power over nature and over ourselves. We study the records of the past and present, first, to understand them; second, to discover facts from them; third (if they are human records), to learn something about their authors or originators; and finally, to make generalizations (hypotheses or conclusions) about them.

What Kind of Document May Be Studied?

The data gathered in documentary research may be drawn from many sources. Chief among these are the following:

1. *Official records.* These may include legal records (such as

transcriptions of courtroom proceedings), laws and other legislative acts, minutes of meetings, administrative reports (for example, the official report of a governmental agency or of a college president to his board of trustees), committee reports in the work of organizations and clubs, the annual reports and proceedings of deliberative bodies, legal instruments executed by individuals (such as contracts and wills), legal instruments conferring powers upon individuals or groups (such as certificates, licenses, and charters), and similar documentary proof of official actions or decisions. These ordinarily constitute excellent sources of exact information because of the care which official bodies must exercise to make certain that such records are accurate, complete, and carefully preserved.

2. *Newspaper accounts.* Although not always accurate in detail (even factual material may be interpreted and presented in more than one way), newspaper accounts, especially as they appear in the standard newspaper of today, often provide essential facts and serve as a more or less permanent record of day-to-day happenings in the world. News may also be found in magazines and various other periodical publications, but a distinction must be made between factual reporting and expressions of opinion (as in editorial writing). Obviously, newspapers and magazines are never as accurate and complete as official source materials; scholars, therefore, use them chiefly when official records do not exist.

3. *Eye-witness accounts of events.* If the investigator cannot witness an event himself (as will usually be the case, especially in dealing with historical matters), a desirable source of information about the event will be the testimony of someone who was a witness. This testimony may be given orally (when the investigator talks with the witness) or in written form. In studying conditions in American schools of a half century ago, it might be helpful, for instance, to talk with a person who attended or taught in a typical school of that era. Or we might seek to learn about present-day education in Germany by consulting a recent immigrant who would be able to give a first-hand account. Because of the uncertainty of human memory, an eye-witness account written down *at the time of the event* will usually prove more reliable than efforts to recall incidents a long time after they have occurred. We might also

say that a written record seems generally to be more trustworthy than an oral report — though not always.

4. *Letters and personal diaries.* Since personal papers like letters and diaries presumably are not edited by their writers with any thought for publication, they may reveal more detailed and more intimate information than public records of events. Data from personal writings are particularly helpful when the scholar is making a biographical study.

5. *Biographies, autobiographies, and memoirs.* If authoritative, these sources will be useful mainly to review the already established facts about a person's life — seldom to establish new facts. Usually more direct and original source materials (like those mentioned above) are preferable, if they can be located. On the other hand, information given in the story of a person's life may be of use in tracing the growth and influence of some historical movement or idea. It would be difficult, for example, to study the development of the American Constitution without knowing a great deal about the lives and ideas of the men who formulated it.

6. *Historical writings and studies.* If based upon scientific investigation, historical writings and studies may be used with some degree of confidence, though examination of the original source materials would be better. Historical summaries are nearly always derived from more direct sources.

7. *Descriptive studies made in the past.* If a scholarly study cannot be repeated (as an experiment can be — or, for that matter, a survey study), it becomes a documentary source of information. In other words, the report of the study is used in much the same way as any other historical document.

8. *Literary and philosophical writings.* Such literary productions as poems, novels, plays, and essays may provide information about actual events, but the scholar is more likely to examine them for their ideas. In literary or linguistic studies, of course, the writings themselves may constitute the only really essential source of data.

9. *Archaeological and geological remains.* These records (the ruins of Pompeii, for instance) are not documents in the same sense as written records; yet they serve much the same purpose in historical research, they are studied in the same way, and they reveal data which are used in forming conclusions or hypotheses.

10. *Miscellaneous.* Works of art, musical compositions, monuments, memorials, and various other miscellaneous sources of information may be important "documentary" sources in certain kinds of research or in the absence of other data.

It can be seen that the supply of source materials for documentary research is extremely varied. The first major task which faces a scholar who has undertaken to solve a problem requiring the examination of documentary evidence is the location and selection of the documents themselves. These may not always be readily accessible, and sometimes it takes much ingenuity and hard work to discover them. A problem entailing documentary research cannot, it is clear, be solved without a direct examination of the materials containing the essential evidence.

The Location of Documentary Data

Heinrich Schliemann about the year 1870 opened a whole new field of research, the field we now call archaeology, by finding and excavating the ruins of the ancient city of Troy. His interest in ascertaining the exact site of the city made famous by Homer led him to explore the coast of Asia Minor until he was able to identify one spot which had all the characteristics noted in Homer's descriptions. The discoveries of Schliemann, in addition to other things, confirmed the fact that Homer had based his story (at least in large part) upon actual historical truth rather than upon pure imagination.[1]

One of the most spectacular occurrences in twentieth-century literary scholarship has been the recovery of an immense quantity of manuscripts left by James Boswell, the great biographer of Samuel Johnson. For years the existence of some of these papers had been suspected, but the bulk of them remained unknown and were thought lost until Professor Chauncey B. Tinker of Yale University began in the nineteen-twenties the detective work which led at length to their re-discovery. Through long and careful efforts, Tinker became acquainted with Boswell's descendants and succeeded

[1] For a fascinating account of Schliemann, his predecessors, and his successors, see C. W. Ceram, *Gods, Graves, and Scholars,* trans. E. B. Garside (New York: Alfred A. Knopf, 1951).

in securing a glimpse in Malahide Castle, Ireland, of a much discussed "ebony cabinet," a family heirloom, in which dozens of Boswell manuscripts were stored. These papers, after much difficulty and expense, were generously purchased and brought to the United States by Ralph Isham, an American financier, who made them available for scholarly study. Other Boswell papers were later chanced upon when an old croquet box was opened, and still more turned up in the attic of an ancient Scottish country house. The detailed history of these discoveries is in many ways as interesting as a best-selling novel.[2]

The point with which we are primarily concerned here is that the documents used in scholarly studies do not as a rule fall fortuitously and haphazardly into the scholar's hands. He must search them out. Like a skillful detective, the scholar laboriously follows clues, recollects his wide knowledge of the materials already known in his field, and frequently calls upon his imagination and ingenuity to track down his quarry. The first step in documentary research must be the location of all the necessary documents.

The Importance of Primary Sources

One can hardly stress too much the importance of getting as near to the original documents as possible. The scholar should never use a copy of a document if he can see the original. True, sometimes this may entail more time and expense than is justified, and a carefully prepared copy may suffice for the purpose at hand. For a scholar working in California, the photostatic copy of a manuscript preserved in the Harvard University Library may be quite as satisfactory as the manuscript itself. But a scholar should not use the published version of, say, a letter if he can conveniently (or even inconveniently!) obtain access to the letter itself. Transcription and publication leave the way open for a whole host of possible errors. Similarly, a picture cannot be just the same as the thing itself, however carefully it may be reproduced.

The document which constitutes a primary source of information is, in most cases, the written record of what its writer actually saw and

<hr>

[2] A large part of the story is excellently related in *The Scholar Adventurers*, by Richard D. Altick (New York: The Macmillan Company, 1950).

heard or the first-hand expression of his ideas. The newspaper account may be a primary source if the reporter himself witnessed the event he describes. Material quoted by an author from the writings of another author, on the other hand, can never be considered a primary source; the investigator, before using such data, should go back to the original published or unpublished form of the quoted material. Textbooks, almanacs, encyclopedias, and similar summaries of information cannot qualify as primary sources (except in a study where a scholar is examining them for their own characteristics), for they usually derive their facts and ideas not from direct observation but from the writings of others.

Like rumors, data which pass through several hands before they reach the investigator may bear little resemblance to the original versions. In studying the poetical works of Geoffrey Chaucer, modern scholars are somewhat handicapped by the unfortunate fact that we do not have extant a single manuscript in Chaucer's handwriting nor even a copy of his poetry written down during his lifetime. Ways in which his lines may have been altered by careless copyists or later editors after leaving his hands or being dictated by him to some scribe have occupied and worried literary investigators for a number of years. A few poems formerly ascribed to Chaucer have been dropped, as the result of extensive research, from the canon of his works. Obviously, no final judgment regarding Chaucer's accomplishments as a writer can be arrived at unless we are certain of just what he wrote. Painstaking scholarship must be exercised in deciding which of the surviving documents are most like the original version of Chaucer's writings. The only solid basis for conclusions reached in documentary research lies, after all, in the use of primary sources — that is, those which are as near as possible to the actual phenomenon under investigation.

Scholars quickly learn the wisdom of preserving all documents carefully. The constant difficulties they meet in the search for materials, their natural annoyance at the careless handling and marring of documents by others, to say nothing of their feelings on learning that valuable source materials have been lost or destroyed — tend to make scholars ardent abettors of all efforts to preserve important records. The scholar comes to realize that a document lost is a page torn from the book of man's history. To him the person who filches souvenirs from a Pueblo cliff dwelling, or who steals a picture from a library book, or who throws away some useful note or letter, seems nothing short of criminal in his conduct. The scholar falls under an immediate obligation to treat tenderly all the documents and records which pass through his hands. In the library he makes certain that the works he borrows go back to the shelves in a condition no worse than that in which he received them. Many such records cannot be replaced if destroyed or damaged. He conscientiously keeps his promises to those who lend him letters, manuscripts, books, and the like, and in every way lives up to the trust which has been placed in him.

Criticism of Documents: External Appraisal

Once the proper documents for investigation have been assembled, the next step is careful and critical appraisal of each item. Such an appraisal usually takes two forms. First there is *external* examination, or an attempt to determine the genuineness or authenticity of the document. Is it what it purports to be? Then there is *internal* examination, which concerns the meaning, accuracy, and general trustworthiness of the statements contained in the document.

As an example of external appraisal, we may take the case of the famous Kensington Stone. This relic, called "probably the most important archaeological object yet found in North America," [3] was dug from among the roots of a tree on a farm near Kensington, Minnesota, in 1898. On one side were carved runic symbols which, when translated, revealed the exciting story of eight Gothic (Swedish) and twenty-two Norwegian adventurers who had been attacked by Indians while exploring the western country. Apparently they left the message carved in stone as a memento of their presence in this wilderness, fearing a second attack by the red men and the possibility of being killed without leaving any trace. Their camp, according to the inscription, had been made on a rocky island. The date inscribed was 1362, though this was not deciphered until much later.

While the stone and its carved writings gave every appearance of

3 By M. W. Stirling in the Washington (D.C.) *Times-Herald*, March 12, 1948.

authenticity, this document was declared by eminent scholars of the time to be a forgery on the following grounds:

1. The farmer who discovered the stone was known to be interested in the early Norse explorations of North America and to be an amateur student of runic writing.

2. No other evidence then existed which would indicate that Norse explorers had advanced as far inland as the Mississippi River valley.

3. The language used in the inscription seemed to be a curious mixture of Norwegian and Swedish.

4. Not being able in 1898 to read correctly the date of the inscription, scholars of the period assumed that an expedition like the one described must have been made (if it was made at all) during the eleventh or twelfth century. In those years, however, Norway and Sweden were at war, and thus Goths and Norwegians would not have been traveling together in the same party.

5. The stone was found not on an island, as the inscription would require, but on a piece of land at some distance from any lake.

There were other arguments as well, and they seemed conclusive. The stone was returned, unhonored, to its finder, who used it for some years as a door-step. Later, however, answers to the objections were advanced one by one. More evidence was gradually unearthed of the presence of early Norsemen in the eastern parts of the North American continent. Further knowledge of the Scandinavian dialects and runic symbols of medieval times seemed to resolve certain supposed discrepancies in the message itself and provided a correct reading of the date. An examination of topography in the Kensing ton area showed that many lakes which had once existed there had long since dried up. By 1948 many prominent archaeologists had become convinced that the Kensington Stone was not a forgery but an authentic document of Pre-Columbian American history, and it was placed for preservation in the Smithsonian Institution at Washington. Here it remains available for further study.

On the other hand, external appraisal may sometimes reveal that a document, while seemingly genuine, is not what it appears to be. Hoaxes and forgeries have been rather numerous in human history. Besides, there is always the chance of an honest error. One of the most famous hoaxes in Western history was the so-called Donation of Constantine, an eighth-century forgery, presumably by some ardent churchman, which purported to give the Pope temporal and political power over all the states of Italy. This and numerous other forgeries known collectively as the False Decretals were exposed in the fifteenth century by the great humanistic scholar, Laurentius Valla.

In our own century, in the nineteen-thirties, a spectacular scholarly scandal came to light when John Carter and Graham Pollard, two young English book dealers, discovered evidence tending to show that certain rare and expensive books by well-known British authors, books presumed to have been published in limited or small editions about the middle of the nineteenth century (and, because of their extreme rarity, commanding fabulous prices in the rare-book market), could be exposed as forgeries printed somewhat later by a clever bookseller. Since relics, letters, mementoes, and various other documents of the sort, such as first editions, have great monetary value for collectors, the temptation always arises to produce a skillful forgery which will be financially profitable. In the case mentioned here, the suspected bookseller, a man of unquestioned learning and enviable reputation, seems to have carried on his business of publishing false documents rather quietly over a period of many years and with immense personal profit. When openly accused, however, he denied his guilt. While admitting that forgery had been accomplished, he attempted to shift the blame to others.

Letters attributed to famous men have frequently appeared on the market with errors so crude and obvious that they are easily proved forgeries. In one such letter offered for sale as coming from the pen of Lincoln, the ineptitude of the criminal forger was revealed by a reference to Kansas at a period some twenty years before that territory was known or settled. These attempts to cheat a gullible purchaser or a slipshod scholar can be defeated by calm and thorough external appraisal of every document used in a study. This rule, of course, applies chiefly to *new* documents — that is, to those which have not been carefully appraised in the past. In every academic field there exist countless documents whose authenticity has been well established. If there can be the slightest question, however, the scholar should adopt the most skeptical attitude. It is a rule of scholarship not to take anything for granted.

Some of the more effective techniques for detecting spurious items have been described by Captain Arthur J. Quirke, a handwriting analyst for the Department of Justice in the Irish Free State.[4] His book makes excellent reading for scholars. Although his discussion applies chiefly to handwritten documents, a number of the techniques he presents may be used also in the analysis of other unauthenticated documents.

No doubt every scholar who has ever studied written records, especially those of an unofficial nature, recognizes the necessity of comparing an autograph manuscript (that is, one written by hand) with one or more known examples of the presumed author's handwriting. Sometimes the difference or similarity will be immediately apparent. A scholar familiar with an author's handwriting from long study of many examples learns to know the individual marks and peculiarities which distinguish it. Nevertheless, it is not always an easy matter to identify the writer of a particular document beyond any shadow of doubt. Even a signature may present problems. Are the signatures of William Shakespeare (or Shakespere, Shaxspere, or Shagspere) which have survived until modern times really those of the great English playwright? We simply do not know; there do not exist a sufficient number of authentic documents indisputably in Shakespeare's handwriting to offer the chance of comparing them carefully and ascertaining their distinctive characteristics. Unless there can be absolutely no doubt as to the authorship of a given manuscript, the scholar verifies it whenever possible by comparing it carefully with authenticated examples of the supposed author's writing. While the analysis of handwriting is too complicated a matter for treatment here, its importance to any conscientious investigator of documentary materials must be recognized.

Other techniques for assessing the genuineness of a document include such procedures as physical and chemical analysis of the

---

[4] Arthur J. Quirke, *Forged, Anonymous, and Suspect Documents* (London: George Routledge and Sons, 1930).

substance upon which it is written. The art of paper making has changed gradually over the years, and a document sometimes may be dated by determining when and where the paper was made. The same holds true for the ink used. Often the printer's type from which a published page has been set can be identified by its design or by certain special characteristics or imperfections, such as broken or worn letters. By studying the type face and by finding other books printed in the same kind of type, Carter and Pollard were able to trace the origin of the forged pamphlets which they were inspecting to a particular printing press and a particular font of type in a London printing office. Typewriters, too, have distinctive and individual characteristics which can be ascertained by close scrutiny. The magnifying glass, the microscope, and the camera prove competent allies in this process of authenticating or condemning source materials.

Recently some interesting new methods of examining documents through the use of ultra-violet rays and fluorescence photography have been developed. These have proved especially helpful in detecting alterations and erasures. When Randall Stewart (now a professor of English at Vanderbilt University) examined the personal journals of Nathaniel Hawthorne in the Pierpont Morgan Library, he discovered that numerous changes had been made in the original material by Mrs. Hawthorne after her husband's death. The author's uninhibited comments on persons and events had been considerably toned down to make them sound more genteel or inoffensive, and in some instances they had been heavily blacked out in ink. By employing modern police devices Mr. Stewart was able to read even the blacked-out portions. Consequently his editions of Hawthorne's journals reveal Hawthorne as a man of real vigor and some bluntness of expression, who was not quite the idealized figure that Hawthorne's widow had succeeded in placing before the world.

Examination of a document's contents may sometimes expose discrepancies that prove it unreliable as a witness. (Documents to the scholar are as courtroom witnesses to the lawyer — sources of information from which the pertinent data must be extracted. Before accepting the testimony of a witness, the court must know his identity and appraise his reliability.) Questions have to be raised by the scholar which, if satisfactorily answered, establish the item as genuine, and if not satisfactorily answered, cause it to be rejected as a source of evidence. Besides determining whether the handwriting corresponds with other examples by the purported author of the documents, whether the paper and ink meet the tests which are applied to them, and whether the document has been changed in any way by another person, the scholar must also check minutely into such details as the date, the signature, the statements themselves, and the general tone or style. If a letter, for example, has been dated from Paris on a day when its purported author is known to have been speaking before an audience in San Francisco, either the document cannot be what it seems to be or some error has crept into the records. The discrepancy must be explained or the document rejected.

A few of the questions which the careful scholar puts to himself almost automatically when he looks at a document are the following: Who was the author? Is the connection between him and the document a natural and plausible one? Is the subject one with which he could be expected to have some degree of familiarity? Could he have been in the place indicated at the time indicated? Was the information given in the document original with him, or did he copy it from someone else? Are the statements made in the document consistent with the known level of intelligence, education, experience, and individual temperament of the purported writer? These and many other questions of the same searching quality help the investigator to arrive at a sound judgment with respect to the genuineness of the document.

Criticism of Documents: Internal Appraisal

Whereas external appraisal is concerned with what the document is, internal appraisal is concerned with what it says — that is, with the meaning, accuracy, and general trustworthiness of the statements made in it. Once the document has been proved genuine, we must ask what significance it may have as a source of information. What sort of data does it supply for the task at hand, for the solution of the problem?

In working with a document of the distant past, the question of meaning or interpretation often comes to mind first. Suppose that an ancient stone implement is picked up on the New Mexico desert. Before its probable significance in the study of ethnology can be determined, the scholar must understand what the object is meant to be. For what purpose was it intended? How was it used by its makers? Once questions of this nature have been answered properly, the scholar can say he knows the *meaning* of the relic and can proceed with his investigation of the other facts concerning it.

In dealing with *written* records, first of all the meaning of the words and the symbols needs to be ascertained. The language (Old English or Anglo-Saxon) in which the only remaining manuscript of the epic poem *Beowulf* was written is one that we no longer use; therefore the scholar must learn it before he can study the text of the poem. Even the words of the King James version of the Bible do not all have the identical meaning today which they had in 1611. *Let* now means *allow*, whereas in the time of King James it meant *prevent*; and instead of *turtle* (for the name of a bird) we would now say *turtle dove*. Before the statements in a document can be correctly understood, then, each word, phrase, and symbolical expression in it must be interpreted. This may involve the reading of a foreign language, the deciphering of a special code, or the translation of some form of communication now no longer used.

The diary of Samuel Pepys, for instance, was originally written down in a form of shorthand which had to be deciphered by modern literary scholars; in fact, a few portions of this famous diary in an obscure private cipher still have not been read successfully. To cite another example, when strange marks and pictures were discovered on stone monuments and on papyrus rolls in Egypt, and others of a different kind upon baked clay tablets in Mesopotamia, they were believed at once to be writing of some sort; but for years they remained untranslated. About 1800, Georg Friedrich Grotefend through careful reasoning found the clues necessary to read the cuneiform writing of ancient Persia; and Jean François Champollion some twenty years later, by his work on the Rosetta Stone, made it possible to translate the Egyptian hieroglyphics.

In literary scholarship especially, though in other fields as well, interpretation has an important place. Many literary, philosophical, and religious works have allegorical or secret meanings which have to be discerned. Bitter satires like Jonathan Swift's *A Modest Proposal* (in which he proposes to relieve the overpopulation of Ireland by serving Irish babies as food) or Daniel Defoe's *The Shortest Way with Dissenters* (in which religious intolerance is described in a sober but shocking manner as highly desirable) have been mistaken by some persons for serious and straightforward recommendations. Individual words and phrases in some works have been laboriously studied in order to reach the author's intended meaning — sometimes without success (e.g., Milton's "two-handed engine at the door" in line 130 of his poem *Lycidas*). Occasionally a thorough investigation of an author's times and the country in which he lived may be necessary in order to understand what he has written. Ideas and phrases (as well as contemporaneous references) easily comprehended by the people of one century may be unintelligible to those of the next. In Chaucer's day — to give one illustration — such terms as *twenty*, *fifty*, and similar round numbers were apparently used freely to indicate merely *a large number*. Thus, when Chaucer spoke of owning "twenty books," we can interpret this to mean not that he had made an exact count but that he owned a substantial library. Today we still use a term like *a thousand and one* when we wish to represent a large but indeterminate number.

Interpreting the meaning of a document may be a very simple thing or a very complicated one — requiring, in some instances, a thorough knowledge of history, linguistics, politics, economics, sociology, psychology, and other disciplines. Common sense tells us, however, that understanding the true meaning of the statements contained in a document is essential if the scholar intends to rely on them as data in the solution of his problem.

Accuracy and Trustworthiness of Documents. If the meaning of the statements within the document has been clearly determined, the next part of the procedure in evaluating a document internally is an appraisal of the accuracy and the trustworthiness of these statements. The investigator must raise various questions about the author's competence and integrity. How good an observer was he? Did he have ample opportunity to observe the matters he described? Did he possess a reputation for truthfulness? How well could he have known the facts of the case? Was he personally interested in presenting a particular point of view? Was he prejudiced? Was he trying to deceive? Were his observations made at first hand, or did he receive the information from others?

Two persons who see the same incident may interpret it in wholly different ways. People who have witnessed an automobile accident from opposite sides of the street may be unable to agree on the details because they were observing from different perspectives, or because one was more observant than the other, or because one was standing still while the other was walking along rather hurriedly, or because of any number of chance circumstances. If the events in a labor dispute are investigated, the representatives of labor and of management usually can be counted upon to disagree not only on the interpretation of the events but even on a factual description of them. Writers of books about such controversial political figures as Franklin Roosevelt will present vastly different impressions. Thus the scholar cannot afford to accept blindly the statements made in even the best authenticated of documents. He must employ every legitimate means to decide upon their probable accuracy and trustworthiness.

Official news releases or prepared public announcements of individuals or groups, works written to please a special person or group (such as a flattering biography), striking reminiscences or interesting but unsubstantiated legends (like the story of George Washington and the cherry tree), historical works which are subsidized by interested parties (families, patriotic organizations, or individuals) for the purpose of obtaining favorable notice for their own activities or ideas (like the histories of California written to counteract the unpleasant information about certain early California settlers in the works of George Bancroft) — such sources as these must all be regarded with extreme suspicion. Actually, no document is likely to prove absolutely accurate upon close examination. Human errors creep in almost everywhere. Some documents, however, will be found far more accurate and trustworthy than others.

How much of the story does a given document tell? This question must always be considered in internal evaluation. Every document necessarily is incomplete; that is, the whole story of any event, in all its diversified details and possible ramifications, never is completely recorded. It would be beyond the realm of human possibility, for example, to reconstruct in every detail from documents the full story of even one day in the life of one person. The scholar is interested, however, only in *significant* information — in those data which help him specifically to solve his problem. Thus he is more concerned with those documents which reveal the significant facts accurately and reliably than he is with having every conceivable detail set forth. On the other hand, the scholar should have some idea of how thoroughly the document in question covers the matter at hand. If its information proves barren or vague, the temptation to read into the document things which are not really there may lead him astray. Books have been written and extensive theories propounded about data not contained in a document at all, but merely *suggested* to the imagination of the investigator. While such excursions into fancy may be decidedly interesting, they cannot be classed as true scholarship.

Dangers in the Use of Documents

Thus far we have been mainly concerned with dangers that lie in the documents themselves — with pitfalls relating to their authenticity, their suitability as evidence, their accuracy, and so on. It may be well to remind ourselves at this point of the two chief dangers to be avoided in the *use* of documents for problem-solving purposes. These are: (1) insufficiency of data, and (2) improper selection of data.

As an example of a conclusion drawn from an insufficient amount of data we may cite any of the several attempts made over a long period of time to prove that someone other than Shakespeare actually wrote the plays attributed to him. The era during which the Bard of Avon lived is shrouded in considerable mystery so far as private lives are concerned. We have just enough information about Shakespeare and his contemporaries to make us wish we had a great deal more. It is known, of course, that a London actor named William Shakespeare came originally from Stratford-on-Avon, where he received a not very extensive education. Because it seems unreasonable that one with little formal education could become England's greatest literary figure, some scholars believe that Francis Bacon or Christopher Marlowe or some other university-educated person must have written the Shakespearean plays. The evidence adduced, however, is chiefly negative. As one of the most prominent recent editors of Shakespeare points out, in each case "the arguer has constructed a thesis or hypothesis, and has gone out and searched for matter which can be reconciled with that hypothesis. His whole case is thus built up within itself. Such arguments have no controls, and, as Bacon says, the fact that a system of thought is consistent with itself is no proof of the truth of that system. A true hypothesis is one supported by proof independent of the presuppositions of that hypothesis." [5]

Similarly, a Shakespearean scholar not many years ago advanced the hypothesis that Shakespeare's plays are not necessarily to be divided into five acts. The playwright himself, he argued, had never clearly intended such divisions, and it would be just as logical to divide them into three acts or four acts, or even to consolidate them into single acts, as to retain the presently accepted five-act division. But in rounding up his evidence this investigator had forgotten one extremely damaging piece of information — damaging, that is, to his hypothesis. Shakespeare's *Henry V* has a prologue at the beginning of each act and thus clearly establishes the playwright's intention of separating that play into five parts. Thus, not only was the evidence in favor of the hypothesis inconclusive, but there was conclusive evidence in existence to confute it.

As an illustration of the second and perhaps more subtle danger (faulty selection of evidence) we may cite the study of Thomas Chatterton made in 1842 by Robert Browning. A poet rather than a scholar, Browning was nevertheless fond of literary detective work, and he did not hesitate to express his ideas and theories, right or wrong, about people and events in literary and political history. In particular, he enjoyed espousing the cause of anyone he considered mistreated by public opinion.

[5] Hardin Craig, *An Interpretation of Shakespeare* (New York: The Dryden Press, 1948), pp. 4–5.

Chatterton, a brilliant young English poet of the mid-eighteenth century, had foisted upon the English reading public a group of ballads which he himself had written in antiquated language, but which he claimed to have discovered among some old manuscripts dating from the Middle Ages. By certain errors of wording and other signs detected only by careful scholars, the hoax had been exposed. After being unmasked, Chatterton had committed suicide at the age of eighteen. His pity and romantic sympathy aroused by the boy's tragic fate, Browning wrote a supposedly scholarly article in which he exaggerated some facts and ignored others, thus drawing the picture of an abused genius who had been driven to suicide by unjust persecution. This picture does not at all agree with the total weight of the evidence available. Browning thus demonstrated one of the commonest scholarly failings — the temptation to plead a special case by closing one's eyes to part of the evidence. Thinking with the heart rather than with the head, however admirable from certain points of view, cannot be called scholarship.

Types of Documentary Study

Since all information about the past comes to us from documents and records, this method of research, as we have said, is the only one likely to prove useful in historical studies. But the documentary method also plays an important part in other academic fields as well.

Every academic field, for instance, has a history that needs to be studied in scholarly detail. Investigations along these lines will include such areas of study as (1) biography, (2) histories of institutions and organizations, (3) sources and influences, (4) editing, (5) the history of ideas, and (6) bibliography.

Biographical research means, as the term implies, determining and presenting truthfully the principal facts about the life, character, and achievements of an important person in one's field of study. The literary scholar will investigate the lives of literary men and women, the student of education will study educators, the scientist will be interested in the lives of other scientists, and so on. All must use the method of documentary research; the facts necessary for a biography cannot be gathered by means of an experiment, a survey, or a case study. When studying the history of an institution (for example, a university) or of an organization (or in some cases, an unorganized group, such as the "metaphysical poets"), the same general method applies as for the study of an individual's life.

The investigation of sources and influences ordinarily entails the attempt to learn how the ideas, writings, and special achievements of a person or group have been influenced by such factors as education, associates and friends, reading, incidents of everyday life, and environment in general. Frequently this sort of thing is done by discovering in a person's written and oral statements or in his conduct clear evidence of such influence. In literature, for instance, a writer may borrow a plot, a character, or a rhyme scheme from some earlier writer. In science, a research man may be led to a new concept by an intentional or unintentional suggestion received from somebody else. We may recall that the theory of the "struggle for existence" was first suggested to Darwin by his reading of Malthus.

Editing the works (or a particular work) of a chosen author to produce a readable modern version or a definitive annotated one, or making available to the world some rare document of interest and significance in one's field — these and similar scholarly activities under the broad classification of editing constitute another beneficial type of documentary study. Sometimes this means only reprinting, as the faculty of the Colorado State Teachers College (now Colorado State College of Education) in 1929 reprinted Henry Barnard's *Normal Schools,* a milestone in the growth of the American educational system, which had appeared in 1851 and had been out of print for a long time. Usually, however, editing consists in much more than simply reprinting. It entails, first of all, establishing the correct text of the item being edited. Among older publications, especially those not protected by copyright, and among works which were copied down by hand (that is to say, manuscripts), variations in the text may abound. Among half a dozen variants, the editor may have to decide whether one is the best and most accurate copy and thus the one from which the text is to be reprinted, or whether all extant copies were made from one or more earlier copies, now lost, and thus need to be used collectively in order to piece together the original intention of the author. Sometimes works are added to or revised by their original authors, and such changes ought to be accounted for by the conscientious editor. Obvious and probable errors or misprints in the text must be corrected. The author's meaning as well as his words must be ascertained and his allusions explained if they are obscure or unfamiliar. As an example of a typical editorial problem, we may cite the task of reproducing the text of Shakespeare's plays. Many editors have worked on this problem, and no doubt many others will do so in the future. Because of the state in which the surviving copies of Shakespeare's plays have come down to us, it is well-nigh impossible to produce a modern edition of the plays which we can be certain represents them as originally written. The same can be said of many other works in various fields.

Editing may sometimes mean, along with other things, translation. Several years ago there turned up in an Italian castle a long manuscript in a complicated cipher, upon the margin of which some unknown person had inscribed the information that the manuscript was a treatise from the pen of Roger Bacon, that unholy and mysterious English friar who spent so many secret hours in the study of alchemy. The writing, after laborious effort, was finally decoded, though some question remains as to the complete accuracy of the translation. At any rate, here was an instance of documentary research where translation was closely related or preliminary to the job of editing.

Studying the history of ideas ordinarily involves the tracing of major philosophical or scientific propositions from their origins or earliest manifestations through their different stages of development or the tracing of changes in popular thought and attitudes over a given period of time. Such an idea as the theory of biological evolution, for example, may be followed from its origins in Greek philosophy to its present status and influence in modern science. Again, recent scholars have advanced the hypothesis that Western man's characteristic attitudes toward himself and the universe have shifted with some degree of regularity from classicism (which views the universe as a static mechanism) to romanticism (which views the universe as dynamic and changing) and back again. Other major ideas may be studied in the same historical way.

Finally, the compilation of a bibliography in any field requires documentary research. Bibliographies provide an essential service to scholarship by listing all works having to do with a given subject, thus immensely shortening the time other scholars conducting studies in the same area must take to locate their materials.

It hardly seems necessary here to go further into the numerous uses of the documentary method for projects of research in the various academic fields. Let it suffice to say that in some fields (such as art, geology, history, linguistics, literature, music, philosophy, and political science) this method is employed perhaps more than any other. In other fields (such as biology, chemistry, economics, education, geography, mathematics, physics, psychology, and sociology) it may be employed less frequently but still is highly useful, both in itself and in combination with other methods.

The Hypothesis in Documentary Research

Lest it should be supposed that research through documents and records must be limited largely to fact-finding and that hypotheses are comparatively rare in this area, we may say again that the most significant and useful results of any research lie in the generalizations or principles which are derived from the factual data. Documentary research has produced generalizations, or hypotheses, in abundance.

One or two well-known examples will be enough to make this point clear. If we turn to the research done in American history over the past half-century or so, we shall at once perceive that two hypotheses or interpretations of historical events (telling how and why they occurred) have achieved far greater prominence and influence than any others. One of these, ably advanced by Frederick Jackson Turner, suggests that attitudes and events in America have been shaped largely by the constant presence of the frontier. According to this theory, the free lands and unrestricted life of the West, by permitting escape from the economic and social pressures of the more settled East, have kept American life democratic and individualistic. The other of these hypotheses, that of Charles A.

Beard, interprets the main incidents of American history as being almost entirely the result of economic factors. Even the early colonists, in Beard's belief, were motivated less by the desire for political and religious freedom than by the attraction of greater economic opportunity in the new land. In the same way the American Revolution and other great crises in our history are interpreted in the light of a continuing struggle for economic advantage. Beard's view thus tends to minimize the possible effect of idealism and moral principles in the development of American life and character. While perhaps both hypotheses to some extent oversimplify the fundamental factors in our historical growth, and while they seem in the broad sense to contradict each other, both represent careful generalizations based upon factual data drawn from an analysis of documents, and both have been extremely influential in shaping the thought of other historians.

These illustrations are cited, without critical discussion, simply as instances of the place of the hypothesis in documentary research. With the other examples mentioned in this chapter, they should point up the prevalence of the hypothesis in this type of research and show that use of the documentary technique involves more than mere fact-finding.

Qualities of the Evidence

Something already has been said about the kind of evidence that is acceptable in scholarship. As in a court of law, the evidence must be relevant, material, and competent. These are the tests we apply to all documents and the data contained in them.

The evidence of a given document can be considered relevant to the problem only if it is demonstrably and unquestionably related and suitable — that is, if it has a real bearing on the problem. If it has no relevancy, it should not be admitted as evidence. Sometimes data may be relevant but still have little or no real weight. In other words, they can easily be dispensed with. Such data are not material and therefore need not (and probably should not) be considered as acceptable evidence. Finally, there remains the question of competence. To be competent as evidence, the document must be proved genuine, and its data must be both accurate and reasonable. Only a competent document is a good witness.

Summary

Documentary research is a method of testing a hypothesis by locating and analyzing data from documents and records of many kinds. These may range in type from official written or printed records to personal comments, both written and oral, and archaeological and geological remains.

The method is widely used in all fields of investigation, but especially in history, linguistics, literature, philosophy, and related areas. After being located, the documents used must be evaluated both externally and internally to make sure of their genuineness, their applicability to the study, and their acceptability as evidence. In general, only primary sources (if these are available) should be used. The dangers of too little data and of the improper selection of data are particular pitfalls in this kind of research. Before deciding upon final conclusions in the study, the scholar should be convinced beyond any reasonable doubt that his documentary data are completely relevant, material, and competent.

11

EXPERIMENT

Early in the twentieth century a Swiss entomologist named Felix Santschi was engaged in studying the behavior of the common ant. Certain of his observations had led him to the hypothesis that ants probably rely upon the light of the sun in determining directions. This might well explain how a single ant, foraging alone in the wilderness without the guidance of any traveled and marked trail, readily finds its way back to the home nest. (Ants using a pathway already traveled by other ants presumably would be guided by chemical traces left by their predecessors.)

To put this hypothesis to the test, Santschi devised a plan of experiment. He selected a patch of grass in a field not far away from some ant hills. On one side he set up an opaque object to serve as a sun shade; on the other, a tilted mirror. Then he waited quietly for the appearance of a lone ant forager on his way back to the nest. As one of these approached, the investigator carefully placed the opaque shield in a position which would cut off from the ant's vision the direct rays of the sun. Next he moved the tilted mirror so that the sun's rays were reflected by it upon the ant from the direction *away from* the sun itself. So far as the ant was concerned, then, the sun, which had been shining from the west, suddenly began to shine from the east. The ant immediately stopped and, after pausing to get its bearings, turned around and started off in the opposite direction — that is, away from the nest. Apparently the ant had been using the sun as a direction finder. When the light abruptly shifted from one side to the

153

other as the result of Santschi's manipulations, the ant seemed to have made up its mind that it was going the wrong way home.

Elements of the Experiment

Santschi's method of observation illustrates in simple form the basic elements of experimental research. This can be described as a means of testing a hypothesis by setting up artificial or controlled conditions for observation. Instead of drawing his conclusions either from logic or from observation under *natural* conditions, Santschi invented new circumstances under which his theory could be tested quickly and accurately. (As a matter of fact, Santschi produced additional evidence by conducting other experiments besides the one described here. The evidence of the observations made by this one process alone would hardly be conclusive.)

Often experimental research involves the construction and use of mechanical equipment, sometimes of a rather elaborate kind. Modern chemists and physicists, for instance, have been extremely ingenious in designing and constructing apparatus for experimental purposes. But equipment is not in itself the essential element in this type of research. The really important factor is the intelligence of the investigator. He must be able to devise and create conditions which he can keep under control at every stage of the experiment. He must be alert enough to follow the development of the experiment as it proceeds and to understand what is happening; otherwise his observations will not be reliable. Some experiments, like those for testing new methods of teaching in the schools, may be conducted without any special equipment at all. Nevertheless, it should be kept in mind that certain conditions, or *controls*, must always be present in any well-conducted experiment. The nature of these may be discerned by recalling some of the earliest experiments recorded in the history of Western civilization.

The Experiments of Galileo. Galileo is frequently called the father of the experimental method. We have already mentioned elsewhere his experiment with falling weights, conducted by dropping cannon balls of different sizes from a height (supposedly the leaning tower of Pisa). Though logic would seem to indicate that the heavier objects ought to reach the ground before the lighter ones,

Galileo's experiment (observation under controlled conditions) demonstrated that objects of the same substance, regardless of their size, fall at identical rates of speed and, if dropped at the same time from equal heights, reach the ground at the same instant.

To demonstrate further what is included in experimental research, we may turn our attention to Galileo's complete investigation of the nature of physical force. Aristotle and his followers, basing their conclusions upon careful observation under natural conditions and upon logical reasoning, had supplied a reasonable and useful definition of force that amply met the needs of early science. According to the physics of Aristotle, force is that which, acting upon any object, causes it to move — which, in other words, produces velocity or motion. When one pushes (or applies force to) any object — say, a table or a chair — the object moves. When one ceases to push it, unless the force of gravity is operating or some other force is applied to keep it moving, the object stops.

By Galileo's day, however, the Aristotelian definition of force had become somewhat less acceptable in that some phenomena had been observed which it could not explain. Galileo and his contemporaries noticed, for example, that the rule did not seem to fit the case of a projectile fired from a cannon. Here all the force is applied at the moment of the explosion and then ceases. Nevertheless, the projectile continues to move in a great parabola over a considerable distance. Here, then, was a situation which apparently contradicted the Aristotelian explanation of what force is and does. Galileo, to resolve the dilemma, set out to find a more universally acceptable hypothesis.

From his experimental observations of objects falling freely, Galileo saw that the motion of a body being drawn to the earth by the attraction or force of gravity is not affected by the weight of the object. Thus force cannot be measured as merely proportional to the weight of the body on which that force acts. This leaves two other logical possibilities, each of which Galileo considered in turn. One of these, the idea that force may be proportional to the distance through which the object being acted upon travels, he rejected on mathematical grounds. The remaining possibility is that force may be proportional to the length of time during which it causes the object to move. In other words, the greater the force, the longer the time during which it operates to produce motion.

Thus far Galileo had proceeded largely through the use of reason and mathematics, except for the "Tower of Pisa experiment" which had caused him to reject one of his tentative hypotheses. He undertook to test the final tentative hypothesis by experimental means.

For this purpose Galileo constructed a piece of apparatus consisting essentially of an inclined board along which he allowed a metal ball to roll. With this equipment he was able to measure fairly accurately the distances covered by the rolling ball during various units of time (or, to look at it in another way, to measure the time necessary for the ball to travel half the distance, two-thirds of the distance, three-fourths of the distance, and so on) and thus to determine quantitatively the effect of the force exerted by gravity. He came to the conclusion, after these controlled observations, that force must be defined not as that which merely *produces* motion or velocity but as that which *changes* velocity. According to this new definition, an object does not necessarily cease to move when the force causing its motion is removed; it only ceases to change its velocity. This amply accounts for the action of the projectile shot from a cannon. Its velocity as it rushes from the cannon's mouth remains constant (except for the effect of air resistance) until the force of gravity draws it earthward. Galileo's hypothesis changed the whole concept of traditional physical theory and is often called the foundation of modern mechanics.

Experimental Studies on the Origins of Living Things. Since observations made under natural conditions proved indecisive in determining whether living things always originate as the offspring of living parents or are sometimes produced by spontaneous generation or other means, controlled experiments were required to settle the question conclusively.

Francesco Redi conducted several interesting experiments during the seventeenth century to determine whether worms and maggots could be spontaneously generated in decaying meat. Suspecting that maggots actually develop from eggs deposited on meat by flies, Redi placed pieces of spoiled meat in a paper-covered container and found that no maggots appeared. When the paper cover was removed and a thin layer of gauze placed over the top of the container, flies were attracted by the rising odor and laid their eggs upon the gauze. By such demonstrations Redi effectively dispelled the notion that maggots could be produced chemically by the decaying meat itself.

When the microscope came into general use in biology, however, organisms never before visible to the human eye were discovered and studied. Since these Infusoria frequently appeared without any apparent source in previously sterile liquids, they caused a strong revival of the old theory of spontaneous generation (heterogenesis). In 1860 Louis Pasteur attacked this problem, using both experimental and other methods. He considered carefully the hypothesis that germs might exist in the air and be carried by wind currents from place to place. This would account for their being deposited in sterile liquids kept in open containers. To test this hypothesis, he first directed a stream of air under forced pressure through cotton filters, then (to avoid possible impurities in the cotton) through asbestos filters. In both instances germs were deposited upon the filters, strongly pointing to the presence of invisible organisms in the air. Next he examined specimens of air collected in different sections of France — in the congested streets of Paris, in the open fields, on mountain heights, and in his own basement laboratory. The clearer and less dust-laden the air, the fewer germs he found. The evidence, then, showed that minute organisms are present in the air, carried by dust.

But did this really prove the air to be the exclusive source of the Infusoria which developed in the sterile liquids? To pursue this question to a conclusion, Pasteur devised a more elaborate experiment. He boiled liquids until all trace of living matter had been destroyed. In each case, when such liquids were left standing in open containers for a few days, the Infusoria gradually re-appeared. When the same process was repeated, however, but with the liquids being placed in flasks with downward-curving necks, to prevent the dust from settling on the surface of the liquid, no germs developed. Only when dust actually came into contact with the liquids did the organisms appear. By demonstrating that only those liquids into which dust had entered contained the Infusoria, while other liquids of the same kind and handled in the same way *except for this one factor of dust* contained no Infusoria, Pasteur at last laid the ghost of spontaneous generation.

Here is an excellent example — in fact, one of the very best — of scientific analysis under controlled conditions. Pasteur succeeded in planning his experiments carefully enough to isolate and observe each factor which might possibly affect the results. His objective, as we have said, was to identify the real *cause* of the phenomenon under investigation. By discovering causes, the investigator is able to gain control over events or to predict them accurately.

Methods of Experimental Inquiry

John Stuart Mill, the great English philosopher, analyzed the search for causes in experimental research in order to identify the various means by which it may be achieved. He identified four major principles or methods of procedure, to which a fifth may be added by combining the first two. These constitute the five famous Mill's Canons, or rules of experimental research.[1] They are useful as guides in the design of an experiment, and they serve as general principles which can be applied in the search for causes, but they should not be regarded as rigid rules applicable in all cases.

Mill, in his book on logic, introduces the first two of his canons as follows:

> The simplest and most obvious modes of singling out from among the circumstances which precede or follow a phenomenon, those with which it is really connected by an invariable law, are two in number. One is, by comparing together different instances in which the phenomenon occurs. The other is by comparing instances in which the phenomenon does occur, with instances in other respects similar in which it does not. These two methods may be respectively denominated, the Method of Agreement, and the Method of Difference.[2]

The Method of Agreement. Mill's *method of agreement* proposes that, if the circumstances leading up to a given event have in every instance only one factor in common, that factor probably is the cause. Or, to express the same idea in the negative, we may say that nothing can be the cause of a phenomenon in the absence of which

[1] See Book III, Chapter 8, of John Stuart Mill, A *System of Logic.*
[2] Mill, *op. cit.* (New York: Harper and Bros., 1873), p. 222.

that phenomenon is found to occur. The principle expressed here has been used effectively in many studies. A few years ago, when an epidemic of a rare disease threatened one of our large eastern cities, investigators, applying Mill's first canon, ascertained that the earliest victims of the disease were all women who had recently purchased a particular kind of cheap fur scarf. When the scarves were discovered to be the one significant common factor in all the cases, they fell under strong suspicion. Upon being carefully examined, they were identified beyond any question as disease-carriers. To be sure, it was not their identification as the common factor so much as the actual finding of disease germs on them which rendered the final proof condemning the scarves. Yet the application of Mill's method of agreement provided the vital clue.

Unfortunately, the various and combining factors in a given set of circumstances are not always so clear-cut and easy to locate as in the instance mentioned above. Perhaps all the victims of a stomach ailment in a country village may draw their water from a common well; yet the water of the well may be pure, and the source of the disease may turn out to be something altogether different. Much of the difficulty in using this canon lies in determining which factors are significant and which are not.

In World War I doctors in the Allied armies were baffled when some wounded men, left lying in the summer sun for two or three days before stretcher-bearers could reach them, recovered from their wounds with no sign of infection. They became well faster, in fact, than others who had received immediate medical attention. The agency of this remarkable circumstance appeared to be the ordinary house fly. Its eggs, deposited in the open wounds, hatched into maggots. Instead of bringing infection, somehow the presence of the maggots promoted healing. Since maggots were present in all the cases reported, such a conclusion, astounding though it seemed, was formed by the application of Mill's method of agreement.

But could this mean that the larvae of the house fly, notorious enemy of human health, ought hereafter to be placed upon open wounds to heal them? For a time some doctors regarded this as a distinct, though shocking, possibility. After some ten years of further investigation, scientists at last were successful in identifying a substance called trypsin as the real healing agent. This chemical (a digestive enzyme) is secreted by maggots but may be obtained in pure form from other sources. It is now extracted commercially from the pancreas glands of cattle as a by-product of the meat-packing industry. Thus in this instance the true cause had to be separated from an apparent cause.

The Method of Difference. The second canon of Mill, which he named the *method of difference*, proposes that, if two or more sets of circumstances are alike in every respect except for one factor and if a given result occurs only when that factor is present, the factor in question probably is the cause of that result. Or, stated negatively, nothing can be the cause of a phenomenon in whose presence the phenomenon fails to occur. Let us say that a group of white rats are fed a special diet from which Vitamin C has been eliminated. Another group of rats are fed a diet which contains ample amounts of the vitamin. We may assume, when we note that the second group of rats grow larger and seem healthier than the first group, that the vitamin in the diet has been responsible. On the other hand, such a conclusion would be justified only if confirmed by a vast number of cases. In this particular instance a factor like the heredity of the two groups or some condition in the environment other than Vitamin C might conceivably affect the results.

Seldom is it possible to find two or more sets of circumstances in which every factor is alike except one. Thus the method of difference can be seen to have distinct limitations. With proper safeguards against error, however, it will prove extremely useful in designing an experiment.

The Joint Method. Perhaps the most generally reliable results in experimental research may be achieved in those investigations in which both the method of agreement and the method of difference are used. Mill called this third canon the *joint method*. According to this principle, if the conditions of the method of agreement are satisfactorily met and the conditions of the method of difference are also met, the identification of the cause should be fairly conclusive. By the joint method we first apply the method of agreement to our testing of the hypothesis (that is, we find the one factor common to all the instances in which the given phenomenon occurs) and next apply the method of difference (we determine that the phenomenon never occurs when this particular factor is absent). If both methods lead us to the same conclusion, the investigator can feel reasonably certain that he has found the cause. It was the joint method that Pasteur used in his experiments on the origins of the Infusoria.

The Method of Residues. Mill also advanced what he referred to as the *method of residues*. This, his fourth canon, recognizes the fact that some problems cannot be solved by the techniques of experiment called for in the first three canons. The method of residues in a sense finds causes by the process of elimination. When the specific factors causing certain parts of a given phenomenon are known, this principle suggests that the remaining parts of the phenomenon must be caused by the remaining factor or factors (that is, by the residue). This might be called, then, a method of last resort, one which we can use when other methods fail.

The Method of Concomitant Variations. For still other instances in which the foregoing methods cannot be applied, Mill offered a fifth canon, his *method of concomitant variations*. This teaches, in effect, that when two things consistently change or vary together, either the variations in one are caused by the variations in the other, or both are being affected by some common cause. As an illustration of this principle, Mill cited the influence of the moon's attraction upon the earth's tides. Because we cannot manipulate the moon experimentally, as by removing it from the scene to learn what will happen when it is not present, the method of agreement and the method of difference will be of no value to us here. Using, however, the method of concomitant variations, we compare the variations in the tides with the variations in the moon's position relative to the earth. We observe that all the changes in the position of the moon are followed by corresponding variations in the times and places of the high and low tides throughout the world, with high tides always occurring on that side of the earth nearest the moon and on the side exactly opposite. With such observations before us, we come to the conclusion that (1) the tides affect the motion of the moon, or (2) the motion of the moon, or the changing of the position from which it exerts its attraction, raises the tides, or possibly (3) the variations in the moon's position and in the tides are caused by some factor common to both. Further consideration of the question makes - us reasonably sure that the variations in the moon's position actually do result in the changes of the tides and thus that the moon's influence is what causes the tides in the first place.[3]

Experiment in the Laboratory

Scientists early discovered that the laboratory provides the ideal atmosphere for experimental research. Not only is it a place isolated from disturbing outside influences; it is also one deliberately designed and equipped for this type of research. If all relevant factors in the experiment are to be kept under control, apparatus must be carefully designed and its effectiveness tested, measurements must be accurately recorded, adequate safety precautions must be taken, and so on. Nevertheless, we should not be misled into equating a roomful of expensive and complicated equipment with successful research. Even with poor materials and makeshift apparatus, an experiment can be a success if the investigator is resourceful, ingenious, and faithful to the principles of experimental procedure outlined above. Students at one small eastern college were able to split the atom and thereby release atomic energy through the use of rather crude equipment made of items rescued from a junk yard. Not laboratory apparatus but the *human mind* is the essential feature of all good experimental research.

No one will deny, however, the advantages of a well-equipped laboratory. For one thing, it makes possible the carrying out of experiments that require unusual equipment or elaborate controls. Sometimes special equipment is so central to an experiment that it could hardly be carried on without that equipment. In trying to discover better methods of teaching pupils to read, educational experimenters devised a motion picture camera which photographs a beam of light focused upon the subject's eye while he is reading a page of print. The motions of the eye itself are thus recorded on film, where they may be studied, and the characteristic eye move-

---

[3] Mill, *op. cit.*, p. 232. Would the above investigation actually constitute an experiment? No, for we cannot control the conditions but merely observe them. Our conclusions are drawn entirely from a survey of the pertinent facts.

ments of good readers can be compared with those of poor readers. Without such a camera, studying the movements of the eye in reading would be extremely difficult.

The interrelation between the hypothesis and the resource of the laboratory is well illustrated by the classic Michelson-Morley experiment conducted in 1881 in Cleveland, Ohio. This was an attempt by two American physicists, A. M. Michelson and E. W. Morley, to learn whether the immense area of space outside the earth actually consists, as Newtonian physics teaches, of an invisible and motionless mass or "sea" of ether, through which the earth travels. If such an absolute substance or entity does exist, the earth moves through it much as a ship moves through the water mass of the sea. Then, argued Michelson and Morley, it should be possible to measure the earth's velocity through this ether by using the ether itself as a frame of reference, in much the same way that a sailor measures the velocity of a ship through the water (using the water itself as a frame of reference) by throwing overboard the log and line and then measuring the distance which separates the moving ship from the floating log after certain intervals of time. By knowing how much line has been played out within a given period (and allowing for drift and currents), the sailor can calculate the velocity of the ship through the water.

Applying this simple idea, Michelson and Morley devised a way of using a beam of light as their "log and line." The ether stream arising in space as the result of the earth's movement through it (like the effect of the ship's passage through the water) should, they reasoned, have a measurable if slight influence on the velocity of the beam of light used in the experiment. A ray of light projected in the direction of the earth's presumed movement through space ought to be slowed down by this flow of ether, like a swimmer moving upstream. A ray of light projected in the opposite direction (that is, downstream in relation to the earth's passage through space) ought to move slightly faster than before.

Reasoning along these lines, Michelson and Morley designed what they called an interferometer, an ingenious and surprisingly sensitive instrument which can detect changes in the speed of light. This instrument has mirrors arranged in such a manner that a single beam of light can be reflected in two different directions at once and thus, in effect, be split into two parts. (Light striking a central mirror is permitted, on the one hand, to proceed straight ahead in its original direction by passing through a thinly silvered section of the mirror and, on the other hand, to be reflected off simultaneously at a right angle. The split beam of light is then reflected by other mirrors back to the central mirror and from there to an eye-piece. The whole apparatus can be rotated at will in order to study the beam of light in all possible relationships to the presumed stream of ether.) After exhaustive tests the two investigators decided, to the amazement of nineteenth-century scientists, that no detectable difference exists in the velocity of light whether it moves *with* or *against* the so-called "ether stream." But theoretically such a difference ought to exist. Thus physicists were left with an embarrassing choice: Either they must abandon the Newtonian theory of ether (which, up to that point, had proved unquestionably useful to scientists), or they must consider incorrect the older Copernican assumption (also useful in many practical ways) that the earth is perpetually in motion. But one fact seemed assured: The earth has no measurable velocity through space. This dilemma finally was resolved by the researches and speculations of Albert Einstein and others, of whom we need say nothing here; at this point we are concerned simply with the laboratory methods of experiment employed by Michelson and Morley to study a complicated problem. Their techniques and equipment, though basically simple in design, were remarkably ingenious and remarkably accurate.

Experiments with People

Since, in general, it is neither expedient nor desirable to subject living persons to the discomforts and humiliations of laboratory experiment (though some admirable individuals have submitted voluntarily to experiences as "human guinea pigs"), non-laboratory techniques have had to be devised for the purpose of experimenting with human beings.

Important experiments of this kind have recently been conducted in the United States on a rather extensive scale in the attempt to test possible preventives of poliomyelitis. In the "gamma globulin" experiment, the first of these tests, public school children (with the consent of their parents) served as the subjects. In dozens of American communities, particularly in some in which there had recently been a high incidence of poliomyelitis, the so-called gamma globulin preparation was administered to as many school children as possible within certain age groups. The object was to compare the number of instances of the disease after use of gamma globulin with the number of instances which occurred in the same communities before it was used. The prevalence of the disease in these communities would also be compared with its prevalence in other communities, where gamma globulin was not used. Finally, a placebo, or ineffective substance, was administered to some of the school children in the experiment (the control group), and these children were to be observed to see whether they became susceptible to the disease and how the results in their case compared with results among those receiving gamma globulin. If the occurrence of poliomyelitis could be shown by these comparisons to be significantly lower wherever the new preparation had been administered, the application of Mill's joint method would clearly suggest that gamma globulin had produced the desired results. If no significant difference in the susceptibility of the different groups were noted, the usefulness of gamma globulin as a preventive of poliomyelitis would not have been proved. Similar tests were made two years later with the Salk vaccine.

Other mass experiments with people have been conducted in recent years by adding fluorine compounds to community supplies of drinking water. Here the purpose has been to determine whether such additions aid in preventing tooth decay. In two communities of about the same size supplied with the same kind of drinking water, the experiment can be conducted with a fair degree of accuracy and objectivity. Fluorine is added to the water supply of one of these communities but not to that of the other community. For some five or six years careful records are then kept in both communities as to the amount of decay found in the teeth of the school children. If there is a noticeable decrease in the amount of tooth decay among children of the community which has used fluorine in its drinking water and not in that of the other community (provided, of course, no other factor affects the operation of the experiment), we may conclude that the addition of the fluorine has aided in protecting the children's teeth.

Another answer to the difficulties of experimentation with people (besides the answer provided by the non-laboratory technique) has been the use of laboratory animals. Edward L. Thorndike and others have tried by experimental methods to discover how human beings learn, and at one time Thorndike actually formulated so-called "laws of learning" largely on the basis of observations made in experiments with rats in a laboratory.[4] Pavlov in Russia studied the physiology of digestion in dogs and applied his conclusions to human beings (including his famous discoveries about psychological association). Other laboratory animals, such as guinea pigs and monkeys, have become quite common as experimental subjects in the attempt to learn new things not so much about the animals themselves as about people.

Perhaps more generally now, however, we are perfecting the various group methods of experimentation, which provide a way of working experimentally with human beings outside the laboratory. The results of experiments with laboratory animals, it seems clear, may not invariably prove true when applied to people, and the group methods offer the means of studying human subjects more directly, though in numbers rather than individually. The principal group methods are usually classified into three types: (1) the one-group method, (2) the parallel-group or equivalent-group method, and (3) the rotation-group method.

The One-Group Method. In the *one-group* experiment a single identifiable factor is added to or subtracted from a group (or, occasionally, an individual), and the resulting change, if any, is measured. For example, a group of students may be given a standard examination in reading. After their scores have been determined, they receive special instruction with remedial reading materials over a period — let us say — of several weeks. Then they are given the same examination a second time, or perhaps a comparable form of it. The scores made on the second examination are compared with those made on the first. If there can be shown to be a noticeable improvement in

4 See, for example, Edward L. Thorndike, *The Fundamentals of Learning* (New York: Teachers College, Columbia University, 1932).

the reading ability of all or most of the students, it would be justifiable to conclude that the instruction in remedial reading has been of some value and, specifically, that it constitutes the essential factor (assuming that no other important change in materials or methods of instruction took place at the same time) which is responsible for the change in reading ability.

On the surface, this may seem like a simple enough procedure. Actually it is, but it may also be susceptible of grave errors. For instance, in the study just mentioned, extreme care must be exercised in making certain that no other factor (such as the teacher's enthusiasm and desire for good results, or the added hours of instruction, or unusual effort on the part of the students) has affected the result. A new method of teaching can sometimes prove effective simply because the teacher uses it with joy and inspiration. In such a case it often happens that the attitude of the teacher and not the method of instruction accounts for the results obtained. The investigator, however, may be deceived into thinking that the method of instruction deserves all the credit.

At any rate, the one-group experimental method can produce highly satisfactory results if all the factors affecting the experiment can be kept under control. In some of the recent experiments with fluorine in drinking water, it has been found possible to achieve generally sound conclusions merely by comparing the amount of tooth decay observed after the fluorine is added (and after a sufficient length of time has elapsed) with the amount of tooth decay observed in the same group of subjects before the fluorine was added.

Because factors operating in a one-group experiment cannot, however, be kept under control in every instance, the parallel-group and the rotation-group methods may be preferred. These methods have been invented for the purpose of securing greater accuracy of observation.

The Parallel-Group Method. In the *parallel-group* or *equivalent-group* experiment two groups of persons are studied simultaneously. These two groups must be as nearly alike as possible — that is, parallel. They must be alike with respect to such characteristics as age level, sex distribution, intelligence level, family backgrounds, previous experience with the materials or subject matter used in the experiment, and so on. The simplest and surest way of securing two parallel groups ordinarily is to find matching pairs of individuals (one member of the pair in each group) who are essentially alike in every characteristic which might conceivably affect the experiment. Having secured his two separate but parallel groups of "pairs," the investigator applies the experimental factor to only one of the two groups (the experimental group). The experimental factor is *not* applied to the other group (the control group). After the experimental factor has been applied, the two groups are studied to determine whether any significant change has occurred in the experimental group as compared with the other.

Some years ago experimenters undertook to learn whether typists could produce more and better work when using the new Dvorak typewriter keyboard than when using a standard keyboard. In examining the question, they selected an actual business office in which a large number of typists were employed. They divided the working force of typists into two roughly parallel groups. The first (control) group continued to work as usual on their standard typewriters. The second (experimental) group received machines with the Dvorak keyboard and instructions in how to use them. The object was to compare the work product of the two groups with respect to both quantity and quality. Under the conditions described, it was assumed that no factors of any real significance would affect this product except the experimental factor itself (the Dvorak keyboard). After a short period of training, the girls using the Dvorak typewriters were able to produce considerably more work and to achieve a higher degree of accuracy than the others. (As a matter of fact, however, the knowledge that they were part of an interesting experiment probably stimulated these young ladies to somewhat greater effort than usual in their work.)

In much the same way, this method of experimenting can appropriately be used to test the effectiveness of some new procedure or device in teaching. Two parallel groups of students are chosen. One group (the control group) is taught by the usual methods or devices; the other (the experimental group) by use of the new device or procedure, but by the same teacher. After a reasonable period of time for instruction (it must be exactly the same for both groups), they may be tested with a standard achievement examination in the subject taught. If the experimental group makes a better average score or shows a noticeably higher degree of improvement than the control group, the conclusion might well be that the new device or procedure has advantages over the older method of teaching. (Again, however, we must recognize the danger of error which may arise out of the teacher's attitude toward the new device. If the teacher is enthusiastic in teaching with the experimental factor but lackadaisical in the use of the older methods, the outcome can probably be regarded as a foregone conclusion.)

But are any two groups of human beings ever really equivalent or parallel? Can identical pairs of individuals be discovered — persons who are alike, for the purposes of the experiment, in every essential detail of character and experience? Probably not. And here lies one of the worst weaknesses of the parallel-group method. Minute and seemingly unessential differences among the individuals of the two groups often have a cumulative effect and result in fairly important differences between the groups themselves. Thus it is necessary, in setting up parallel groups for the experiment, not only to compare and equalize the two groups as pairs of individuals but also to compare them in their general (or average) aspects. If an intelligence test is used in pairing individuals, for instance, the investigator must find pairs who are nearly or exactly equal in their scores and must also make sure that the range of scores and the average score for the two groups are alike. The same sort of comparison must be made with respect to other important characteristics of the two groups. A little thought about this matter will show at once that securing equivalent groups is not only a complicated process but a major difficulty.

Besides the trouble and care involved in securing parallel groups, we face also the necessity of dealing with a large number of human subjects to provide us with reliable data. Ordinarily it is not practicable in one experiment to have groups of more than a few dozen persons. Larger numbers just cannot be handled conveniently. Yet the results obtained with small groups cannot be accepted as reliable until the experiment has been repeated many times. Data from too small a number of cases cannot be trusted. For this reason experiments like those mentioned here must be done over and over again with different groups. Only after observing hundreds or even thousands of human subjects can the experimenter begin to feel sure that his conclusions apply to the population as a whole. What may prove experimentally true of a small group of human beings need not necessarily hold for the general population.

The Rotation-Group Method. The *rotation-group* experiment seeks to avoid many of the dangers of both the one-group and the parallel-group procedures. In the rotation-group experiment two or more groups of subjects may be used, and an attempt usually is made to see that the groups are more or less equivalent. Then the experimental factor is applied to each group in turn. Thus each of the groups in the study becomes by turns an experimental group and a control group during the various stages of the investigation.

By the use of this rotating arrangement the investigator may conduct his experiment with several groups rather than with only two, and these groups do not ordinarily need to be equated as carefully as when the parallel-group method is used. Furthermore, it is possible to apply the rotation-group technique to a single group of subjects by introducing the experimental factor to different groups of individuals within the total group at different times. There are many ways of accomplishing this, and it can be done quite easily if the investigator will remember to maintain the conditions which must always be present in a successful experiment.

Difficulties to Be Avoided

As in all other kinds of research, there are numerous difficulties and pitfalls in testing a hypothesis through experimentation. Perhaps the most common fault is the natural tendency of the investigator to depend upon the results obtained in a single experiment. If this experiment has been conducted properly and its results are valid, the same results will be reached when the experiment is repeated. Repetition will reveal whether this is the case. If it is not, some error will usually be found in the procedures followed. At least one repetition of the experiment is always necessary as the absolute minimum if we are to place any reliance at all upon the conclusions reached, and frequently it is a good idea to repeat the experiment several times. Failure to repeat with identical results tends to invalidate any experimental study.

Poor instruments and faulty equipment used in an experiment may cause inaccuracies and thus completely ruin a study. Such things as minute impurities in chemicals or unsuspected individual factors among animal or human subjects may profoundly affect the results. But this kind of difficulty seems fairly obvious to any careful student. Every scholar soon discovers the importance of absolute accuracy and purity in his materials and equipment; if these conditions are impossible of attainment, he makes allowances and provisions to compensate for his experiment's shortcomings in such respects.

Less obvious, perhaps, is the difficulty of identifying *all* the variable factors which may affect the results of an experiment. In any study of human subjects, for instance, the isolation and control of every factor which might have any bearing on changes occurring during the experiment may prove well-nigh impossible. If an experiment conducted with a human subject requires a month's time, in the very nature of events the subject will have grown and changed in certain respects during that month and will no longer be exactly the same person he was when the experiment began. The changes may be minute, but they are nevertheless present in some degree. Besides, it is hardly practicable to keep human subjects under constant surveillance during the entire course of an experiment. A child upon whom some new method of teaching reading is being tried may, unknown to the investigator, get additional instruction in reading from his parents at home; and this factor can distort an assessment of that child's progress in terms of the experiment. Another person who is required to go without sleep for forty-eight hours in order to provide information about the physiological effects of sleeplessness may, unknown even to himself, indulge in occasional cat-naps and thus unconsciously change the conditions of the experiment and invalidate its results. Needless to say, that experiment is most nearly ideal in which every significant factor (or variable) can be identified clearly and controlled completely throughout the course of the study. Sometimes this ideal simply does not prove possible. The experimenter, it should be kept in mind, always tries to control the variables which may conceivably have some effect on the results of the particular experiment, leaving uncontrolled only those (there are often a great many of them) which would appear to exert little or no influence on the results.

The choice of subjects for study may lead the scholar astray in an experiment. When Thorndike and others observed the behavior of rats under controlled conditions to discover indirectly how people think and learn, they certainly discovered much new information about rats. Whether what they discovered applies to human beings as well as to rats may be a matter for argument. Perhaps it would have been better to study people directly. The degree to which the subjects are representative of a whole group or "population" is another important consideration. In an experiment conducted in a school to determine whether giving milk to children at recess time each day has a desirable effect upon their growth and general health, one would have to make certain that the children selected for participation actually represent the school population as a whole or their own particular age group. If well-fed children from substantial upper-class homes are selected, the milk at recess time probably would have no important effect and, in fact, might merely spoil their appetites for lunch. If, on the other hand, a group of undernourished children from poor homes are chosen for this experiment, the results may be quite favorable, but these results would not necessarily apply to *all* school children or even to the average child. Choice of proper subjects, then, can have a profound bearing upon the success of an experiment, and the whole question must be weighed very carefully before the investigator proceeds with his work.

Especially when dealing with human subjects, the bias of the experimenter may play an unfair part in the results. It has already been pointed out that a teacher trying out some new method or device can make it produce good results merely by enthusiasm, personal interest, or unconscious effort to make it succeed. Bias may also appear in the subjects of an experiment; they may be stimulated by their status as experimental subjects, or they may try harder if they know the purpose of the experiment. To avoid the dangers of bias, every reasonable precaution must be taken. For example, in testing a new medicine, it is customary to give some of the subjects false injections or sugar pills which they believe to contain the medicine. In one experiment involving a new drug intended to cure the common cold, some subjects who received only sugar pills recovered from their colds quite rapidly — in fact, faster than they might have recovered under normal circumstances. The power of suggestion can be very strong in human beings.

Experimentation with persons also suffers from the effects of unconscious signaling or practice. Frequently these dangers are extremely difficult to detect. Anything in the equipment or in the method which tends to tell the subject (or even hint to him) what hypothesis the investigator is testing, or what the significance of his responses is, may color his responses. Furthermore, after a certain amount of practice in responding to the experimental factor or in taking examinations to measure the results, the subject may learn special skills or develop unusual speed (the "practice effect" so often referred to in research) which may enable him to achieve higher scores or in other ways appear to change or gain something through the application of the experimental factor. Such possibilities must be watched for and guarded against with great care.

Finally, we should mention the dangers inherent in the use of an insufficient number of subjects in a group experiment. If the number of subjects is quite small, the results of the experiment will not be likely to apply to larger sections of the population. The actual number of subjects in any experiment will depend, of course, upon common sense and particular circumstances. There are principles of scientific sampling which will serve as useful guides to the investigator; these are described briefly in Chapter 12. For the moment a word of caution will suffice. No investigator should rely upon results obtained with an experiment performed upon too small a group. One of the classic jokes in scholarship concerns the graduate student who attempted to study the effect of certain diets on white rats. At the end of the study he summarized his discoveries by explaining that one-third of the rats had gained weight on the special diet, another third had died during the study, while the third rat had run away.

Summary

The experimental method of research is one in which controlled conditions are established for testing the hypothesis. Often this requires a laboratory and special equipment, but experiments can be devised and performed in which artificial aids of this kind need not be used.

John Stuart Mill analyzed the most important philosophical principles underlying experimental techniques and resolved them into five methods of procedure: (1) the method of agreement, (2) the method of difference, (3) the joint method, (4) the method of residues, and (5) the method of concomitant variations. Mill's five canons deal with experimental techniques in the abstract and are now used chiefly as guides in the planning of experiments.

Since for various reasons it is not always possible or convenient to study human beings in the laboratory, certain methods have been devised for observing them experimentally in groups outside the laboratory. These are classified as the one-group method, the parallel-group method, and the rotation-group method. Though experiments are also undertaken with individual subjects, the need for a large enough sample to yield valid results makes the group methods well adapted for experimental work with people.

Besides the usual dangers of error in research, there are special dangers relating particularly to experimental studies. Every experiment should be repeated several times before its results can be accepted as convincing. Instruments and materials used must be accurate and in good condition. Great care must be exercised in seeking to identify all the factors which might affect the results of the study and in keeping them under constant control. The selection of the animal or human subjects to be observed in an experiment has an important bearing on the results, and the number of subjects should be large enough to serve as a clearly adequate sampling. The bias of the experimenter or of the human subject may spoil an experiment, and unconscious signaling or the "practice effect" sometimes enters the picture.

Thus, while experiment is in many ways the most scientific method of research, it presents (like all other methods) numerous pitfalls. In the last analysis, it is chiefly the intelligence and the ingenuity of the investigator, coupled with an objective attitude and a large amount of care and patience, rather than elaborate equipment or materials, that will guarantee successful results in an experimental study.

12 THE SURVEY

When Caesar Augustus, emperor of Rome, as we are told in the New Testament, issued his epoch-making decree which required every person in the empire to report on a given day to the city or village of his birth and there enroll upon the tax lists, he was actually conducting one of the first major survey studies in the world's history. Facts disclosed by such a survey could obviously prove of considerable practical usefulness, for they not only told the emperor the precise number of people in his domain but also provided the means of assessing and collecting taxes from them.

As in this early census of Caesar Augustus, most surveys involve counting. The data secured in surveys characteristically are *quantitative*.

The survey typically constitutes a way of obtaining exact facts and figures about a current situation (such as, in a census, the number of persons inhabiting a country and their distribution throughout that country). This method (also known variously as the *descriptive study*, the *normative-survey*, or, in some instances, the *status study*) attempts usually to *describe a condition* or to *learn the status* of something and, whenever possible, to draw valid general conclusions from the facts discovered. It should be kept in mind that the survey need not be restricted to fact-finding but may often result in the formulation of important principles of knowledge and the solution of scholarly problems. Nevertheless, the facts established by a careful survey may sometimes be extremely useful in themselves. For example, a school district which makes a child-population study will thereafter have a reasonable basis for planning its future facilities and hiring new teachers. The survey sometimes has been called that kind of study in which the investigator obtains his data from other people.

A Modern Instance: The Cancer Survey. Surveys frequently establish or discover certain relationships between different phenomena which might otherwise not be known. As an instance of this kind of survey, we may turn our attention to a study which is being conducted by the American Cancer Society. Since the survey still is under way at the time of this writing, only the preliminary results can be discussed.

The survey of the American Cancer Society, as reported in the public press, aims to discover whether cigarette smoking is a cause of lung cancer. Medical men for several years have suspected the smoking of cigarettes as a possible cause of this disease, especially because a marked increase in lung cancer has been observed along with a similar increase in smoking. The amount of lung cancer in the United States is said to have increased since 1933 to three times the number of cases observable before that time. Many of the persons who have contracted it (chiefly men over 45) were soldiers in World War I and acquired the smoking habit in the trenches. To determine once and for all whether an actual relationship does exist between cigarette smoking and the incidence of this type of cancer, the American Cancer Society in 1952 instituted a survey of some 200,000 American males between the ages of 50 and 70. These men were questioned to learn how many of them smoked cigarettes and the approximate extent of their smoking habits. The death rate of this group was then to be studied over a period of years, and the causes of death to be determined, so that mortality rate and medical reasons for death could be learned for non-smokers, moderate smokers, and heavy smokers.

A preliminary report issued in 1954 showed that 187,766 had been interviewed up to that time, and of this total 4,854 had since died. When the death certificates were examined to determine the dates and causes of death, it was found that cigarette smokers in general have a mortality rate 63 per cent higher than do non-smokers (that is, they die much younger). There were among the group studied 82 per cent more deaths from heart disease among smokers and 106 per cent more from various types of cancer. Generally speaking, these figures suggest that the more one smokes (only cigarette smoking was considered in this investigation), the more likely one is to die of cancer or heart disease and the earlier one is likely to die. The results, of course, cannot yet be considered as final (or could not when this was written), and several other factors in the picture which have not been included in the Cancer Society study may be in need of careful scrutiny.

Beginnings of the Social Survey

The survey method did not really begin to prove its usefulness until it became a weapon for social and economic reform in the late eighteenth and early nineteenth centuries. As everybody knows, the eighteenth century was a period marked by great social upheaval (particularly in England and other manufacturing countries) as the result of changes brought about by the Industrial Revolution. To correct economic injustices and restore a measure of social balance, a great many reformers appeared on the scene. Their suggestions for change often carried a religious or emotional appeal.

A reformer of rather different kind was the English philanthropist, John Howard. Becoming high sheriff of Bedford in 1773, he started immediate efforts to improve conditions at the Bedford jail. His reforms were opposed on the ground that all prisons of the time operated under substantially the same conditions and that changes were not justified at Bedford unless precedents could be found elsewhere.

To ascertain whether a precedent might not exist for better prison management, Howard set out on a journey through much of England in the course of which he visited jails in many counties. At each one he carefully recorded the location, the number and names of the prisoners, the offenses for which they were being held in custody, their terms of imprisonment, the number of jailers provided, the illnesses of the prisoners, their complaints, and other relevant data. In effect, he made a thorough survey of prison conditions in England.

Armed with precise facts and figures, he presented his testimony before a committee of the British House of Commons, where he made a very forceful impression. The committee, accustomed by previous experiences to emotional testimony unsupported by detailed evidence, received Howard's exact knowledge with much respect. As the direct result of his testimony, two bills were enacted almost at once to reform some of the evils he had pointed out. One provided for the release of all prisoners against whom no "true bill" had been brought. (In the past such prisoners could secure their freedom only by payment of a special fee to the jailer. Now the government assumed responsibility for payment of this fee.) The other act required regular cleaning, whitewashing, and inspection of jails, together with medical care for sick prisoners and various other safeguards for their health and welfare. Thus the survey, while it solved no real problem but only offered accurate and convincingly described facts, proved effective as the basis for corrective action.

Howard next turned his attention to continental Europe. Through various pretexts (like volunteering to contribute alms to the prisoners) he gained admission to prisons in France, Germany, the Netherlands, and other countries. This gave him data for a *comparative survey*—that is, a comparison of the status of prisons on the continent with that of the English prisons. His widely influential book, *The State of Prisons* (to give it a somewhat abbreviated title), was published in 1777, and supplements appeared in 1780 and 1784.

The last five years of his life Howard spent in studying ways of preventing the spread of the plague. To observe how sick people were being treated in European hospitals, he deliberately subjected himself to contagion and thus learned at first hand the true conditions in the lazarettos or (as they were sometimes called) pesthouses of that day. Later he published his *Account of the Principal Lazarettos in Europe* (1789). On a journey to inspect the camp hospitals of Russia he contracted camp fever and died, thus literally giving his life to research.

Howard proved in his remarkable surveys the value of direct field observations, of specific schedules (or planned outlines to guide observation), and of the comparative analysis of conditions in different places.

A French Reformer. Frédéric Le Play, a prominent French mining engineer, professor of metallurgy, government official, and (briefly) politician, in addition to these activities developed an intense interest in studying the economic and social condition of working people.

He spent some twenty-five years making detailed observations of life among the poorer classes in most of the countries of Europe and some in Asia, and gave over the final decade or so of his life to an examination of economic and social conditions in France.

Le Play hoped that his investigations might reveal the basic elements which are necessary for proper family and community welfare. To achieve this, he lived with and carefully studied nearly three hundred individual families of the laboring class in France. His favorite procedure was to live anonymously with such families for a time, compensating them for board, room, and the time they devoted to him. He would study especially their sources of income and their habits of handling their finances. Because nobody had undertaken this kind of study before him, he found no ready-made scientific methodology which he could follow. He was forced, therefore, to invent his methods. The distrust of the families he studied had to be allayed. Many decisions had to be made regarding the items to be selected for observation and the ways in which they could best be observed. Seeking always to be completely impersonal and impartial, he inspected family budgets, discussed with members of the family their financial and social activities, and carefully scrutinized the daily account books kept by housewives. After some two decades of study, he published a partial report of his observations in 1885.

The following year Le Play founded an international organization for the study of social economy and thus encouraged participation by others in this area of research. By introducing the technique of observing representative families directly and in detail, he opened an entirely new approach to sociological problems. His chief contributions to scholarly method lie in his use of exhaustively detailed outlines to guide his observations, his development of a technique for personal interviews, his questionnaires, and his laborious checking of account books and other such records as a means of verifying his data. He also made considerable use of the case study, or objective description of the history and status of an individual or group.

While the studies of Le Play did not actually solve any problem, they provided much important information about selected aspects of family life. Le Play thought, however, that he detected a strong relationship between the economic welfare of the family and its emotional and social success. Modern researchers in sociology still make use of his methods both in fact-finding and in formulating hypotheses.

Later Sociological Studies

One of the most prominent successors of Le Play in sociological research was Charles Booth, owner and manager of a steamship company in England. Booth originated the comprehensive study of community life when he investigated conditions in the notorious East Side of London.

Previous descriptions of the squalid life in what we should now call the slums had been generally discredited as too dramatic and impressionistic. Booth went about his investigation coldly and dispassionately. His object was to produce a true picture of living conditions among the very poor, and from this picture to show the necessity for economic aid to distressed people. To obtain all the essential data he hired and meticulously trained a staff of young assistants. By renting a room in a district being studied, watching the activities of its inhabitants at all hours of the day and night, acting and even dressing like those whom he desired to observe, and searching out information through long interviews (often lasting eighteen to twenty hours in all) and written records, he was able to bring together an amazing collection of descriptive material.

His reports on the survey, published at intervals between 1889 and 1903, even had elaborately drawn maps indicating the degrees of poverty which he found in the different streets of the area studied. He also tried by statistical tabulations to show "the numerical relation which poverty, misery, and depravity bear to regular earnings and comparative comfort."

Late in life he became concerned about the plight of the aged poor and strongly advocated governmental old-age pensions, as well as other measures to reform the British Poor Law. His greatest achievement, however, was his extreme thoroughness in studying various aspects of a community's life.

B. S. Rowntree aimed at even greater precision than Booth had obtained when he compared the status of laborers in a small town with that of laborers in a large city. His procedure entailed the careful study of as many facts as possible relating to a proportion of the population selected at random. This method of random sampling, he believed, gave him an accurate cross-section of the group as a whole. He repeated the same survey about a generation later, finding that living standards for both populations had improved, according to his calculations, about 30 per cent.

The beginning of the twentieth century marked a rapid increase in the use of survey techniques, especially for economic and sociological studies. The Experimental Bureau of Municipal Research was organized in New York in 1896, the Russell Sage Foundation for social improvement was established in 1907, and in 1909 the first city-wide survey in the United States was conducted in Pittsburgh by Paul Kellogg. Other city surveys followed (such as that in Springfield, Illinois, in 1914), and the movement reached its peak around 1928, when almost 3,000 general or partial surveys of our cities had been completed. Regional surveys also were sponsored by such organizations as the New York Regional Planning Commission. Surveys relating to crime and law enforcement followed as well — for example, the Missouri Crime Survey (1926), conducted by a group of Missouri lawyers, and the work of the Wickersham Commission on Law Observance and Enforcement (1929), sponsored by the federal government.

Surveys in Education

The period between World War I and World War II saw a tremendous development in the use of educational surveys. The growing number of graduate students working in education as a field of study in our universities naturally stimulated educational research, and the survey method seems to have been the one which most of these young people preferred or were encouraged to use. Hundreds of doctoral studies were made relating to school administration and organization, and there were many school district surveys. The result of these investigations was not, of course, to solve educational problems but rather to provide previously lacking *descriptions* of our American school system, to pool many divergent ideas, techniques, and bits of information, and thus indirectly to throw light upon existing conditions that needed change and improvement.

Educational research really began in the eighteen-nineties with the pioneering work of J. M. Rice, editor of *Forum* magazine, who believed that children were being forced to spend more time than was necessary upon certain traditional subjects, and who stumped for the introduction of more science and social studies into the curriculum. Between 1895 and 1910 such scholars as Thorndike, Strayer, and Ayres were making detailed surveys of children's progress in the grade schools.

Continuing surveys, as well as educational research in general, have brought about many fundamental changes in our schools. Teaching methods have been improved, school buildings have been redesigned, and school districts (especially in rural areas) have been reorganized into larger units — all as the result of research. Methods of teaching reading skills and of writing children's books have been vastly revised, for instance, because educational scholars took the trouble to count and record the words actually understood and used by children at the various age levels. The growth pattern of children has been scientifically observed and minutely described in studies made by Gesell and his associates at Yale University and by others. These and many similar examples prove the practical usefulness of the survey study.

Public Opinion Surveys

Within the past few years a very important use for the survey has been discovered in public opinion polls. These are widely employed both as a means of determining public opinion on national and international issues of the day and as a means of conducting market research.

Business firms have learned that profits can be increased and mistakes avoided in the marketing of their products if the reaction of the potential purchaser and his need for the product can be determined in advance. Before a new detergent washing powder was introduced on the market recently, several months were spent in demonstrating its effectiveness in a campaign of door-to-door interviews with housewives. This research revealed, surprisingly enough, that housewives liked the new powder when it was colored blue, but the same powder colored red, green, or purple produced a negative response. Business firms also seek to analyze the results of their advertising programs through this kind of research.

Market surveys, then, are public opinion polls conducted usually to test the public's reaction to a new product (or one which is being developed), to discover the relative effectiveness of different ways of packaging a product, to identify consumer preferences for various brands or variations in form of similar products, and to analyze the actual or potential market for a given piece of merchandise. This last often includes prediction of the probable sales, determination of the best selling price, analysis of a company's sales policies, measurement of the effectiveness of its advertising, and the like. Large manufacturing companies today maintain bureaus of research that gather data relating to such matters as these, and there exist a considerable number of advertising and consulting firms which make a business of reporting financial and marketing trends, making many types of special tests and surveys, and furnishing advice on marketing problems.

Sampling Procedures

In public opinion surveys, as in other types of surveys as well, the investigator may find it impossible or unfeasible to make direct contact with all the individual sources of his data — that is, to question every single one in the group whose reaction he is attempting to measure. The market researcher investigating the response of housewives to a new product cannot, without spending an excessive amount of time and money, visit every housewife in the whole country. The canvasser seeking to learn how people are planning to cast their votes in the next election cannot interview each voter. It is necessary, therefore, to select with some care those representatives of the total group (or population) from whom the desired information will be obtained.

A sample may be described simply as a part of the larger number, and the process of sampling in a survey means gathering the information from sources which tend to form a cross-section (or representative sampling) of the entire group from which, if time and expense permitted, it would be desirable to obtain data. Probably the easiest method of sampling is to take a list of all the persons who might supply the required information and then select from it every tenth name or every twentieth name or whatever proportion of the total is desired, this choice depending somewhat on the number of names on the list. Such a process is known as random sampling.

Before the Presidential election of 1936, the *Literary Digest* magazine conducted a poll to determine whether Alfred M. Landon or Franklin D. Roosevelt would be elected President. The method used was random sampling. Ballots for a straw vote were mailed several weeks before the election to persons whose names had been picked at random from telephone directories in all parts of the country. When the returns were tabulated, the *Literary Digest* confidently predicted Landon's election by a substantial majority. But the official election was won by Roosevelt. The amount of error in this poll totaled nearly 22 per cent, and it was apparently caused by the unrepresentative character of the sample. Various explanations may be offered as to why the sample was unrepresentative, but the important fact here is that it failed to give a true picture of public opinion as a whole. At the same time *Fortune* magazine conducted a poll in which the sampling was made by other methods, and its error amounted only to about one per cent.

The sample, then, should be as nearly representative of the whole group as possible. It should also be large enough to have real reliability. If we ask ten architects which magazines they read regularly in an effort to learn which magazines are favored by architects in general, we may secure a representative sampling of the different kinds of architect among our sampling of ten, but clearly the number of individuals questioned, in relation to the whole, is too small for us to place any reliance upon the results.

Size and Nature of the Sampling. In general, the larger the sample (in proportion to the complete population which is to be observed), the higher its degree of reliability. This will depend somewhat, however, on the size of the entire group from which data are desired. If the group, or population, does not number more than a few hundred, a sampling of at least 50 per cent might prove necessary for sufficient reliability. If, on the other hand, it numbers well in the thousands, a sampling of as low as 10 per cent or even less may be satisfactory. These estimates, of course, must be regarded as rule-ofthumb figures. There are statistical means of deciding upon the proper size of the sampling which ought to be used in any given survey. The essential thing for the scholar to recognize is that both size and representativeness of the sampling have an important bearing on the results he obtains.

The simplest procedure in sampling ordinarily is one which gives an equal chance or probability for every individual in the entire group to be selected as part of the sample. This may be accomplished by drawing up a list of all names in the group and then selecting every fifth or tenth or whatever interval yields the number of names necessary to achieve reliability. Or the names may be written on slips of paper and pulled out of a hat. Such procedures are called unrestricted random sampling. All members of the group are equally likely to be selected, but the investigator does not know in advance which ones they will be; he knows only how many he wishes to select. If a scholar were seeking information from the approximately 1,800 colleges and universities in the United States but came to the decision that a sampling of only 500 of them would prove sufficient for his purposes, he might select this number by writing each of the 1,800 names on a card, shuffling the cards, and then taking 500 cards from the deck at random.

To make certain that the sampling is truly representative, on the other hand, the scholar mentioned above might justifiably argue that the sample must contain at least one institution of higher learning from every state in the union and that it should include also the correct proportional number of universities, liberal arts colleges, technical schools, junior colleges, and so forth. For this reason he might find it advantageous to make a selected or judged sampling rather than one which is arrived at purely through a chance distribution.

Before beginning to select his sample, an investigator must have absolutely clear in his own mind the exact nature of the population he wishes to observe or measure. Just what population the scholar has in mind will naturally depend on the problem he has chosen to study. If, for example, he should undertake to learn whether training in methods of research has proved beneficial to teachers in American public high schools, his population would logically be all those high school teachers in the United States who have received this kind of training. But since making contact by interviews or questionnaires with all individuals in this fairly large population would no doubt be an impossibility for him, and since what he might find to be true about an adequate cross-section of this group could be assumed to hold true for the entire group, his best procedure would be to select a representative and reliable sample for direct study.

The ideal sample is an exact replica of the larger group of which it forms a part. When working with studies that involve human beings, however, it seems never entirely possible to find samples which can be called exact replicas of the population to be observed. People vary too much to permit achievement of this ideal sample. It is considered sufficient, therefore, if the sample can be ascertained to possess in the identical degree as the total group that special trait or characteristic which is under consideration in the study. Thus a sample of the high school teachers mentioned in the previous paragraph would consist of teachers who had received some instruction in methods of research, but these same teachers might vary considerably with respect to other characteristics.

The scholar must watch, to be sure, for secondary traits which might affect the results of the study. With regard to such a matter as old-age pensions, the attitude of young people may be rather different from that of older people, or the attitude of indigent persons from that of persons with savings accounts and insurance policies. To make sure that the opinions and attitudes measured are actually those of the entire population or group studied, it would be essential for the sample to contain the correct proportion of young people, older people, indigent persons, and financially secure persons. This process of dividing a population into constituent parts for the purpose of making the sample truly representative is partly a matter of the investigator's good judgment and is often called *stratification*. The sample, then, would be a stratified sample; and when the sample is made up of random samplings from each part or stratum, the method may be termed stratified-random sampling. Factors often considered in making up a sample for a public opinion poll include such things as age, location of residence(in a wealthy or poor section, in a city or on a farm, etc.), color, sex, religion, national origin, education, present citizenship, occupation, socio-economic status, and political affiliation. In many cases the stratified-random type of sample will prove more nearly representative than that selected by the purely random method.

In sampling, the representativeness of the sample must be determined first, then its optimum size. If a sample is unrepresentative, merely increasing the size of it will not necessarily make it a better sample. While we have previously remarked that, in general, the larger the sample is, the more accurate it is likely to be, this principle holds true only if in becoming larger the sample also becomes more nearly representative. The *Literary Digest* poll did not become representative simply because it was large. We may say, however, that the more homogeneous a group is, the smaller will be the sample required.

Statistical calculations can give us an idea of the degree of confidence which can be placed in the accuracy of a sample of a given size and can suggest the degree of sampling error which may be present in a particular case. By and large, however, the accuracy of any sample can only be estimated. The scholar must simply take steps to guarantee in every reasonable way that the sample he selects will be both representative and reliable.

The Interview

In a survey one of the most common and most effective means of obtaining the necessary data is the personal interview. To an inexperienced person the interview usually seems a rather simple thing. Actually it is far from that. The technique of interviewing amounts to something much more than merely approaching a number of people and asking a few casual questions. The interview for a scholarly study cannot be conducted in the indiscriminate manner of the sidewalk interviews that we hear on the radio.

The first important step in an effective interview is to seek the confidence and cooperation of the respondent. This often requires making a definite appointment or at least winning permission to call upon him. The second step is to prepare in advance a detailed outline or plan of the complete interview. This ought to include a list of specific and carefully worded questions to be asked. Such questions must always be asked of each respondent in exactly the same way, and reading them from a written list may help the interviewer to fulfill this requirement of the interviewing technique.

Having prepared his plan and made mutually agreeable arrangements for a meeting, the interviewer should always try to be alone with the respondent throughout the interview, since the presence of other persons may influence or interfere with the responses and may make it difficult to keep the respondent's full attention. At the beginning of an interview, the purpose and scope of the study should be fully explained, as well as the type and number of persons who are being approached for information.

Every question must be clearly stated and its full import understood by the respondent. This may require a fairly detailed explanation of what the question means, and the interviewer should be willing to repeat or explain until he feels quite certain that the respondent understands what he is being asked. Clear diction and proper enunciation are, of course, essential here. Above all, the interviewer must exercise patience. If the respondent has difficulty in comprehending a question, it may have to be rephrased. If he hesitates to give personal or confidential information, an effort must be made to reassure him and thus to encourage an answer. The interviewer must be careful at all times to avoid injecting his own bias or viewpoint into the phrasing of a question or even into the intonation of his voice. The good interviewer never creates the impression that he expects a particular answer or that it matters to him what answer is given. He also refrains from asking questions that might embarrass the respondent. (For the Kinsey survey on sex matters this problem was met by providing an atmosphere of great objectivity and by carefully describing the nature and purpose of the study before any questions were presented.) He does not ask the kind of question that implies an accusation ("Why do you attend church so irregularly?") or that in any way puts the respondent on the defensive.

The interviewer succeeds best when he has the ability to meet people easily and to win their confidence, when he demonstrates complete honesty and dependability, and when he has trained himself to be entirely objective. A pleasant and efficient approach to the respondent will go farther than one which is either timid and overly solemn or blatant and overpowering.

Finally, the interviewer should learn to record accurately and *at the time of the response* the answers given by the respondent. Preferably these answers ought to be recorded in the respondent's very words. Should this not be possible, at least the record should be so definite and unequivocal that no doubts about what it means will occur later. If the interviewer cannot read his notes intelligently at the end of the interview and recall afterward exactly what each response was, he has wasted his time and that of his respondents as well.

One other suggestion may be added. When an interviewer begins his work, he should learn in advance everything he can about the persons he is to interview. If they are housewives, he will not gain their confidence unless he understands the rudiments of household economy. If they are Spanish-speaking families, he ought to know something of their language, their customs, and their ways of making a living. The less like a total stranger the interviewer appears to the respondent, the more easily will he win cooperation in the study.

The Questionnaire

The written questionnaire may be regarded as a substitute for the personal interview. Because of the relative ease and speed with which it can be distributed by mail over a large geographical area, the questionnaire has definite advantages in survey research. It saves both time and expense. To visit all 1,800 colleges and universities in the United States for information would require months of time and a considerable expenditure of money for travel, but a mailed questionnaire will reach them all within a few days and at relatively little cost. The disadvantages of the questionnaire lie partly in the uncertainty of obtaining replies and partly in the difficulty of extracting personal and confidential information from the respondents.

A questionnaire consists typically of a series of written questions similar to those which an interviewer might ask, but perhaps even more carefully formulated (because the interviewer will not be on hand to explain what each question means). This questionnaire (usually printed or typewritten) is mailed by the investigator to the persons who comprise his chosen sample. Each questionnaire must be accompanied by a brief letter of transmittal and explanation, requesting the respondent's aid in the study and outlining the purpose and scope of the research. There should also be enclosed a self-addressed, stamped return envelope. The scholar should remember that he is asking the respondent to do him a favor by supplying the information desired, and his manner of making the request should always be courteous and sincere as well as persuasive. Humor is out of place in the covering letter sent with a research questionnaire.

In general, the effective questionnaire will follow these rules:

1. It should be as brief as possible.

2. The information asked for must be otherwise inaccessible to the investigator. (Else why ask someone to take up his time in supplying it?)

3. The subject inquired about must not be a trivial one but must have importance enough to justify the time and effort involved.

4. The questions ought to be aimed at obtaining factual data, rather than opinions, impressions, or estimates.

5. The wording of every item ought to be understandable and familiar, in order to insure the respondent's comprehension of what is being asked.

6. For the same reason, the items should be arranged in a neat and logical order.

7. The questionnaire should be conveniently planned and set up to take a minimum of the respondent's time.

8. Clear instructions must be included as to the way the answers are to be indicated.

All these points are important in the design of a good questionnaire, but special emphasis needs to be placed on the use of clear, simple, and understandable terms. Words which normally have more than one meaning should be defined. Lack of understanding of the terms obviously leads to errors, often very serious ones, in the results of the study. One should seldom use technical words or the special vocabulary of some vocation, even when the persons receiving the questionnaire might reasonably be expected to know these terms. Usually the meaning of any question can be stated very simply.

Questionnaires can be classified under either of two general cate gories: the open form and the closed form. In the open form, the questions are asked in such a way that the respondent replies in his own words. In setting up this form of questionnaire, the investigator leaves blank spaces or empty lines on which the answers are to be written. The closed form, on the other hand, suggests the possible answers for each question, and the respondent replies merely by checking or circling or underlining the answer with which he agrees. Many closed questionnaires call for only a "yes" or a "no" answer. In such a case, however, one should always provide a third possible answer (such as "uncertain," "undecided," or "?"). Because of the relative ease of answering the items in a closed questionnaire (and also the greater ease of tabulating the results), the preference is for this form wherever possible. A variation of the closed form is the pictorial questionnaire, in which possible answers are indicated by simple sketches. The pictorial questionnaire is helpful in stimulating interest in the questions and in making the questions clearer for people who are not very good readers. The use of pictures is, of course, to be recommended only if the investigator finds that it will serve a special purpose and, even then, only if he possesses artistic ability or can obtain the assistance of a clever artist.

Sources of Error in Questionnaires. As an instrument for acquiring correct information, the questionnaire is far more delicate than the inexperienced scholar might suspect. The chief among many sources of error are summarized below:

1. The questioner's bias or desire for answers of a certain type can readily color the questions asked. This may be because the scholar has a strong wish to prove his hypothesis true — a most unhealthy attitude in research. The failure of objectivity invalidates many questionnaires that are currently being used.

2. The bias of the auspices or sponsorship will almost inevitably affect the results. When a group openly committed to a known point of view or a company interested in the sale of a particular product conducts a questionnaire survey to measure the popularity of that point of view or of that product in comparison with competing products, the results can rarely be accepted as completely unbiased. Thus a questionnaire sponsored by an organization (hypothetical)

called the Society for World Citizenship will receive answers (if the study is typical of others of its kind) which are overwhelmingly in favor of "world citizenship," that is, with the known point of view of the group. Respondents, whether out of courtesy or timidity, tend as a rule to answer in the way they think they are expected to answer. Moreover, those who disagree with or are indifferent to the sponsoring group's views are less likely to reply at all, and thus the answers tend to be weighted on the side of those who do agree.

With these words of caution in mind, the scholar should, however, · secure an official sponsor for any questionnaire, since questions asked by an unidentified and lone investigator frequently will be ignored. The best sponsor is a scholarly organization, a college or university, or some other reputable group whose disinterestedness is unquestioned.

3. Imperfections of design may cause inaccuracies in the replies. Haphazard arrangement of items, lack of instructions on how to indicate answers, and failure to explain the purpose and scope of the study — these and many similar imperfections can confuse the respondent and make his replies false or meaningless.

4. An unrepresentative sample, as already noted, can destroy the value of any survey study. But with a questionnaire, the problem is heightened further by the probability that not all those who receive the questionnaire will reply to it. Thus, while the sample selected may be accurately representative, it can become grossly unrepresentative if replies are sent back by only a fraction of those from whom they are expected. It is very important, therefore, that every reasonable effort be exerted to encourage responses. A follow-up letter to request the completion and return of unreturned questionnaires frequently helps to increase the number of responses received. Unless the respondents have been promised absolute anonymity, it is usually wise to keep a record of the replies as they come in, so that (after a lapse of three or four weeks, at the very least) those who have not replied may be reached by a follow-up letter or by direct personal contact. The follow-up request should always be direct and straightforward and should stress both the need for the data and the significance of the study. It should never be an appeal for sympathy, nor should it be angry or humorous.

5. Even when factual information is requested, the various re-

spondents will have different ways of interpreting and even of looking at the same events. Thus descriptions of rather simple incidents may vary greatly. If information is desired regarding a labor dispute, very likely the representatives of management and the workers themselves will disagree markedly over the actual facts.

6. Often the same question answered again by the same person after the lapse of even a short period of time will be answered in a slightly different way. These individual variations apparently cannot be avoided, and they demonstrate the common tendency of human beings toward inaccuracy and changing beliefs in spite of the most conscientious effort at accuracy and consistency.

7. A whole host of additional sources of error might be mentioned. Pure carelessness, accidents of circumstance(the way the respondent happens to feel on the day he reads the questionnaire, for instance), ambiguous questions ("Do you favor world citizenship?") which may be understood differently by different people, or even by the same people at different times — these are a few, and the list could be greatly extended. Not the least of the investigator's worries is the possibility that the respondent may answer unthinkingly and in a perfunctory manner, merely to finish the questionnaire and be done with it.

Reactions Against Questionnaires. Innumerable questionnaires appear to be cramming the mail bags these days. The United States has been called "a nation of questionnaires." Many are sent for purposes of research, but others are intended primarily for advertising or propaganda. A businessman who receives a questionnaire asking about his preferences in magazines, automobiles, or imported liquors may learn to his discomfiture that a salesman will arrive later to sell him the product for which he has expressed a preference. Or a questionnaire may precede a solicitation for funds. At the very least, answering a questionnaire takes up a good deal of time that often might be spent more profitably. Furthermore, a vast number of questionnaires have been carelessly put together or in other ways represent a waste of time and effort. Finally, people may consider the questionnaire as an unwarranted attempt to meddle in their affairs. Such experiences and reactions have to be taken into account by the scholar.

Some organizations deliberately protect themselves against unwelcome questionnaires by refusing to accept them at all or by answering only those which can meet minimum standards of quality. The scholar who keeps these minimum standards in mind while preparing his questionnaire will have a much better chance of receiving replies. The following check-list will give an idea of the criteria by which the questionnaire may be judged:

1. Is it sponsored by a reputable organization or institution?
2. Is the purpose of the study fully and clearly stated?
3. Does it concern a topic of sufficient importance to justify it?
4. Is it carefully and logically organized?
5. Are the questions clearly and briefly worded?
6. Can the questions be answered briefly?
7. Is the information asked for available elsewhere? (If so, the investigator should have used the published or otherwise accessible sources.)
8. Is the questionnaire in good mechanical form — that is, printed or typewritten and easy to read?
9. Are the demands upon the respondent reasonable ones? (He should not be asked to spend hours of time and effort in running down records.)
10. Is a summary of the results promised?

If the questionnaire falls below the standards indicated in this check-list, one should not be surprised if it goes unanswered.

The respondent should always be given the opportunity of seeing a summary of the study's results if he is interested in it. He may, of course, be directed to the publication in which the results will appear, or he may be promised a summary when the study is finished. When a summary has been promised, it must be sent without fail. Too many young scholars forget this little courtesy. It is also a helpful and courteous gesture, in sending out the questionnaire, to provide two copies, one to be retained in the respondent's files.

Validating the Questionnaire. How can one be certain that his questionnaire is a reasonably satisfactory one? If it proves ineffective in bringing back accurate and reliable data, the time and money spent on it have been wasted.

First of all, the investigator should examine his questionnaire in its preliminary form with all the above suggestions in mind. If, in his opinion, it successfully meets this test, the next step is to try it in personal interviews with a few of the persons who have been chosen to receive it. This can usually be done quite easily. The trial of a questionnaire in this manner will often reveal items which are misunderstood and other faults in the design also.

After discovering how typical respondents understand and react to the various items in his questionnaire, the scholar should now consider the difficulties he may meet in tabulating and interpreting the responses. Ease of tabulation is a desirable attribute in an instrument of this kind, particularly when one is dealing with replies numbering in the hundreds or thousands. A little experience plus an inspection of successful questionnaires used by others will do more than anything else to uncover the pitfalls which must be avoided.

In the final analysis, the validity of a questionnaire depends largely upon judgment. Nevertheless, the conscientious investigator will take every possible precaution to develop as objective an instrument as possible for gathering reliable data.

Collecting information through the use of questionnaires or interviews is far less difficult than interpreting and summarizing what the information means. This fact points up the basic weakness of the survey method. Although the survey, properly conducted, provides an efficient means of learning details about a current situation or problem, the scholar still must arrive, through straight thinking, at generalizations and principles which follow from the facts established. It is not really facts that solve problems, but the conclusions scholars draw from these facts through reflective thought.

Fact-Finding vs. Generalizing

The fact-finding survey, to be sure, has its uses. As we have previously said, it accurately describes a given situation and may bring attention to conditions and needs that might otherwise go unnoticed. But of much greater significance for scholarship is the survey that can identify a relationship of cause and effect between two phenomena or that can produce valid general principles upon which to base future action.

Are comic strips an effective means of transmitting ideas from business and industrial management to adult workers? Many executives have wondered whether such a lowly device as the comic strip might not be offensive to workers as puerile and insulting to their intelligence. But a survey made by the Department of Communications in Education at New York University has shown that comic strips rate very high with readers at practically every age level. Apparently they are being read by four out of five adults (84 per cent of the men and 79 per cent of the women). They are enjoyed not only by those with little schooling but even by those who have a college background, and almost as many professional workers read them as do unskilled laborers. From such discoveries as these, it would seem reasonable to conclude that properly prepared comic strips will find acceptance among most workers and need not be rejected as a vehicle for the transmission of ideas.

Does the presence of tonsils help in resisting poliomyelitis? The School of Public Health at the University of Minnesota made a survey of some 2,500 victims of this disease and learned that patients who still had their tonsils fared markedly better than those who had tonsilectomies. Only one out of every 12 persons in the group who retained their tonsils contracted the bulbar form of polio. Among those whose tonsils had been removed, one out of every three suffered from this dreaded form of the disease, which frequently results in death. The survey, spreading afield into Egypt, Chile, and Japan, where few tonsilectomies are performed on children, ascertained that bulbar polio is extremely rare in those nations. If the facts are correctly interpreted by those making the study, they seem to indicate that the presence of tonsils helps in resisting at least the bulbar form of poliomyelitis.

The survey, then, should not be mistakenly thought of as merely a fact-finding device. It may — and often does — result in important hypotheses or conclusions that solve serious current problems.

The survey is useful also in providing information for comparison studies and in identifying trends. A survey completed fifteen or twenty years ago may be repeated today, and something will be learned about changes which have taken place in the meantime. If these changes can be shown to occur at a definite rate of speed and in a certain direction, a trend can be identified and future conditions predicted. The Bureau of the Census predicts the future population of different areas by comparing survey figures of the past and present. Thus movements and changes of many kinds can be detected while they are taking place. In a sense, this really entails combining the survey with documentary research; studies of the past become documents which contain criteria to be used in learning in what respects the present and the past may be different. The scholar soon finds, of course, that any classification of research methods into various types is an artificial and arbitrary one and that there need be no hesitancy about using the different methods in combination. The object of all research, after all, is to discover truth by the best means possible.

Summary

The survey, or descriptive study, is a process for learning pertinent and precise information about an existing situation. In the hands of the scholar, it has been particularly useful as a tool in sociological and educational studies.

Since in dealing with large groups, or "populations," an enumerative study of each single member is rarely feasible or even necessary, the typical survey entails the selection of a sample, or cross-section of the whole, for purposes of direct, minute observation. This sample should be clearly representative of the population to be studied; ideally it is an exact replica of the larger group of which it forms a part. At the same time, the sample must be large enough, in terms of the whole group and of the problem being studied, to yield reliable results.

The principal devices for gathering data from other people through the survey method are the interview and the questionnaire. Each of these must be carefully planned, for there are many pitfalls in their use. Besides the errors stemming from faulty sampling, there are seeds of possible error in the construction of the questionnaire itself. The bias of the investigator, the bias of the sponsor, the use of ambiguous language, the failure to explain the full purpose and scope of the study, and other failures in objectivity and in communication may distort the results.

In general, it is easier to obtain data through the survey method

than to draw valid conclusions from the facts discovered. But the
survey need not be purely a fact-finding device. It can also provide
a means of testing and establishing principles, of comparing the past
with the present, of identifying trends, and thus of presenting a
sound basis for action.

13 THE LANGUAGE

OF STATISTICS

Anyone interested in understanding or conducting research must learn something about the language of statistics. In one sense, we may say that statistics provides a way of describing the data which have been gathered in a study. For instance, a person engaged in medical research might wish to measure the weight and height of all boys in the United States at the age of 11. After weighing and measuring thousands of 11-year-old boys, he is able to tell us, by the use of statistical methods and language, the average weight and height of American boys of this age. He can also tell us the extent to which some of the boys *deviate* from this average. In other words, he can use the descriptive terms of statistics to tell us what the sample which he has gathered looks like with regard to those characteristics which he has measured.

Statistics, as everybody knows, involves mathematics. Rightly considered, mathematics constitutes a language in the same way that English or French or Latin does. We have a group of symbols whose meaning is agreed upon, and the symbols are organized into a usable system or structure for the purpose of communicating information from one person to another. It has been said that Einstein's theory of relativity cannot be understood or described in words and that familiarity with mathematical symbols and concepts is necessary to grasp it. Thus we can justly speak of statistics as a descriptive language.

Another purpose in the use of statistics is to determine how accurate the data and conclusions of a study appear to be. One of the commonest rules of experience declares that errors occur in almost every type of measurement. In research it may be extremely important to know just how large an error has occurred. How can one discover this? Through the use of statistics. When astronomers talk of the distance between the earth and the sun, they state it as 93,005,-000 miles, plus or minus 9,000 miles. This is an example of the calculation of *probable error*. If we could actually travel from the earth to the sun and measure the distance as we go along, the substitution of careful physical measurements for the calculations now used might result in a much smaller margin of error, though some degree of error no doubt would still occur. The statistician would be able to tell us the probable limits of this error by comparing all the physical measurements made of this distance, and then applying statistical formulas.

Statistical methods applied to the data of research, then, help the investigator chiefly to (1) analyze and more accurately describe the data and (2) calculate the relative accuracy of the measurements used. It need hardly be added that the materials to which statistical methods can be applied effectively are usually those of a quantitative nature. For this reason a knowledge of statistics would prove particularly useful in a survey, but the method is important for other types of study as well.

The Theory of Probability

Statistical methods and formulas in general are based upon a fundamental theory. This theory, in turn, hinges upon observation of what we often speak of as the "law of chance." According to this law of chance, if a person should toss a coin enough times, it would come down "heads" half the time and "tails" the other half of the time. We cannot, of course, ascertain in advance whether it will be "heads" or "tails" on any one particular toss, but we can predict with reasonable accuracy the outcome of a sufficiently large number of tosses. Experience and experiment have told us what we can expect in such a situation. Whenever a coin is tossed, provided there is no false manipulation and the law of chance operates freely, we can feel sure that the chances of "heads" or "tails" are exactly even, or fifty-fifty. To say this in another way, the probability of "heads" is one out of two tries, or ½.

Similarly, in a true-false examination which has 100 items, the person whose answers represent pure guesswork has theoretically an even chance of giving just as many right answers as wrong answers. To reduce this statistical advantage and keep the student from achieving a higher score than he deserves by guessing at many answers, the teacher may charge double for wrong answers when scoring the test (Score = Rights minus Wrongs).

In research the theory of probability has numerous and interesting uses. Rhine and his associates at Duke University, for instance, base their belief in extra-sensory perception largely upon the fact that, in some of their experiments, the results do not follow probability (that is, they are not what one would expect if chance alone were involved) and thus cannot be explained as mere chance results.

One of the first minds to explore the theory of probability in any detail was Blaise Pascal. A great mathematician, Pascal reportedly became interested in the subject while discussing gambling odds with a French nobleman, the Chevalier de Méré. The latter enjoyed some notoriety as a gambler. One day he proposed a theoretical problem to Pascal. Suppose (he said) there are two men playing dice. Each wagers a certain amount of money, the victor to be the one who can win three out of five throws. Each man throws the dice twice, and one of the gamblers wins both of these first two throws. At this point the game is interrupted and cannot be finished. Now the question is: How shall the stakes be divided? If the game had been completed, one or the other of the two men would have won all the stakes, but instead a fair division must be decided upon. Obviously the gambler who had already won two throws out of five would have had the better chance of winning the game finally, but just what were his chances, calculated mathematically?

To any mathematician, the solution offers no serious difficulty. Pascal, however, carried the matter much further by studying the nature of probability as a whole. He noted that, except for minor comments on the subject by such men as Aristotle and Kepler and

Galileo, the field remained practically unexplored. For some time he investigated the question of mathematical probability in his correspondence with another great mathematician of his day, Pierre de Fermat, who added some thoughts of his own to the investigation. Pascal recorded many of his conclusions regarding the calculation of probability in his posthumously published *Treatise on the Arithmetical Triangle* (1665). Later scholars pushed the studies further and found many ways of applying the principles he had developed.

Applications of the Theory of Probability

The "laws of chance" or probability, now formalized in the science of statistics, have become extremely important in many phases of modern life. As one example, they provide the foundation for the insurance business as we know it. By analyzing the mortality records to discover the various ages at which people die, the insurance actuarian calculates the relative chances of death at the different age levels and thus determines what insurance premiums must be charged. In a similar way other types of risk may be calculated very accurately.

In directing the firing of artillery, the army's battery commander uses the mathematics of statistics to compute the correct settings of the guns and the number of times they must be fired before he can be certain of hitting the target.

The schoolteacher, in grading test papers, makes use of statistics to assist him in classifying the different scores made by the students. He knows that, according to probability, the "average" student will achieve approximately a middle score and that there will be in the usual school class many more of these "average" scores than there are higher and lower ones. Consequently he will mark those papers falling into the most common (average or middle) group with a grade of C (or some other grade that means "average"), those which are noticeably higher with grades of B or A, and those which are distinctly lower with grades of D or F. He constantly keeps in mind something known in statistics as "the normal curve." This concept of a normal curve of distribution derives from the theory that, when a large quantity of examples of any phenomenon (such as the scores in tests) are considered, they will be seen to group themselves around a certain average or mean and also to distribute themselves more or less evenly in both directions from this central point.

Statistical calculations are more common in everyday life than most of us would suspect, and many of the terms are familiar to everyone. We frequently hear and use such expressions as "in all probability," "on the average," "relatively constant," "very exceptional," and numerous others of a similar nature — all derived from statistical descriptions. In addition, we are now thoroughly accustomed to the everyday uses of statistical statements in relation to such things as automobile accidents, birth and death records, inches of rainfall, estimates of crop yields, miles flown by airplanes, unemployment figures, cost-of-living indexes, and so on. We are less familiar, perhaps, with the fact that such a theory as Darwin's concerning the process of biological evolution depends for its reasonableness upon the application of statistical principles. (This would be true generally of any study in which the relationships of large masses of data are being determined.) Underlying all statistical calculations is one indispensable idea. Simply stated, it is this: *Events may be expected to move in the direction in which it is most probable they will move.* The statistician usually seeks to discover the probabilities connected with any given event under observation.

But the data to which the statistical method may be applied, as we have noted, must be quantitative. That is to say, a fire insurance company may not be able to predict whether a certain house in a certain city will catch fire and burn down during the coming year, but it can tell with surprising accuracy just how many houses in that city will succumb to fire in that period. The company can, in other words, predict the *total* fire loss which is likely to occur. Events which may prove unpredictable for a single individual can be predicted with reasonable assurance for a group. While nobody knows exactly when John Jones, who is 40 years of age, will die, an actuarian is able to state almost precisely how many 40-year-olds will die this year, how many next year, and so on. When dealing with an individual case, the statistician can determine from group statistics the probabilities relating to the individual. He thus can tell a 40-year-old what his life-expectancy is — which means merely the average age at which people who are now 40 years of age can be expected to die. This knowledge, we can clearly see, has many practical uses.

Measures of Central Tendency

While no attempt can be made in this chapter or elsewhere in this book to teach in detail the various methods of statistics (these must be studied with considerable care, ordinarily in a separate college course entirely devoted to the subject), it may prove of some help to describe briefly a few of the more common kinds of statistical calculation and, in a very general way, their applications to research.

In one widely-used type of calculation, the scholar seeks to discover certain *measures of central tendency.* What, for example, is the average age of college presidents in the United States today? What is the average rainfall in New Mexico? What is the distribution of scores received by a group of students who have taken a test in mathematics? These are a few of the many things which the language of statistics might help one describe. If he can arrive at a number, or measurement, which represents the arithmetic *mean* (or average) of all the many items which have been measured (ages of all college presidents, day-to-day measurements of rainfall in New Mexico, the score of each student on the mathematics test, and so on), the statistician can express in a brief and convenient form the central value of a whole array of data.

The mean can be calculated in the following manner. First, measure each item. Then multiply each measurement by the number of times it occurs (its frequency). Add up the total of these figures. Finally, divide this total by the number of items measured. This is the usual way of calculating an arithmetic mean or average from ungrouped data. The method may be expressed mathematically by a formula. If we let the symbol M stand for the mean, Σ (sigma) for "sum of," X for the amount or quantity represented by each measurement, and N for the total number of measurements, our formula would be as follows:

$$M = \frac{\Sigma X}{N}$$

When measurements or scores are grouped into a regulated series called a "frequency distribution," the formula for calculating the mean may be changed slightly. All the measurements first are grouped into a table containing equal intervals. The frequency (f)

of the measurements falling within each interval is multiplied by the mid-point of the interval before being divided by N. Our formula then reads:

$$M = \frac{\Sigma fX}{N}$$

(For more detailed information, consult a textbook on statistics.)

Suppose we are trying to determine the average (or mean) age of American college presidents. First, we determine how many of them fall into each age goup (how many are 60 years of age, how many are 61, and so on). We multiply each age (60, 61, etc.) by the number of presidents of that age (the frequency). If there are ten presidents aged 60, our total for that group will be 600. We then add all these totals together and divide the result by the number of college presidents whose ages have been included in the study. The arithmetic mean in this case might prove to be a figure like 58.76 years. This would be the average age — for statistical or theoretical purposes — of American college presidents. Perhaps there would actually be no presidents of exactly that age; they might all be older or younger than the exact figure obtained. Nevertheless, the arithmetic mean still would be a useful and understandable figure.

In a recent study seeking to learn how large the families of college graduates are, it was discovered that, on the average, women who graduated from college in 1928 have produced 1.73 children. Obviously, no such thing exists as .73 of a child. Yet for statistical purposes the number is highly accurate. It gives us a central value which describes the facts under study in a way that helps us to draw certain conclusions and make vaious comparisons. We might use the figure above to determine whether women graduates of colleges today produce larger families than did those of 25 years ago. (Actually they do. The mean, according to one recent study, is 1.76 children per family.)

Besides the mean, a statistician may wish to determine other measures of central tendency, such as the median or the mode, of any group of measurements. The *median* is a figure which tells us which measurement in the total group is most typical. It means "the middle number." To determine the median, we arrange all the measurements in order, from the largest to the smallest (usually in a list). We then count from either end until we come to the middle. This middle number is the median. Applying this method of calculation to the ages of college presidents, we might list all the presidents in rank order by age, from the oldest to the youngest. If we have — let us say — 999 names on our list, all arranged according to age, the median will be the age of the person listed as number 500. This would be a whole number like 55 or 56 and would represent the actual age of at least one of the college presidents on the list.

The *mode* simply consists of that category of measurements which has the greatest frequency. That is, it is the measurement or number on the list which occurs the largest number of times. We might find in our study of the ages of college presidents, for instance, that there are more presidents whose age is 59 than there are presidents of any other age. This figure (59) would then be called the mode. In ordinary language, we might refer to it as the *most popular* measurement. In some lists of measurements there may be two modes (we would speak of such a distribution as bimodal) or even more.

Principles of the Normal Curve

Identifying the mean, median, or mode of any group of measurements can give the scholar useful information — information, that is to say, which describes the data in terms of the central tendencies. A statistician usually is interested not only in the central tendencies of data but also in the way the various measurements are dispersed or distributed in relation to each other. For this purpose he makes use of a device known as the *normal curve.*

In almost any kind of measurement, slight but noticeable differences occur. Two people timing a foot race with stop watches will find that their measurements of the time which elapses during the race do not exactly agree in spite of the most careful attempts to obtain absolute accuracy. In astronomical research the measurements made of the distances between heavenly bodies and of other factors will differ somewhat if made by different astronomers or even by the same astronomer at different times or with different instruments. Mathematicians who noticed these variations in the measure-

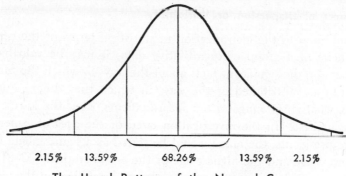

2.15%   13.59%   68.26%   13.59%   2.15%

The Usual Pattern of the Normal Curve

ments recorded by equally careful astronomers found that, when they were all charted on a graph, they formed a bell-shaped curve. A similar pattern occurred when measurements of other natural phenomena were treated in the same way.

For a long while scientists held the mistaken idea that the bell-shaped figure formed by charting almost any distribution of measurements represented some sort of natural law. They called this figure a normal frequency curve. Later it was ascertained that such a figure is normal chiefly for the distribution of those factors which are controlled entirely by chance. (The combinations which occur when dice are thrown can be charted in just such a pattern.) Thus the bell-shaped figure came to be known as the *normal curve of probability*, or simply as the *normal curve*.

Strictly speaking, the normal curve ought to be regarded as a mathematical ideal. It pictures the theoretical result of all chance distributions. While it tends to describe the ideal distribution rather than the actual distribution of measurements in any given case, a comparison between the actual and the ideal often reveals important information. When one is considering the possible effects of chance factors in a survey or some other type of scholarly study, for instance, the usefulness of the normal curve as a standard of comparison cannot be overemphasized. Not only can the investigator compare the distribution of the measurements he takes with a theoretically perfect distribution, but the probable amount of the error present in his measurements can be accurately calculated.

Measures of Dispersion or Variability

In addition to the identification in statistical terms of the central tendencies of a group of quantitative data, it may be valuable to discover also the significant facts about the ways in which the various measures are distributed or the ways in which they differ. For example, what is the *range* of our measurements, from the lowest one to the highest? In the investigation cited of the ages of American college presidents, the range would be stated as a figure giving both the lowest age and the highest age of the group studied (32–81, for instance). The range can be small or large, depending on the nature of the data gathered, and this fact might affect the conclusions reached in the study. In comparing ages of college presidents to-day with ages of college presidents of half a century ago, it might prove possible *by comparing the ranges* to show that more young men are being chosen for college presidencies today (or *vice versa*), even though the average or mean might be very nearly the same for both groups. (This example is purely suppositional.)

The range, however, constitutes only a crude statement of measurement, since it merely tells us the limits below or above which our measurements do not extend. Of greater usefulness in research is a calculation called the *standard deviation*.

Here again we have a measurement of dispersion which is a kind of ideal invented by the mathematician. In the theoretically perfect distribution which we find in the normal curve, statisticians have identified as most nearly average or typical that group of measurements lying within a certain distance (one standard deviation) from the mean, or center of the curve. These measurements are the ones which fall in the area immediately to the right or left of the center line (see the diagram of the normal curve, page 207). The area of the standard deviation constitutes 68.26 per cent of the total area of the normal curve, or 34.13 per cent of the area on each side of the center. Thus, when we speak of one measurement in a certain distribution as being within one standard deviation of the mean, we indicate thereby that it belongs to the group of measurements which are most nearly typical or average for the population being measured.

Those within the second standard deviation are farther from the

THE LANGUAGE OF STATISTICS

mean and are therefore less typical. A measurement, for instance, that falls outside the area of one standard deviation but still within 47.72 per cent of the area directly adjacent to the mean on either side is said to be within two standard deviations.

Measurements in the third standard deviation are those lying farthest from the mean in either direction. The area designating the third standard deviation consists of 2.15 per cent of the total area of the curve on each side of the center line. It is that area which lies at the extremities of the curve, nearest the open ends. In any distribution of measurements the average group would theoretically comprise 68.26 per cent of all the measurements recorded. (We are speaking now of a theoretically perfect or ideal distribution.) Another 27.18 per cent of the measurements would be considered as either just above or just below average. The 4.30 per cent farthest from the mean would be regarded as exceptionally high or low.

A schoolteacher grading tests would probably assign marks of C to all students achieving scores within one standard deviation of the mean. Those who scored in the second standard deviation above the mean might receive the grade of B, and those in the second standard deviation below the mean, the grade of D. Finally, those excellent students achieving grades in the third standard deviation above the mean might be given the grade of A, while those falling the corresponding distance on the opposite side of the normal curve would no doubt be counted as deserving an F. This is not to say, however, that such a distribution is necessarily the one to follow in grading. In the first place, if grades on a classroom test fell into the exact pattern of the normal curve, such a result could obviously occur only as pure chance and would probably indicate weaknesses in the test itself. In the second place, teachers who try to grade "according to the curve" usually assign the grade of A (or its equivalent) to approximately 7 per cent of the class, B to 14 or 15 per cent, C to about 56 per cent, and D and F in the same proportions as B and A, respectively. It must be recognized that this method of grading, though based on statistical ideas, in some respects remains an arbitrary one.

In research the calculation of the standard deviation can prove useful in a number of ways. In a survey the investigator may compile data from several different samples of the population he is questioning or examining. After calculating the mean score for each group, he charts these mean scores in a curve of distribution to determine how large the differences are among them. Comparing his curve of distribution with a normal curve will tell him the probable amount of error in his figures; in other words, it will tell him approximately how close he is to the correct mean score for the entire population represented by his various samples. This comparison will indicate how much reliance can be placed on the accuracy of the data gathered. When used in this way, the standard deviation is known as the *standard error*.

A simple method of determining the probable amount of an error in calculating a mean score from several samples would be to examine the range of the different mean scores from the different samples and to divide this range in half. But this method depends partly on the investigator's judgment (under certain circumstances) and is a rather crude measurement at best. The *probable error* simply means a limit within which the true measurement is likely to fall. When we say that the sun is 93,005,000 miles from the earth, with a probable error in that measurement of 9,000 miles more or less, we mean that our measurement of this distance is not likely to be wrong by more than about 9,000 miles. Statistically speaking, the chances that this measurement may be wrong are regarded as 50–50, or about equal to the chance of its being right. We should always keep in mind, however, that this figure is arrived at through estimates and that there still remains the possibility that the estimated probable error could be wrong. The laws of probability, on the other hand, give us a certain degree of confidence in the figure as stated above.

Calculations of the standard deviation may help us to determine the relative *significance* of certain types of data. We might ask: "Is there any significant difference between the efficiency of teachers trained at a teachers college and that of teachers trained at a liberal arts college?" The answer to such a question would clearly hinge upon just what we mean by the term *significant*. How large a difference between the two groups would we have to find before we could call it an important one — that is, important enough to result in any justifiable conclusion? To ask the same question in another way, with how much confidence could we predict, after making a thorough survey, the superiority of one of these two methods of training teachers over the other (if any)?

Suppose we ask the same kind of question with regard to a simpler and more clear-cut matter. Let us say that we wish to learn in advance whether the Democratic or the Republican candidate will win the governorship of a certain state in the next election. To seek the answer we poll a representative group of several thousand voters. Assume that the sampling of the voters' preference thus obtained favors one of the candidates by a ratio of 55 per cent of the sampling to 45 per cent. How sure can we be that this difference did not occur merely by chance, by the fact that in our survey we merely happened to interview more voters from one party than from the other? Is the difference of great enough significance to predict with any degree of confidence the real outcome of the election? To determine this by statistical methods, one would have to calculate the standard deviation which would be theoretically normal for the sampled group and then compare it with the amount of preference expressed by the voters in the sample. (In this case, the preference would amount to 5 per cent, which is the difference between 55 per cent and an even split of the votes.) If the amount of preference indicated by our sample falls outside the area of one standard deviation, we can rely upon it as having a certain amount of significance, the exact degree of significance depending on how it compares with a theoretical difference which might occur entirely by chance.

In science the same or a very similar technique is often used in learning whether a given result in a test or experiment has been caused by chance or by the factor being tested. While trying out or experimenting with a proposed remedy for some disease, the medical researcher must always consider the possibility that the cures he observes may have been effected by some random factor other than the drug or treatment he has administered. This assumption is frequently referred to as the null hypothesis — that is, the supposition that chance rather than an identifiable cause has produced the results observed. In order to be reasonably certain that chance as a causative factor has been eliminated from the study, the investigator applies his knowledge of statistics and makes a *test of significance*; in other words, he examines his data mathematically and seeks to determine whether they fall into a pattern very much different from that which would result merely from chance.

Since in this book no attempt is being made to offer instruction in the mathematical calculations required by statistical treatment, the reader is referred to the standard textbooks on statistics for further information about probable error, standard error, significance of differences, level of confidence, and other terms used in statistical work.[1] He should become familiar through the same sources with at least the simpler mathematical processes which are involved in calculations made for the purposes described above.

Correlation

The investigator often wishes to learn how much relationship one factor has to another in a given study. Students in the field of education have examined the relationship between IQ scores and the marks received in school subjects. A business firm, hoping to improve its procedures, might seek to discover whether there is any relationship — and how much, precisely — between the length of a salesman's visit with a client and the size of the order the salesman is able to obtain from that client. A public opinion analyst may be interested in the connection (if any) between a man's occupation and his political preferences. The relationship between the number of years of formal education which a person has had and the annual income which he is able to earn has been calculated many times in different studies.

How can a nutritionist make sure that a particular element in the diet actually produces good or bad results in health or growth? One favorite method used in determining such a question has been to experiment with litters of white rats. One litter of rats will be fed a diet which does not contain any of the element under study. Another litter will receive substantially the same diet, except that the extra element (a vitamin, for instance) will be added. By comparing very carefully the rate of growth, condition of the fur and teeth, and similar physiological characteristics of the two litters of rats after a sufficient period of time (or, more usually, by means of a day-to-day comparison), the effectiveness of the dietary element under consideration can be more or less measured. A useful measurement

[1] See Bibliography, pages 275 ff., for some relevant titles.

of its effectiveness can then be expressed in terms of the amount of correlation which has been found to exist between the presence or absence of this factor in the rats' diet and the pattern of growth and of general health which results. If the ratio of correlation turns out to be fairly large, one can predict with some degree of significance (or with a certain level of confidence) that the addition of this element to the diet of rats (and thus of human beings as well!) will always have the same or similar results.

Amount or degree of relationship is commonly expressed as a *coefficient of correlation*. If no correlation exists between the things which are being compared, this coefficient is said to be zero. From this neutral point, the ratio may vary in either a positive or a negative direction. It may go as high as plus one $(+1.0)$ in a positive direction, which means that when one factor is present the other is also present in every case. On the other hand, it may go as low as minus one (-1.0), which means exactly the opposite: that when one factor is present the other is always absent. A positive correlation of .30 or higher ordinarily may be considered sufficient evidence of a positive degree of relationship, though sometimes this may be partly a matter of judgment. In fact, before one decides whether a strong or weak relationship exists between two factors, it is necessary to calculate the amount of error present in the figures used.

In establishing any measure of correlation, care must be taken to ascertain beyond any reasonable doubt that the two or more factors compared really have some relationship to each other. A high correlation between economic prosperity and the brevity of women's skirts, which one researcher discovered, hardly proves that the latter causes the former or that they are necessarily related other than by pure coincidence. Furthermore, a positive relationship between two factors may continue only up to a certain point. If one were to measure the annual rainfall in Iowa and compare it with the amount of corn grown each year in that state, a certain degree of relationship no doubt would be discerned. In general we should probably find that the greater the rainfall, the larger the corn crop. Yet an unusually heavy rainfall in any one year might conceivably ruin much of the corn being grown in that year by flooding the farmlands. Such dangers must be foreseen and avoided in searching for correlations and drawing conclusions about causal relationships.

In dealing with statistical calculations, we should keep in mind at all times that the figures represent only approximations and probabilities. Although statistical measures may appear exact, they seldom are. The belief that "figures never lie" can deceive one into accepting statistical "proofs" which plain common sense will tell him are not true. The scholar must always be on his guard against this tendency. The language of statistics has many excellent uses in research, especially in helping to determine how accurate certain types of quantitative data seem to be, but it is always a means to an end rather than the end itself.

Summary

No attempt has been made in this chapter to describe statistical processes in detail. This function must be left to the many textbooks available on the subject. What has been attempted is a brief discussion of statistics as a language which may be used in describing certain types of data and in applying the theory of probability to the data which have been collected in order to determine how accurate and complete they appear to be. In addition, ways of arranging data into understandable patterns are discussed, including measures of central tendency (mean, median, mode) and measures of dispersion (standard deviation, probable error, the normal curve, and so on).

Besides measuring and describing the quantitative data of research, statistics can also be used to reveal their significance. Correlation, for example, concerns the use of statistical methods to determine relationships between factors which are being studied.

The scholar is reminded that the data to which statistical methods may be effectively and confidently applied are quantitative. He is also warned against mistaking the figures arrived at in statistical calculations for exact measures. They constitute, rather, approximations and estimates. The language of statistics can easily mislead the unwary, and this fact suggests the advisability of acquiring a thorough knowledge of statistical methods before attempting to make use of them in research. Anyone in education, psychology, sociology, economics, and the natural sciences can benefit by the study of statistics and can find it an irreplaceable tool in research.

14

THE CASE STUDY

When Plutarch wrote his *Parallel Lives* of some of the great men of ancient Greece and Rome, he was really producing what we might call, in one sense, "case histories." His object was not merely to give interesting information in these biographies but to learn and present for the benefit of his readers the sources and nature of important human qualities of character.

The scientific case study, or case history, amounts in essence to a careful and thorough examination of the life and behavior of one individual, or "case." The same techniques used with individuals may be applied with similar effect in the study of groups of individuals (families, communities, or identifiable geographical regions) or to a particular aspect of social behavior.

Sigmund Freud, originator of psychoanalysis, formulated most of his theories regarding the inner consciousness of men and women by conducting lengthy case studies of his subjects. While there may very well be a good proportion of the subjective element in this type of study, the method nevertheless tends to uncover information which might otherwise be overlooked.

As will be recalled from a previous chapter, Frédéric Le Play made some use of the case history method while studying the economic life of lower-class French families. No doubt he realized that a statistical survey, no matter how complete it may be, never gives a wholly understandable picture of the entire situation studied. Quantitative data alone do not always appear to be enough. When human beings constitute the subject matter of a study, actual examples of the experiences and the development of individual histories add reality to the picture. Quantitative data tend generally to make the description abstract; case histories can make it human.

In sociological and psychological research in general, the survey and the case study often are used as complementary to one another, for there is a close relationship between them. The case study especially seems to be more effective when used in conjunction with the survey method. At the same time, because of its resemblance in some respects to the documentary method of research (particularly when the documentary technique is applied to historical studies), the case study has also been called a historical-genetic type of investigation.

Materials Used in the Case Study

The investigator usually identifies as a "case" for his investigation any person or group of persons (such as a family, an institution, or a community) which he wishes to study in great detail. (Under certain conditions, the method may be applied also to animals.) He then proceeds to gather all the available information which has any possible connection with the life history and the development of the subject. When he has finished this extremely detailed gathering of minute facts, the investigator will be able to put together a fairly complete and continuous picture of the subject's experiences and thoughts over a period of time, and to make an interpretation of these experiences and thoughts. To a certain extent this may sound very much like documentary research. As a matter of fact, it is, except that we are dealing in the case history with living individuals and social groups.

The data gathered in a case study may be derived from a multitude of sources. Chief among these are the personal testimony of the subject (like Freud's method of asking his patients to probe their memories in order to recall their past experiences and feelings), personal documents (letters, diaries, journals, and so on), and biological, psychological, and sociological measurements. The documents examined may well include not only letters and diaries but autobiographies, the accumulated records of schools and social service agencies, medical histories, transcripts of conversations and clinical interviews, and many similar materials. These must be inspected and analyzed in much the same way that we test any other documents to determine their authenticity and their correct meaning.

What the investigator ordinarily aims at in the case study is not only a thorough description of the individual or group under scrutiny but also the identification of the principal causes leading up to the individual's or group's present status. By analyzing very carefully all the data which can possibly have a bearing upon the present status of the subject, reasons for it (as well as the exact nature of it) may sometimes, though not always, be discovered. Of course, the investigator, having turned up all the significant facts regarding the subject's development and status, may try to use this knowledge in improving that status or in correcting an undesirable condition. That is to say, the result of a complete case study may be reform or cure. This, however, lies properly outside the province of research and constitutes therapy or treatment — another problem entirely.

In a social service agency, for instance, a worker may conduct an extensive case study of a client who has been classified as a juvenile delinquent. In this setting the main purpose of such a study would not be served unless the behavior of the young delinquent could be corrected and his talents reclaimed for the good of himself and society. This would be the ultimate and practical reason in such a set of circumstances for seeking to learn the nature and causes of the delinquency. Yet the problem of cure cannot be regarded as one of the functions of research itself. The case history method merely ascertains the facts and analyzes them in order to draw inferences and establish general principles from these facts. Using such information for psychiatric treatment or for social reform is a different activity altogether, though it may follow directly from the discoveries made in the course of research. We have already noticed the same characteristic, it will be recalled, in the typical survey.

The difference between the survey and the case study lies chiefly in the fact that the survey is a quantitative study, gathering its data or measurements from a large number of individual units (usually persons), whereas the case study thoroughly examines one or more of these units (called cases), preferably those which appear to be most representative or typical. Thus, a survey of delinquency in a high school might reveal the total number of offenses, the different kinds of offense, the physical and psychological characteristics of the offenders (their age, family background, mental ability, sex, amount of education, health, etc.), and the increase or decrease in delinquent acts over a period of time. The case history method, on the other hand, would attempt to search out the causes of delinquency by making very elaborate investigations into the development and general background of a few typical offenders in the group. Most social workers appear to believe that, for their purposes, the second approach is likely to prove the more useful and revealing of the two. But as a research technique the use of the two methods together is often more fruitful than the use of either one alone.

Some Techniques Used in the Case Study

The research worker who looks into the case history of a subject carefully refrains from *judging* either the character or the motives of the person he studies. That is, he maintains a scientific objectivity toward the subject's behavior. Although perfect objectivity may be impossible to attain, he strives to record the facts as he finds them, neither condemning nor praising. The investigator who brings to the study his personal prejudices and preconceived standards of morals or beliefs may see facts imperfectly or distort their meaning. Here, as elsewhere, the function of the research worker is to seek the true nature of reality. His work in the case study method of research is diagnosis rather than reform.

Perhaps the most commonly employed technique in a case study is the personal interview. This means eliciting information directly from the subject being studied. The conditions under which the interview is conducted can vary considerably and will depend upon the circumstances of each investigation, but as a rule these conditions are more informal in the case study interview than in the survey interview. A free flow of talk is encouraged. The relationship established between interviewer and subject becomes a very important condition of the interview, though the experienced interviewer will know how to keep his own position as objective and unobtrusive as possible. We have seen how Le Play, a pioneer in the use of what we now call the case method, literally moved right in with the working-class families he studied in his survey of economic and social conditions in France. Similarly today, a sociologist interviewing hoboes might find it strategic to live among them for a time as a pseudo-hobo, or he might simply visit and question them in hobo jungles, at missions, on freight cars, or in other places where they might be more likely to feel at ease than in the investigator's office. Under such informal conditions, to be sure, accurate note-taking may prove difficult.

Good note-taking is an essential part of the case study method. Notes ought to be taken at the time information is received (e.g., during the course of the interview), or, if this is impossible, they should be written down immediately thereafter. Preferably, the actual words of the speaker or speakers, rather than a paraphrase or approximation, should be recorded. Even in a very informal interview the trained research worker can sometimes record his notes unobtrusively and in a way that will not make the person interviewed feel uneasy or self-conscious. Needless to say, all notes ought to be as complete and correct as possible. Since the interviewer does not always know in advance precisely which data will prove most significant and useful after analysis of all the information gathered, he cannot afford to overlook any fact that may bear upon the development and status of the subject under investigation.

In a case study investigation the use of a prepared questionnaire or schedule does not always produce the best results. In an interview it is likely to inhibit the free flow of talk or even to encourage evasion and lying. For another thing, questions about a life history cannot well be answered with an easily tabulated "Yes" or "No" or check mark. The really helpful answers will tend to be rather detailed and therefore long. Finally, as we have noted before, the characteristic materials of a case study are not primarily quantitave; they lend themselves more to study through the documentary method of research than to quantitative techniques such as the survey questionnaire.

Combined with interviews will be the search for and the exhaustive study of written records. Information acquired in the interview should be verified, if at all possible, by this means. But the written records can provide other data as well. The investigator must be prepared to examine diaries, letters, account books, medical records, church, school, and social agency records, newspaper notices, and the like, keeping in mind constantly the question of which data seem likely to be most significant for purposes of the study. In recording data for the case history, it is, of course, desirable to formulate a systematic approach. Each record should contain at least the following information: the date (especially for the interview) on which the data were obtained, the names of persons giving statements, the actual words used in the statements, a brief description of the conditions under which the interview or other form of interrogation took place, a summary of the specific techniques used in any given part of the investigation (such as direct personal observation, interview, questionnaire, and the like), identification of the person or document supplying the information, and supplementary remarks. The whole point (and this can be learned best through experience) is this: A record made of any step in the case study should be so complete that none of the investigative work, once done, will have to be done over again.

The properly conducted case study usually requires a fairly long period of time. Instead of one interview, a whole series may be necessary to obtain the type and amount of information desired. Constant probing of the same ground is often essential in order to find the significant factors in the study. Since the case history describes the subject's development not at a single given point but over a considerable length of time, neither memory nor the available records can be counted on to furnish complete information immediately. The investigator in the case study needs patience. This kind of work is both intensive and inclusive. That is, instead of selecting a few items about which to seek data from a great many sources, as in the survey, the case history investigator puts all his attention on learning everything he can learn with certainty about a limited number of cases.

But how shall one determine which cases are typical? In choosing his cases for study, the investigator may be misled into selecting those which appear most interesting or spectacular. He must avoid this temptation by trying to be absolutely objective, by looking honestly for representative subjects, and by conducting whenever possible a preliminary statistical survey before making his selection. Nevertheless, the element of subjectivity, of personal judgment, cannot be entirely absent either in choosing the cases or in assembling the data. This tends to keep the case study method of research from being wholly scientific. No doubt new and more objective techniques will be developed as time goes on; meanwhile, the method has proved so productive that its weaknesses need not prevent its use if the investigator exercises due discretion. As a matter of fact, it has in recent years been more and more widely employed in certain fields, such as education, and with marked success. If nothing else, the use of the case history can decrease the tendency to misinterpret statistical data. The relationship of isolated factors often can be seen more clearly through intensive case study than through mere quantitative analysis.

Summary

Essentially the case study method comprises a careful and comprehensive analysis of the development and status of one individual, group, or institution. The method can be used effectively in combination with a survey.

The materials used in case study research include information obtained from such sources as personal interviews, personal documents, and medical, educational, and social agency records. The personal interview is perhaps the most important tool, but the data obtained from interviewing should be verified by comparison with written records whenever possible. Notes made in personal interviews must be full and accurate, and preferably written down during the interview itself. In eliciting the materials for the case study, the prepared questionnaire is less effective than in the survey. The well-conducted case study requires time and patience because of the detailed nature of the investigation.

In analyzing the evidence gathered, the investigator usually searches for causes of the current condition or status of the subject studied. The case study differs from the survey in that it constitutes a detailed examination of a few typical cases rather than an accumulation of quantitative data from a vast number of respondents.

The case history investigator must earnestly try to maintain objectivity and refrain from passing moral judgment upon the cases he studies. His object is to learn the truth by diagnosis.

The method suffers from several defects. One of these is the difficulty of selecting cases for study which are known to be definitely typical. Another is the strong element of subjectivity which, thus far, seems unavoidable in this kind of research. Nevertheless, the case study, especially when used in conjunction with a quantitative survey, often draws attention to information that cannot be obtained successfully in any other way and thus can be justified scientifically.

15 THE ROLE OF ACCIDENT

IN RESEARCH

It frequently happens that major discoveries in research are made almost entirely by accident. These may come about either through chance observation of some unsuspected phenomenon or through the sudden appearance on the scene of documents, artifacts, or other sources of information whose existence previously had been unknown.

The Chance Appearance of Source Materials

The erosion or shifting of soil, the drying up of lakes, and other natural alterations in the face of the earth may expose hitherto unknown archaeological or geological data. During the "dust bowl" days of the nineteen-thirties in the western plateau district of the United States, the wind removed several inches of topsoil in many areas and laid bare spots which had been covered for years. At these places geologists and archaeologists picked up Indian relics that probably would have remained hidden forever under different circumstances. What we know of the so-called Folsom Man we may owe largely to another such major shifting of topsoil a decade earlier in New Mexico.

Accidental circumstances have brought to light a number of important documents that would otherwise almost surely have been destroyed. In 1765 Bishop Percy in England one day noticed a housemaid attempting to start a fire with a bundle of old papers.

On an impulse he stopped her and examined the papers. To his great surprise, they turned out to be a manuscript collection of old popular ballads. They interested Percy as the surviving remains of early folk literature, and he began to study them. Later he published them as *Reliques of Ancient English Poetry*, one of the landmarks in English literary history. Had he not been both perceptive and alert, these priceless materials might easily have been destroyed forever.

A similar stroke of fortune saved for scholarship a number of important papers by James Boswell, the noted English biographer of the eighteenth century. In 1850 Major Stone, an officer of the East India Company, made some purchases in a little shop in Boulogne-sur-Mer, France. Upon his return to his lodgings, he chanced to observe that the wrapping paper which the shopkeeper had used was part of an old letter and that this letter bore the signature of James Boswell. Returning to the shop, Major Stone learned that the wrapping paper had been recently purchased from an itinerant vendor. In those days it was not an uncommon practice to use waste paper in this fashion. Stone immediately offered to buy up the entire stock of paper from which the Boswell document came, and he thus recovered for scholarship a most important group of letters written by Boswell to his close friend, William Temple.

The precious and perishable source papers of scholarship often owe not only their discovery but their very preservation to luck. The charred edges of the one extant manuscript of the Old English epic poem *Beowulf* show how nearly it once missed destruction in a fire in the library where it was housed.

Chance Observations of Phenomena

Familiar to every schoolboy is the tale of Archimedes' dramatic discovery of the law of specific gravity. According to legend, the discovery was at least partly accidental. Requested by Hiero, the ruler of Syracuse, to determine whether the royal crown had actually been manufactured of pure gold, as asserted by the goldsmith, or whether cheaper metals had been mixed in as alloy, Archimedes reportedly stumbled upon the principle of specific gravity while taking a bath. Noticing the displacement of water caused by the weight and bulk of his own body, he is said to have leaped excitedly out of his bath and run down the street shouting, "Eureka!" By calculating the amount of water which would be displaced if the crown were pure gold, Archimedes was able to expose the fraudulent goldsmith and prove that a quantity of silver had been mixed with the gold in making the crown.

The history of scientific research abounds with instances of the chance observation which acts as a catalyst on the trained mind. Galvani's discovery of "animal electricity" in Bologna, Italy, is supposed to have come about because his wife happened to be preparing some frogs' legs for his dinner. A pupil of Galvani's, operating an electric friction machine close by, accidentally touched one of the legs with a knife he was holding. Much to his amazement, he saw it make a spasmodic twitch. Galvani, when informed of this, promptly undertook to investigate the strange phenomenon. Hanging several frogs' legs from copper wires on his balcony, he noted with surprise and interest that the muscles of the legs twitched whenever the wind blew them against the iron railing of the balcony. From this observation Galvani reasoned that an electrical fluid must be present in the frogs' legs which became active when it was brought into contact with the copper and iron together. Volta later used Galvani's discovery (though they disagreed about the principle involved) in producing the first electric battery. Incidentally, we still recall the significant contributions of Galvani to the study of electricity when we employ such terms as "galvanometer" (the instrument used in measuring small amounts of electrical current) and "galvanize into action," an expression which perhaps can be traced back to the stimulus-and-response phenomenon of the frogs' legs.

The discovery by Louis Pasteur of the means for turning disease germs into agents of immunization may be credited chiefly to accident. Pasteur had been studying cholera in chickens, and in the process had been producing cultures of cholera germs which he used in his experiments. On one occasion he took a few days' vacation. When he returned he inoculated a number of chickens with a germ culture which had become old and which he had meant to destroy. Unexpectedly, these chickens, though they became ill, survived the disease. Then when they were inoculated with fresh germs, they resisted the disease entirely. Apparently the old germs, through lack of oxygen, had been so weakened that the natural resistance of the chickens prevented their having a fatal effect. Thus Pasteur learned that immunity may be developed by inoculation with a mild form of the disease, using weakened germ cultures. The principle of the vaccine has been applied successfully with several diseases.

When Röntgen discovered the X ray he was experimenting with electrical discharges in vacuum tubes and attempting to detect invisible rays of light through the use of a photographic plate. One day he noticed that a photographic plate covered with black paper which had been lying on his work bench beside the vacuum tube was glowing with fluorescence. He had not previously suspected that there might be certain light rays which could penetrate black paper. To verify his observation, Röntgen covered the vacuum tube completely with black paper and darkened his work room. When the electrical current was turned on, the photographic plate held near the tube glowed luminously, thus proving beyond question that the mysterious rays could penetrate opaque objects.

Unsatisfactory conditions in a dirty laboratory are said to account for Sir Alexander Fleming's discovery of penicillin, one of our most remarkable drugs. The continued handling of certain cultures of staphylococci with which Fleming was working caused them to become contaminated. In one instance he noticed that all the germ colonies on a particular plate except those near the center had died. This suggested to him the possibility that one type of germ colony had killed the others. He identified this colony, a mold, as penicillin and wrote a report of his observations. Years later another experimenter, Howard Florey, read Fleming's report and asked himself whether this unusual substance might not prove useful in the cure of diseases. The result is well known. The odd fact seems to be that Fleming probably would not have made his discovery had he been working in a spotless laboratory under sanitary conditions.

Making Use of Chance Discoveries

For every chance observation which has resulted in some new addition to knowledge, thousands of opportunities have probably passed unnoticed. Certainly others before Röntgen had had similar opportunities to observe the phenomenon of the X ray. Medical men before Fleming knew that certain molds kill disease germs. Needless to say, the scholar cannot depend upon accident as a method of making discoveries or solving problems. But it is important for him to be alert and ready to profit by unusual occurrences or observations made in a study. The true scholar, seeing something unexpected occur in the course of his investigation, wants to know why it occurred.

As Pasteur so aptly stated: "Chance favors the ready mind." When Charles Goodyear accidentally dropped some raw rubber on a hot stove and thus learned that heat will harden and strengthen rubber, he could put the knowledge to practical use because his mind was prepared as the result of his previous work. If such an incident had happened under other circumstances, the person spilling the liquid rubber on the hot surface might simply have been annoyed by his own clumsiness. Nothing of importance would then have been derived from the accident.

Almost every year discoveries in research take place whose ultimate importance nobody seems at the time to recognize. Though it was asserted as early as 1840 that cod liver oil can be beneficial to children with rickets, the advice went almost unheeded for nearly a century. Fleming's report on penicillin lay on the shelf gathering dust until Florey chanced upon it in a routine inspection of scientific literature.

Thus the effective scholar must remain ever on the alert for fortunate accidents. While he cannot reckon upon these, he must possess both the perspicacity and the common sense to take full advantage of them when they occur, as they frequently will, during the progress of a study.

Summary

The scholar should prepare his mind for the possibility of accidental discoveries in research. He will do well not to ignore strange and unusual phenomena which he observes during the course of a study but, instead, to search out the explanation. To do so requires an alert and prepared mind which will seize upon every opportunity to inform itself and which looks beyond the merely obvious. As Pasteur said, "Chance favors the ready mind."

PART FOUR

Presenting the Results of Research

16

PREPARING THE

WRITTEN REPORT

Writing should not as a rule be attempted until after a study has been completed. Some people have the false idea that the written report *is* the study. Not at all. The report is merely the means by which a scholar informs his colleagues of the work he has done — his conclusions about the problem studied, his method of solving it, and the evidence he has been able to find in support of his hypothesis.

The scholarly report should not be written to entertain the reader. Fiction, popular essays and articles, poems, and many other types of writing serve that purpose. A report of research has only one function: it must *inform*. It propagates knowledge. This does not mean, however, that the research paper needs to be dull and uninteresting or that the scholar is exempt from the requirements of "good" writing. The report *can* be extremely interesting, and it *can* be well written. Nevertheless, interest and style are not primary concerns of the scholar in reporting the results of his study. The flight of rhetoric, the subtle ambiguity, the anecdotal digression — these have no place in the scholarly research paper.

Nor should the report be an attempt to impress the reader with the writer's erudition. Even though the subject matter may be difficult and specialized, it should not be made more difficult through the manner of writing. Wordiness, indirection, and pompous language are barriers to communication — and to scholarly achievement, for

231

the effective scholar is one who can communicate his findings. Correctness, precision, and clarity should be the scholar's watchwords. Always, in putting his report into written form, he should keep in mind the one essential of a research report: to tell, without pretension or hedging, exactly what was done in the study and what conclusions have been reached.

The Best Way to Proceed

The best way to proceed is to go directly to the point. If the scholar will forego all efforts to make an impression of unusual erudition upon his readers, if he will try to make his paper not as long as possible but as short as possible, if he will conscientiously refrain from adding comments which have nothing at all to do with the study, he will have escaped the principal vices of report writers. After all, the worth of a paper should be measured not by how much it says but by what it says. A great many inept writers waste so much time and space putting down pompous but purposeless remarks or extraneous information that they never seem to arrive at the main issue — a description of what was accomplished in the study. *Get to the point* is probably the first rule of good report writing.

Presumably the scholar who has just completed a thorough and successful study of some problem in his field knows almost everything there is to know about that problem. His brain is full of information. He has formulated his hypothesis and has found the evidence to support it. He knows exactly why he believes his hypothesis to be the correct one. Since he *knows* what he has done in the course of the study and *knows* what evidence there is to support his conclusions, he should be able to write down what he knows. After all, he need only put what is in his mind into words. Lack of practice in writing may hinder the inexperienced scholar somewhat; but, by and large, anyone should be able to express in clear and understandable words anything about which he is firmly sure in his own mind. Thus we might say that the second rule of good writing is to *Know thoroughly the subject about which you write*. For the scholar who has done a satisfactory piece of work in solving his problem, this ought to present no real difficulties. He has only to describe what he has done and to present the evidence for his conclusions.

Perhaps the writing of a report will not seem quite so simple as is implied here for the person who has had little experience with written communication. For him a third rule of procedure may be suggested: *Learn to organize the information you have on the subject you have studied.* In other words, make some orderly pattern of your thoughts. Probably the scholar's quickest and best way of accomplishing this is to ask himself what arguments he has developed in favor of the hypothesis which he believes to be the right one. If each favorable argument is set down in turn, together with the evidence proving it, an almost perfect structure for the research report will result. This structure might be symbolically represented by the outline drawing of a Greek temple, whose roof is supported by pillars, which rest upon a firm floor or foundation. The floor of

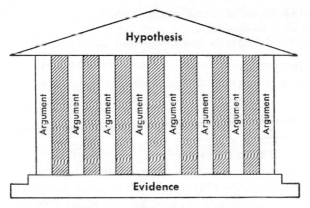

The Structure of the Greek Temple
as a Model for Organizing a Report

the structure would represent the evidence or data on which are built the arguments (or reasons) that support the conclusions (or hypothesis). If data are handled in this way, the hypothesis will clearly be supported by a strong system of what we might call mental architecture.[1]

To make certain of organizing his thoughts effectively and of showing a definite and unquestioned relationship between his evi-

[1] Although we have mentioned the formulation of evidence into supportive arguments only, the scholar may wish to argue in refutation (usually at the outset) of all the possible arguments which might be advanced *against* his hypothesis.

dence and his hypothesis, the scholar will find it helpful to draw up a written outline of his study. This will serve the purpose both of clarifying the picture of the study in his own mind and of helping him plan and write the report. An outline represents the skeleton of the entire study. It shows how the data have been organized into effective arguments and how these arguments lead logically to the conclusion reached. The scholar who cannot outline the main points of the study and gather his data into a pattern of arguments may find that he simply does not have in his mind a firm and clear picture of the study on which he has been working. At the same time, the outline is a mechanical aid in organizing and presenting the materials effectively. As each part of the study (or topic of the outline) is written up in turn, the outline helps the scholar maintain, throughout the writing, a consciousness of the relationship among all the parts and of the cohesiveness of the whole.

The Distinction Between the Essay and the Research Report

Since the requirements of the essay differ markedly from those of the research report, the scholar must never mistake the one for the other nor confuse the two styles when writing a paper of his own.

The research report is never anything but the *description of an actual study* which has been carried to completion by the scholar. The essay, on the other hand, is a *discussion* of some subject or problem, usually expressing the writer's opinion, interpretation, or point of view. The scholarly essay does not necessarily add anything new to the sum total of knowledge; it may simply summarize existing knowledge or suggest possibilities. The research report always constitutes an addition to knowledge.

In writing the essay the scholar is not bound by the same strict rules that govern the presentation of materials in the research report. For example, he may refrain from fully documenting his statements. In the research report, the exact sources of information *must* be clearly and accurately indicated, so that other scholars will be able to find the identical materials by checking the sources named and thus verify, if they wish, the statements and conclusions presented. The writer of a research report is expected to do much more than express his opinions, however logical and appealing these may be; he must offer conclusions based upon sound factual evidence which has been honestly appraised.

Perhaps it is a sufficient indication of the difference between these two types of scholarly writing to say that the research report must always demonstrate that an actual problem has been studied and solved or that new facts have been discovered. In the essay the writer may simply show that he has thought about the problem, or he may describe his personal observations and experiences with it, or he may analyze and classify the opinions and the scholarly discoveries of others regarding it. What the essayist offers, then, cannot be considered a thoroughly substantiated solution of a problem. He may offer penetrating insights, and he may even argue for a solution which has every indication of being true (and which may later, upon further study, really turn out to be true); but he cannot offer a definitive solution (in the scientific sense) of the problem because he has not conducted a scientific study. A scholar who has completed a study along scientific lines does not report his findings in an essay but writes instead an accurate and factual description of the sources of information, the method used in searching for and analyzing data, the hypothesis reached, and the evidence that supports the hypothesis.

The essay may be written partly to entertain as well as to inform. In any case, the writer of an essay usually tries to write in an interesting manner. The research report attempts to present the truth in as direct a manner as possible. Above all, it must remain objective. Scholars writing reports of their studies find that they can maintain their objectivity best by speaking in the third person. The scholar speaks of himself not as *I* but as *the author* or *the present writer*, thus keeping the personal element out of his report as much as possible. In an essay the personal element, together with a certain amount of informality, may be perfectly in place. Most essays, whether they are what we would call scholarly or not, consist mainly of personal observation or opinion or speculation which is not restricted by scientific requirements. In other words, conclusions in an essay are likely to be based upon uncontrolled observation, often supported by selected facts (sometimes only those on one side of an issue) and by the opinions of authorities. The essay serves a good purpose in its dissemination of ideas and opinions, but its purpose is clearly different in kind, not simply in degree, from the much more precise purpose of the research report.

The Outline of a Report

In planning how materials gathered in the course of a scholarly investigation are to be presented, certain useful customs are to be observed. For one thing, the reader must be informed at once what the problem is that the scholar has undertaken to solve. Ordinarily the statement of the problem is one of the first things the scholar needs to present in his paper. If his readers do not understand what problem was worked on in the study, they will hardly be able to read the report intelligently.

A *brief* description of the problem ought to appear in the title of the paper, but this need not be a full or lengthy statement of it. The title indicates for the benefit of the prospective reader something about the nature and substance of the paper. This information can be presented, however, in abbreviated form — one or two lines, at most. There does not seem to be much point or sense to the eight- or nine-line title sometimes encountered. Often a title of only half a dozen words is sufficient to give the prospective reader an adequate idea of the subject.

The Introductory Part of the Paper

A *full* description of the problem (including any delimitations) ought ordinarily to come in the first paragraph or two of the paper and not, except in very rare cases, in the title. The scholar should be sure to describe his problem clearly and completely, so that there can be no misunderstanding regarding the exact subject matter of the study and the question that the study seeks to answer.

We may say, then, that the opening section of every scholarly report should carry an accurate statement of the *problem* studied. In addition, there should be at once an indication of the solution reached in the study — that is, the scholar's final *hypothesis*. Unsatisfactory hypotheses which were tried out and discarded during the course of the study need not be mentioned in the paper at all, unless the scholar wishes to mention them simply to refute them. The actual solution of the problem, however, must be revealed before the data are presented. This is necessary in order to help the reader follow the argument properly. The scholar does not build up suspense and save the solution of the problem for the very end of his paper, as if he were writing a mystery story. Rather, he does everything essential to enable his readers to follow the development of the thought and argument upon which the proof of the hypothesis rests.

Often it proves effective to open the paper with a statement of the hypothesis — of what the study has proved. This, of course, is purely a matter of judgment on the part of the scholar when writing his paper. Whether the problem or the hypothesis is first stated really has no basic significance. The important thing to remember is that *both* the problem and the hypothesis must be thoroughly understood by the reader if he is to grasp the argument and see how the data fit logically into the pattern developed by the study. This requires that both the problem and the hypothesis be clearly stated at the beginning of the report.

Another item that should appear very early in the report is a description of the *method* used in solving the problem. Obviously if the method selected has been a poor one, the results cannot be depended upon. The critical reader will carefully consider whether the scholar has followed an approved scientific method and whether the method chosen really fits the problem. Thus a description of the steps taken to solve the problem constitutes one of the most important elements in the introductory portion of a scholarly paper. Too often such attempts to tell how the study was done turn out to be vague and unedifying. The scholar who has difficulty describing the techniques used in conducting the study might very well ask himself whether he really selected suitable techniques and whether he knows what they were. If his techniques were good and if he understood what he was doing in the course of the study, he should have no serious difficulty in telling his reader what method he used. Merely naming the method (calling it a survey, experiment, case study, or the like) does not answer the purpose, of course. The scholar must put down carefully and specifically just what steps were taken to solve the problem. He should tell where the sources of information were found and how they were selected. He should identify the type of data which were gathered and the ways in which they were analyzed and classified. He should indicate in detail just how he went about the job of testing his hypothesis and (perhaps) why he thinks the method he followed was effective.

In addition to stating the problem, announcing the hypothesis or conclusion, and describing the method used, the scholar may wish in his opening paragraphs to say something about his purpose in conducting the study, and he may wish to define some of his terms. Statement of purpose and definition of terms, however, are not found in all reports and cannot be considered as important as the first three items mentioned.

The purpose of the study is the reason why it was undertaken. In what ways was the study justified? What use will there be for the results? How may the results change the status of knowledge in the field in which the study was undertaken? What is the scholar's special interest in the particular problem studied? These questions indicate something about the purpose for which a study may be made. The scholar may deem it essential or advisable to explain the purpose while making other introductory statements. Many scholars do. Ordinarily, however, one should not spend too much time on these preliminary matters but should move as quickly as possible into the main body of the paper.

In some instances, though not invariably, the scholar may find it necessary to explain in detail the meaning of certain words and phrases he is using in the paper. When special terms are employed or invented by the writer, they should ordinarily be defined at the time they first appear in the paper. If there are many such terms, however, they may well be defined in a special paragraph (or more, if needed) near the beginning of the report. A technical term which may be interpreted in more than one way should always be defined, so that there can be no question of the exact sense in which it is being used. In general, however, the scholar should avoid words which require special definition. It would be best if he could get along without any definitions at all. Unfortunately, this does not always prove possible. To sum up, when definitions are necessary, they should be carefully supplied, and the introductory section of the paper sometimes is the proper place for them. This kind of thing, on the other hand, should never be overdone.

The opening paragraphs of the usual research report, then, should contain a clear and complete statement of the problem, an indication of the solution which the scholar proposes for this problem (that is, his hypothesis), and a brief but understandable description of the methods used in the study. There may also be something on the purpose for which the study was conducted and perhaps definitions of special terms, if necessary. Anything else in the introductory section of a research paper is likely to be extraneous. In particular, the all-too-frequent habit of opening the paper with oratorical bombast should be avoided. A straightforward clarity and conciseness are basic to effective presentation.

The Main Body of the Paper

Once the preliminary matters have been disposed of, the main part of the report can be presented. This consists in the development of the *argument* — that is, the description of the evidence and of what it shows.

Merely presenting the evidence is not enough. The scholar must interpret it for his readers; he must show what he thinks it proves. To illustrate: A teacher once brought into his classroom three balls of metal. They were all about the same size, and they all looked more or less alike. Holding them up one at a time before the class, he remarked as he displayed each of the balls, "This is aluminum. This is lead. This is iron." The demonstration meant very little to his class, however; for he did not indicate what it was intended to prove. Finally he asked members of the class to hold each of the three metal balls in their hands and compare their weights. "Notice," he said, "that the iron is heavier than the aluminum and the lead heavier than either of the others." Thus he interpreted for his class the meaning of the evidence. He told them what he thought the evidence meant. This is exactly the sort of thing which the scholar must not fail to do. Stating the evidence does not serve his purpose unless he demonstrates in a logical manner that the evidence presented actually substantiates his arguments in favor of his hypothesis.

Only when he interprets as well as presents the evidence can readers weigh it and follow his reasoning through to the conclusion.

The main body of the paper may very well be divided into sections in which the various arguments are taken up in turn. Whether these sections are one page long or three pages or complete chapters or only single paragraphs will depend upon the relative strength of each argument and the amount of evidence which has been uncovered to support it. At any rate, a paper always falls into natural divisions if the material is handled in this manner. Every section should be more or less self-sufficient; that is, it should have an introductory statement which tells what the section deals with, and it should have a summarizing statement at the end which reviews the argument and reminds the reader of what the evidence has demonstrated. Sections of a short paper do not require subtitles, although in a long paper (over twenty pages, for instance) the use of a few subtitles may make the task of understanding the argument and the data an easier one. Young scholars probably tend to overdo the use of subtitles, perhaps to make it clear that they have included everything in the paper which ought to be there. Giving a section of the paper a title or a separate chapter number may make it seem a little more important than it might otherwise appear; but if a subtitle serves only this purpose, it is pure bluff. A paper cut up into too many small sections loses in coherence and continuity. For a paper of twelve to fifteen pages, probably no subdivisions of any kind are necessary; the paper runs through from beginning to end without a break. Longer papers may be broken into numbered sections. A very long paper may have chapters and chapter titles. A chapter, to justify the name, ought to be several pages long in every case. Divisions which are shorter than this do not really deserve to be called chapters.

The Final Summary

The practice of writing a short final summary after all the evidence has been presented and the argument is complete has much to recommend it. Such a summary should not contain any new information but should recapitulate in brief the entire content of the paper. It is as if the scholar were asked by a colleague what problem he had studied and what results he had obtained. He would reply briefly and to the point, sketching all the important points of the study, describing the conclusions and how he had arrived at them. This, in essence, is what the summary does.

It should be possible from reading the summary alone to learn from it just what the study has demonstrated and how, though without any of the details and without any documentation of the evidence. The summary restates the entire argument, showing how the hypothesis has been substantiated, but it emphasizes the main points rather than the details. It amounts to a condensation, a brief description of the whole study. Whether it is one page long or a complete chapter depends upon the length of the total paper, but in general it should be as short as possible.

Recommendations for action are not normally a part of any research study and thus ought not to be included in a summary. The function of the summary is to tell what was accomplished in the study, especially what new principles or facts of knowledge were discovered. Recommendations as to how such new discoveries may be applied are always a matter of opinion — in a sense, an afterthought. For this reason, if recommendations are made by the scholar, they should be made in a separate chapter or section of the paper and should never be confused with the study itself. The study was made in order to learn certain facts or principles which add to knowledge; it is complete when the investigator solves the problem he set out to solve. Recommendations resulting from the study are not additions to knowledge; they are suggestions as to how the knowledge, or information obtained, may be put to use. This is not primarily the scholar's job, though there is no reason why he should not offer any suggestions and recommendations if he cares to do so. The only thing he must keep firmly in mind is that these recommendations are not a part of the study itself, but something extraneous, something added. If the scholar suggests how the results of the study may be useful in a practical way, he goes beyond the limits of the study itself and enters the realm of opinion. As long as this distinction is understood, there can be no confusion between the summary and the recommendations made (if any). What the scholar needs to avoid is the tendency to think of recommendations as a part of the study proper.

The usual research report, then, consists of three parts. The first of these is an introductory section which tells what problem was investigated, how it was attacked, and what results were obtained. (The order in which these points are covered in the report is up to the scholar and may vary from paper to paper.) The introduction may also discuss the purpose of the study and perhaps define certain special terms. It ought never to be a mere exercise in rhetoric or a tissue of vague generalizations. The second and main part of the paper gives the various arguments which have induced the scholar to accept his hypothesis or solution as the correct one, together with the factual data upon which the proof of each argument rests. This part of the paper, comparatively speaking, is the essential one. The summary, in the final portion of the paper, gives a description of the study in condensed form and thus, in a sense, draws all the arguments together.

Some General Advice

Perhaps the most pertinent advice that may be offered a young scholar is to use clear and simple English invariably in his writing. By and large, this ought not to prove difficult of accomplishment if he has a clear and accurate conception of the study which he has just completed. Long words, unusual words, and, in particular, vague words hamper an understanding of any paper. While special technical terms may be necessary to convey certain meanings in a few academic fields, they frequently turn out, upon mature consideration, to be much less vital than one might suppose, even in the most involved scholarly paper. One is tempted when reading some papers to conclude that a great many technical words and phrases are pure affectation and that the same ideas could have been expressed more directly and more forcefully with simpler language. Undoubtedly the reports of some studies make the investigation seem unduly complicated and abstruse because the writer of the report lacked the ability to describe his work intelligently. Difficult and specially invented words do not reveal the profundity of the scholar's thought as much as they reveal the barrenness of his ideas. We may speak of thoughts expressed in vague or technically complex language as being "disguised in verbiage."

The scholar while writing his paper should be able to identify every statement he makes (in effect, every sentence) as one of the following: (1) a direct statement of fact, (2) a basic assumption, (3) an expression of expert opinion, or (4) an opinion of his own.

In setting down a known fact, the scholar must be sure to state how he knows it to be a fact. Ordinarily this is accomplished either by describing the way he observed this fact (if he got it by first-hand observation) or by indicating the source of his information (that is, by documentation). Sources, if they are books, may be described in footnotes. Other sources — like interviews, manuscripts (especially those of unusual importance), or experimental processes — may well be described in the body of the paper itself. The point at issue is precisely how the scholar has made certain that the statement given as fact really is fact. A sentence written to state something which the scholar knows to be true must offer its reader some way of verifying its truth, and usually the quickest and best method of doing this is to identify the source of the information. The scholar must be sure, then, that what he states as fact is not mere opinion. That a respected authority says a thing is true does not make it true. On the other hand, principles and facts discovered by someone else in the course of careful, scientific research may be stated as demonstrated truths. In referring to the results of a good research study by some other scholar, the person writing a report uses words like the following: "Jones [i. e., the other scholar] has shown. . . ." This indicates that the scholar has read a research report written by Jones, has found the research methods used by Jones entirely adequate, and accepts the results as clearly demonstrated. If Jones had written an essay rather than a research report, however, and had stated his results or hypothesis without explaining how his problem had been solved, his conclusions would have to be regarded as opinions rather than as proved facts or principles. Any reference to the conclusions reached by Jones would then be stated somewhat in this manner: "Jones believes. . . ."

A basic assumption has the status of an accepted fact or principle. It is something which informed people so generally recognize and believe that no documentation is necessary. For example, a statement in a scholarly paper that the earth is spherical in shape would hardly be subject to challenge, although perhaps the fact cannot be proved beyond any shadow of doubt. Similarly, if one assumes that a chair thrown out of a third-floor window will fall downward rather than upward, there is little need for any indication of the source of such an assumption or for any substantiating evidence. People in general will agree to such a statement without requiring any further discussion of the phenomenon. Thus, any fact or principle which can be regarded as true because it has long been understood and accepted or because it is proved by common experience can be stated as a basic assumption without the need of documentation. No reference or source need be mentioned for the information that summers are warmer, as a rule, than winters. The matter is common knowledge. In writing his report the scholar will find that he uses many basic assumptions almost without being conscious of doing so, but he should learn to recognize them for what they are. They are statements of fact or of known and accepted principles; yet they require no documentation in the paper.

In the discovery of truth, opinions ordinarily carry little weight as compared with factual data. Nevertheless, there may be instances in which no evidence can be found except expert opinion. In a court of law, for instance, an expert medical examiner may be called upon to render his opinion as to the cause of some person's death. Although an expert opinion could be wrong, there is a better chance that an opinion will be right if the person giving it is an expert than if the person were chosen at random. Experience and constant study count for something. On the other hand, opinion cannot ever achieve the force of actual fact. When an expert's opinion is quoted or referred to in a scholarly paper, it should always be introduced by a phrase such as "In Smith's opinion. . . ." In other words, the reader should be informed that the statement given is an opinion and not a statement of fact.

The writer's own opinion would probably best not be mentioned at all in a research report, except perhaps in a footnote. Opinions often are based upon impressions rather than upon real evidence, and generally can have no bearing on the results of the study. It seems hardly worth while to express them, other than as a matter of interest. Anything the scholar wishes to say to his readers which he thinks will prove interesting but which has nothing to do with the proof of his hypothesis ought to be relegated to a footnote and not made an integral part of the paper. Personal opinions tend sometimes to bring the subjective element into a study — an element which the scholar always makes every effort to keep out. Opinions prove nothing of a factual nature, though they may suggest further hypotheses. Occasionally the expression of a personal opinion may constitute a misleading factor in the paper. At best, it can add very little, if anything, to the real objective of the report, which is to inform the reader of the solution the scholar has been able to discover for the problem studied and of the evidence he as unearthed in making sure that his proposed solution is the correct one. In any case, if the writer expresses his opinions at all, he should clearly so label them, in order to distinguish them from statements of fact.

What the Critical Reader Looks For

The scholar when writing a report of a study should constantly keep in mind the reader for whom he is writing. It may help to consider briefly what the critical reader looks for when he reads a scholarly paper. First of all, the scholar should remember that his reader will not be the average person (who would prefer to be entertained) but an especially well informed and critical person who is probably an expert in the field in which the study has been made. This reader can be expected, therefore, to read the paper with unusual care, to be skeptical of its assertions unless they are proved by real evidence, and to make certain efforts to assess the accuracy of the scholar's materials. He may look up the references given in the footnotes to determine whether (1) the footnotes themselves are absolutely correct and (2) the scholar has interpreted his sources correctly. In the case of an experimental study, the reader may even repeat the experiment as described in the paper to see whether he obtains the same result.

In addition to this routine checking, various questions will be raised in the critical reader's mind that must be answered satisfactorily if the report is to be regarded favorably. Is the title an accurately descriptive one, brief and not misleading? Is the problem properly defined and the scope of the study delimited, so that no misunderstanding can develop regarding just what was studied?

Were appropriate methods chosen to test the hypothesis? Are these methods adequately described — so well described, in fact, that another person could repeat the study? Is the problem one which has never been solved before? Has previous research on the subject been found and examined by the scholar, and has he used its results in solving his present problem? Have all the pertinent data been found? Have the data been analyzed intelligently and classified logically? Have sufficient examples and illustrations been given to show how the evidence leads to the conclusions proposed by the scholar? Is the presentation of the arguments clear and logical (so that every step in the argument can be followed)? Has an objective, open-minded attitude been maintained throughout the study? Does the hypothesis follow logically from the facts? Is the thesis a worthwhile contribution to knowledge? Is good form or style (as to grammar, footnotes, etc.) used throughout the paper? Does the scholar show evidence of original thinking in his handling of the problem?

These are some of the questions which come to mind when the critical reader examines a research report. It follows, then, that these questions must also be asked by the scholar of himself when he is writing his paper.

Graphic Presentation of Data

Any full treatment of graphic presentation comprises a book in itself, and the reader who seeks detailed information on methods and materials should consult one of the several very satisfactory textbooks devoted to the subject.[2] What is attempted here is merely to suggest some of the possibilities of the graphic way of presenting data and to urge its use when appropriate.

The writer of a research report need never hesitate to include in his paper explanatory graphs, charts, illustrations, and similar ex-

---

[2] See, for example, Bruce L. Jenkinson, *Bureau of the Census Manual of Tabular Presentation* (Washington: U. S. Govt. Printing Office, 1949); R. R. Lutz, *Graphic Presentation Simplified* (New York: Funk & Wagnalls Co., 1949); Rudolf Modley, *How to Use Pictorial Statistic* (New York: Harper and Bros., 1937); Mary Eleanor Spear, *Charting Statistics* (New York: McGraw-Hill Book Co., 1952); Helen M. Walker and Walter N. Durost, *Statistical Tables: Their Structure and Use* (New York: Teachers College, Columbia University, 1936); or Hans Zeisel, *Say It with Figures* (New York: Harper and Bros., 1947).

hibits *if they facilitate understanding of the data.* Such devices, however, should not be used only because they seem interesting. Illustrations that stimulate interest may be extremely effective in a popular book or article, but they have no place in the scholarly paper if their only function is to arouse interest. The purpose of graphic presentation in writing up the results of research is not entertainment but elucidation.

Before attempting to produce a chart or drawing or photograph as a part of his paper, the scholar would be well advised to avail himself of the practical suggestions offered in a good book on graphic presentation. Most persons of intelligence, with a little aid of this kind, can produce understandable (even if not highly artistic) charts and graphs. If, however, a scholar finds that he has no ability whatsoever in this line, there would surely be no violation of scholarly ethics in his hiring a person with artistic training to do this portion of the work for him from data which the scholar supplies. A photograph made by an expert photographer will prove eminently more satisfactory for illustrative purposes than one bungled by an inexperienced amateur. An artist will know more than the average scholarly investigator about the materials and techniques for an effective chart or graph. Nevertheless, graphic presentation of an elementary kind can be accomplished satisfactorily by almost anyone.

Among the simpler charts which have proved highly effective in giving statistical information one may list, first of all, the *line graph* (also called the rectangular graph, the rectilinear graph, the curve chart, or the Cartesian coordinate graph). Other common types include the *bar chart*, the *pie chart*, the *area* or *volume chart*, the *component* or *belt chart*, the *pictorial chart*, the *flow chart*, and *maps* of several kinds. These ought to be familiar to every scholar and may be studied in detail elsewhere. For purposes of this book, a brief description of the principal ones will suffice.

The Line Graph. The line graph, perhaps the commonest and most easily contrived of all these types, shows relationships between two factors and appears especially appropriate for presenting changes that occur in a certain factor over a fairly long period of time. Suppose that the average attendance in a classroom over several months is being charted. The attendance may vary from as few as twenty to as

248 PRESENTING THE RESULTS OF RESEARCH

many as forty pupils throughout this period. After the record has been compiled and the average attendance for each month calculated, the information can be presented in very simple graphic form by using a chart like the following:[3]

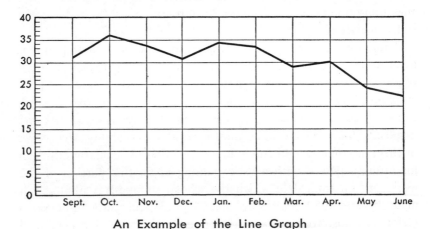

An Example of the Line Graph
Average Monthly Attendance in a Classroom, September to June

In this chart the vertical lines (drawn from equidistant points on the horizontal axis or base line) represent the months of the school year and are so labeled. The horizontal lines (drawn from equidistant points on the vertical axis) indicate the average number of pupils attending the class at various times. Where the lines intersect one may read the average attendance for any given month, and the total pattern quickly provides an idea of the variations which occur throughout the school year. Other possible ways of presenting the same information in a line graph might have been tried. For instance, the average monthly attendance might have been shown by dots placed in the spaces, rather than at the intersections of lines. Or, instead of using units of 5 for the segments on the vertical axis, the scholar might have preferred units of 10, 15, or even 20.

[3] Since the examples shown here are synthetic ones, presented primarily to show the form of the graph or chart and the type of data to which each is suited, rather than to present data in themselves, no documentation is given. In a scholarly research paper the source or sources of the data in a chart must always be fully documented.

This relatively uncomplicated example shows only one of the many ways in which the line graph may be used to present data, but it should serve to illustrate the basic nature of this type of chart, with which the student is no doubt already familiar. On the whole, the line graph should never be complicated by too much detail; usually the simplest pattern turns out best.

The Bar Chart. The bar chart, another form of presentation which has the virtue of being rather easily understood, is effective chiefly for comparisons. A number of similar items are measured with respect to some quantitative factor. Bars which represent these different quantities are then drawn to a convenient scale and placed in an arrangement which provides a rapid means of comparing the quantities visually. Often these bars are arranged in descending order of size, the longest bar (indicating the largest quantity) at the top. Suppose the salaries of public schoolteachers in several states are being compared. After information has been collected and averages calculated, the comparison may be made clear in a chart like the following:

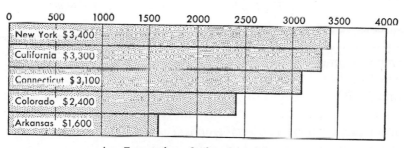

An Example of the Bar Chart
*Average Annual Salaries of Public Schoolteachers
in Selected States*

When the bars of such a chart are vertical rather than horizontal, the form is known as a *column chart*, but the same principles apply.

The Pie Chart. The pie chart has particular advantages when proportions or divisions of a whole are to be shown. In describing how the tax dollar is allocated in a state budget, for example, a chart of this kind may prove helpful.

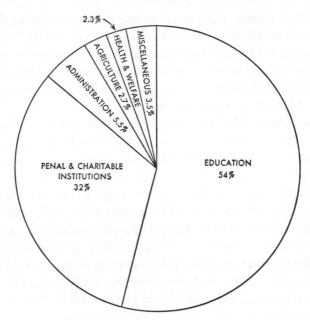

2.3%

MISCELLANEOUS 3.5%

HEALTH & WELFARE 2.7%

AGRICULTURE

ADMINISTRATION 5.5%

PENAL & CHARITABLE
INSTITUTIONS
32%

EDUCATION
54%

An Example of the Pie Chart
Allocation of Tax Funds in the Current Budget of a State

Other Types. In addition to the types of graph mentioned and identified briefly above, the scholar might well become acquainted with the nature and uses of *maps* (to show geographical relationships), and of a number of other useful diagrams such as *flow charts* (to trace the channels of authority and the divisions of responsibility in an organization) and *pictographs* (in which simple pictures or cartoons are used to help the reader grasp quickly the meanings of the symbols). Various forms of the *statistical table* (when used for illustrative purposes) may also be studied profitably in this connection.

Clear, Accurate, Self-contained Diagrams. Whatever chart or diagram is used, the scholar should be careful to make it clear, accurate, and self-contained. *Clearness* can best be achieved by keeping the design simple and by limiting the types and number of symbols used. Nothing very complicated should ever be attempted in a single chart, for complexity leads to confusion. When the material to be shown is complicated, the difficulty of presenting it clearly can often be overcome by making more than one chart and thus distributing the burden of information which each one carries.

Accuracy is especially important because an inaccurate chart can easily convey a false impression. The scholar must always ask himself whether his diagram actually gives an honest impression of the facts and makes the true meaning of the facts apparent. (As everybody knows, there are ways of stating facts which amount really to telling lies.) Moreover, graphic representation has many unexpected pitfalls for the amateur. If, for example, you represent a certain quantity by a square whose side is one-quarter of an inch long, you could not accurately represent twice that amount by a square whose side is twice that length, or one-half inch long, because the second square would then actually show *four* times, not twice, the area of the first square.

To be *self-contained* the chart must have a title which identifies it, an explanation of the symbols and of how the information is to be read, a description of what the chart is supposed to show, and a statement (ordinarily in a footnote) giving the sources of the data. The data presented in a chart or table must be documented in exactly the same way as any other quotation or citation in the scholarly paper.

If two or more charts or exhibits are used in a paper, it is customary to number them for ease of reference. (The scholar can refer to them as Figure I, Figure II, etc.) When several charts are used, they should generally be placed in an appendix at the end of the paper; otherwise they may interrupt the continuity and thus interfere with an understanding of the arguments. A style manual will answer most questions that arise over the mechanics of numbering, identifying, and placing the graphic materials in the report.

Graphic presentation does not, of course, take the place of careful verbal explanation. This is an extremely important point. A chart illustrates the evidence discussed in the paper and thus aids in understanding it better or supports it in more detail, but the written presentation should be so capably handled that adequate understanding is possible and adequate support given without illustrations. In other words, the scholar when writing his paper should not lean too heavily upon graphic presentation alone. He must clearly and fully describe his data in verbal or mathematical symbols and then employ illustrations only as an additional means of elucidating the subject. Graphic presentation can add much to the effectiveness of the written report so long as it is not made a crutch or a substitute for the essential business of presenting information in words.

Some Common Faults in Scholarly Papers

Perhaps the most serious of the faults more commonly found in scholarly papers is the tendency to make broad, sweeping statements without sufficient evidence and sometimes without any documentation. However impressive these may sound, they are dangerous because they mislead not only the reader but the scholar himself, and they are often based upon either thoughtlessness or prejudice.

Another common fault is lack of precision in statements — a tendency to generalize or to state ideas vaguely. This can be corrected by making certain that the scholar really knows what he means and that he is saying exactly what he means.

A third fault is weakness of organization and arrangement. This occurs chiefly when the scholar begins to write without having thought through the total structure of his argument. To write without advance planning can be disastrous.

A fourth fault is failure to describe fully and clearly the method by which the hypothesis was tested. The scholar should never leave his reader in doubt regarding the method used in the study.

A fifth fault, and one which occurs frequently, results probably from the scholar's misunderstanding of his problem; it consists in a lack of direct connection between problem and hypothesis. In other words, the hypothesis really applies to another problem than the one which was supposed to have been studied. The scholar should be sure that his proposed hypothesis constitutes a solution to the problem as he has defined it.

A sixth fault is that of summarizing materials from some source without clearly showing how they are derived from the source and without some introductory statement about the source and the summary which the scholar has made. These omissions may lead to confusion over the nature of the material.

A seventh fault frequently encountered is failure to distinguish between problem and purpose. The statement of the problem tells *what* was studied; the statement of purpose tells *why* it was studied.

Finally, there is the fault of introducing new elements into the summary. When a new piece of information turns up after the report has been written, it should be placed in the body of the paper (even if this means some rewriting) or in a footnote, never in the summary alone.

Summary

The scholarly report is the means by which the scholar informs others about his work. It is not ordinarily written until after the successful completion of the study itself. The report and the study are two different things and must not be confused.

A scholarly report is written to inform rather than to entertain or to impress. The writer should avoid oratory and circumlocution and go directly to the point. Before beginning to write he should carefully organize and outline the whole report.

While the scholarly report cannot be said to have any fixed pattern, there is normally an introductory section that describes the problem and the method of study and states the hypothesis or conclusion reached. Following this are presented the reasons or arguments confirming the hypothesis, together with all the evidence in support of these arguments. At the end of the paper it is customary (and also helpful) to summarize briefly the entire study. Recommendations for action based on the results of the study are not properly a part of the scholarly study itself, but may be appended in a separate section if desired.

The scholar should use clear and simple English in writing. He should give the source of every factual statement and should conscientiously identify basic assumptions or mere opinions. He should keep in mind what the critical and intelligent reader will be looking for when reading the report. The tried and proved methods of graphic presentation should be studied and used whenever they may help in elucidating the data. Graphs, charts, tables, and other illustrations and arrays must be understandable, accurate, and self-contained. They should not, however, take the place of a full verbal (or mathematical) explanation of the data.

17 PUBLICATION:

THE ULTIMATE GOAL

Discoveries of new knowledge can be of little consequence to the world unless they become known to people who will actually use the information. Without any doubt, much valuable information on hundreds of important current problems lies useless and gathering dust on the shelves of our university libraries in the form of unpublished masters' theses or doctoral dissertations. Other data remain locked in the pages of scholarly reports which the authors never have taken the trouble to publish.

Publication is the means by which the scholar officially makes his discoveries known to his colleagues and to the world in general. Without publication his work may be of use to himself but can hardly be useful to anyone else. Thus publication is not so much a desirable achievement for the scholar as it is a definite obligation upon him. He must release the results of his investigations to the world as a part of his professional duty. There are, of course, research men working for private commercial companies whose discoveries are kept secret for the exclusive use of one company; and there are dictatorial governments which do not allow freedom of publication to their scholars for fear some other country might profit from the information. (In fact, nearly all governments today place restrictions of one kind or another upon the circulation of new knowledge which has important military value.) By and large, however, the scholar seeks truth so that, when it is discovered, it can be given freely to the world for the betterment of mankind and man's condition. This is an essential portion of the great academic tradition which we have inherited from the scholars of the past.

One of the questions frequently asked by the beginning scholar is: How much can I expect to be paid for a published article? The answer is (with a very few exceptions): Nothing. Perhaps this may prove difficult for the beginner to comprehend. He knows many persons, no doubt, who write articles and stories for money, some of whom even make a living in this way. But such writers produce their works for commercial publication and write chiefly to entertain the general public. They write for profit, and thus publication becomes an end in itself. To a scholar, on the other hand, the writing and publishing of a report cannot be regarded as an end in itself but rather as the means by which he informs his colleagues of his discoveries. He writes in order to make some contribution to the world's knowledge. Often he actually pays for publication out of his own pocket. Publication must be recognized, then, as a scholarly duty rather than as a method of profiting from research.

Furthermore, publications which print the results of research usually are not read (and would not be understood) by the public in general. They can be of use only to the informed scholars of one academic field. Thus they necessarily have a very limited circulation and often must be subsidized by some university or research foundation in order to exist at all. Even if they desired strongly to do so, they could not afford to pay for the work published.

The scholar, therefore, must set aside any ideas of monetary gain from publication of his reports. If a report is book-length, he may even find that he must pay a substantial share of the cost of publication himself. The relatively small number of university presses which issue scholarly books are unable to finance all the volumes they would like to publish. They tend for this reason to restrict their efforts to books which they consider of major importance. A few publishers have experimented with cheaper methods of book production (such as lithoprinting) to make it possible to print works of a scholarly nature which might not otherwise appear in published form.

The Scholarly Article

The manuscript of a scholarly article which is being prepared for submission to the editor of a periodical should, by and large, receive the same treatment as any paper carefully prepared in the course of one's required graduate work. It should be typewritten neatly and legibly on standard-sized typewriting paper, using only one side of the sheet. The typing should be double-spaced throughout (except for quoted materials of three or more lines, which are single-spaced and indented). Naturally, the grammar and spelling ought to be impeccable, and any typographical errors should be carefully and neatly corrected with pen and ink. In general, with the exception of special information which a graduate school or a professor may desire the student to include on his title page, the publishable article need not be noticeably different in its outward form and appearance from the usual carefully prepared class paper.

The scholar who prepares an article for publication should supply, as his first manuscript page, a suitable title page that contains the full title of the paper (in capital letters), the name and address of the author, and the name and address of the publisher (or of the periodical) to whom the manuscript is being sent. These items really are all that are needed on the title page. On the second page of the manuscript, the scholar should leave three or four inches of space at the top, then write the title as he wishes to have it appear in the printed article (which is just as it appears on the title page also), and skip three or four spaces below the title before starting his first paragraph. Usually no table of contents at the beginning, nor index at the end, is necessary for an article. Beginning at the first page of the article, not counting the title page, every page must be numbered consecutively through to the end, preferably in the upper right-hand corner. It sometimes helps to typewrite across the top of each page an abbreviation of the title and the author's name, in addition to a page number. This identifies the page if it ever becomes misplaced or mixed with other papers.

Footnotes may be placed at the bottom of the page, just as they will appear in the printed article; though some publishers prefer to have them placed at the point of occurrence, immediately under the line in which the reference and footnote number occur. In this case a solid straight line must be typewritten above and below the inserted footnote in order to separate it from the body of the paper. This, of course, is done mainly for the benefit of the typesetter. In the usual article the footnotes are numbered consecutively throughout the entire work — that is, the author does not begin a new numbering system with each new page.

Because a bibliography does not ordinarily constitute one of the parts of the printed article (although many exceptions to this rule can be found), full information about each work referred to in a footnote should be supplied within the footnote itself. The precise title of the cited work, its author's full name, the place and date of publication, and (especially if it is a fairly recent book) the publisher's name — all these bibliographical facts ought to appear in the footnote if there is to be no bibliography. A few periodicals, however, do encourage the inclusion of a bibliography, and in such instances the amount of detail given in the footnote may be substantially reduced. Nevertheless, there still remains an absolute minimum of information which the footnote must contain: the author's name, the title of the work, and the page number or numbers.

Once the entire manuscript has been typewritten in good form and is ready for mailing, it may be placed unfolded in a large mailing envelope. The pages can be held together with a paper clip; they should not be fastened together with a staple or similar device. Insertion of a sheet of stiff cardboard for backing will prevent wrinkling or folding of the manuscript in transit. The cardboard should fit into the envelope snugly. A manuscript is first-class mailing matter, and it is best sent by registered mail. Or it may go by prepaid express. It should be firmly sealed. Occasionally items do go astray in the mails, and it is always advisable to retain a carbon copy. Before sealing and mailing his manuscript, the author should place inside the envelope sufficient postage for the paper to be returned if it is not accepted for publication. The scholar should never expect the editor of a periodical to bear the cost of mailing back a rejected manuscript. (An exception to this rule might occur, however, if the manuscript was originally sent by *request* of the editor. An unsolicited article must always be accompanied by return postage.)

Young scholars perhaps ought to be cautioned never to send papers to editors merely for criticism — without the intention of offering the material for publication. This kind of thing may be done occasionally by inconsiderate persons, but it only causes annoyance. To make absolutely clear what his intentions are, it is customary for the author to include a short explanation like "Submitted for publication" or "Offered for publication" on his title page or, better, to enclose a brief covering letter with his article. Such a covering letter should never praise or attempt to "sell" the article. The author should simply explain that he is sending his article to be considered for possible publication. He may also point out that return postage has been enclosed, but usually no additional information of any kind is necessary. In rare instances the author may wish to draw special attention to certain matters of unusual importance or interst pertaining to the paper, and he may even invite suggestions for changes which might improve his presentation. As a rule, however, the less he says, the better. His article will stand on its own merits and will undoubtedly receive a thorough and impartial reading by one or more informed scholars in his field before being either accepted or rejected.

Once a manuscript has been sent away to an editor, several weeks may pass before the author will receive any word about it. Some editors — though not all — acknowledge a manuscript as soon as it arrives in the office. A careful reading by those who must pass upon its merits may take weeks in some cases. Eventually the author will be notified that his article has been accepted or will have it returned to him.

If the article has been accepted, publication may not actually occur for as long as a year. Editors plan the various issues of their periodicals well in advance, and scholars must control any impatience to see their work in print. On occasion the editor may report that all space in the periodical has been allocated for more than a year ahead, and in such a situation he may offer the writer a choice between delayed publication or the right to seek a place for the article in some other periodical.

If the article is conditionally accepted, certain changes must be made before it can be published. The author may not care to make the changes proposed; in that case he should ask to have the manuscript returned. If he agrees to the changes, either he or the editor may do the necessary rewriting. (It has been this writer's experience that alterations proposed by editors almost invariably help to improve the paper.)

If the article is rejected, the author should not expect elaborate critical comments or a detailed explanation of the reasons for non-acceptance, though some considerate editors are kind enough to supply such information. The author should very carefully reread a rejected manuscript before sending it on to the editor of some other periodical. No writer need be discouraged by one or two rejections (or even several), for a rejection does not always imply lack of merit in the paper. What one periodical cannot use may be snatched up eagerly by another. Yet rejection by one editor, especially when the reasons for it are explained by critical comment, should bring to the author's mind immediately the possible need for revision. He should never try his paper on another editor until he has thoroughly convinced himself that rewriting (or even restudy of the problem) would not considerably improve it.

Proofreading, Offprints, and Other Matters

Some weeks before an accepted article is to be printed and issued, galley proof will be forwarded to the author for correction. This will come to him in the form of long sheets of inexpensive paper on which the article has been printed without any page divisions or other attempts at proper spacing. The purpose of a galley reading is to locate and mark all errors which were made by the printer in setting the type. Proofs should be read with extreme care, and every error must be indicated in such a way that the printer can correct it before setting up the article in page form. A scholar who has never before performed the task of proofreading may consult a good modern dictionary for information about the symbols commonly used in the correction of printer's proof.

It should be emphasized that galley proof is sent to the author only to make certain that he has the opportunity of preventing typographical mistakes from appearing in the final printing. He should never, except by special advance arrangement with his editor, seek to rewrite any substantial portion of the article once it has been set up in type. Changes made at this point in the proceedings are expensive and should be unnecessary, and many editors flatly refuse to permit them unless the author is willing to pay the costs. Because an article is presumed to be in final and perfect form when submitted by its author, there can hardly be any justification for very much rewriting unless new evidence has unexpectedly turned up in the meantime. The author who insists upon the privilege of rewriting and improving his work after he receives the galley proof only demonstrates his lack of maturity or his failure to understand the practical aspects of publishing.

At the same time that he corrects proof, the author of an article usually is offered the opportunity to purchase offprints. An offprint is a separately published copy of the article, printed just as it appears in the periodical, and ordinarily available to the author (but to no one else) for distribution among his friends and colleagues. It may be supplied with or without covers. Most authors of scholarly articles will want 50 to 100 offprints (which, by the way, can be had only while the type is still standing and not later when it has been broken up); the cost of these will depend upon the length of the article, the number of copies ordered, and whether covers are supplied. Offprints are sometimes referred to as reprints, a word which means pretty much the same thing; though *reprint*, strictly speaking, signifies a second printing or a facsimile edition of a work.

The scholar can help to reduce the number of errors which occur in setting type if he will study carefully the periodical for which he is writing before he begins the preparation of his manuscript. The style of presentation in one periodical may be slightly different from that in another. The scholar should acquaint himself with stylistic differences and adapt his own style to them. For example, his manner of handling footnotes must be patterned conscientiously after those of the other articles printed in the periodical for which he is writing. Since every periodical has its own way of treating certain details, the only method by which one can be sure of conforming to the requirements of a particular periodical is to study that periodical beforehand. Any deviations in the manuscript will have to be changed by the editor, and such changes and corrections always open the way to errors.

The Scholarly Book Review

One type of writing which the scholar frequently finds himself called upon to do for publication is the scholarly book review. Whenever a new book of scholarly interest appears, it is customary for its publisher to send a few review copies to the editors of periodicals in the field with which the book deals. These editors then seek out prominent and respected scholars in that field who are willing to read the book and render their judgment of it.

Sometimes, on the other hand, reviews may be written and submitted voluntarily by individual scholars. There is nothing at all wrong with this latter practice, though it is less usual than the assigned review. Before submitting a book review, the scholar should, of course, make certain that the editor to whom he sends it has not already made arrangements in the matter with somebody else. By and large, a review should not be submitted later than one year (or, at the very most, two years) after the book has been published.

Unless the book seems to be of more than ordinary importance in its field, a review seldom needs to be longer than 500 to 800 words. Occasionally a review of somewhat greater length may be permissible. No special title for the review is customarily required, though some periodicals prefer to have one. The basic bibliographical information about the book serves in place of a title for the review. Such items as the book's full title, its author's name, the date and place of publication, the publishing firm's name, the number of pages, and the price must be set down in the regular form sanctioned by the periodical for which the review is being written.

The review itself should always do more than merely describe whether the reviewer liked or disliked the book. In general, it should seek to accomplish four major purposes. First, it should clearly and succinctly state the main thesis of the book. What has the author attempted to prove? What problem did he study, and what hypothesis did he formulate? What has he contributed to knowledge? Second, it should analyze and assess the materials presented as evidence. Is the author's argument convincing? Do his data bear the test of critical scrutiny? Third, it should consider whether the materials have been well and effectively presented. Are the ideas developed logically? Has the author succeeded in conveying his information with both clarity and forcefulness? Is the material in the book properly organized? Is the style of writing understandable and pleasing? Finally, the review should contain the critic's judgment as to the general value of the book and the type of reader for whom it will prove useful or interesting. If it contains these four essentials, a review can serve an important purpose for other scholars; for they can save precious time, as new books in their field appear, by determining from a perusal of scholarly reviews which books they must read at once, which books they may reserve until a later time, and which books they need not read at all. For the most part, it may be considered less vital for the scholar who is reading a review to know the critic's judgment or impression of the book than to be accurately informed of exactly what is in the book. Like all scholarly writing, therefore, the review ought to be informative rather than merely entertaining.

Summary

To make his discoveries known to the world, the scholar must accept the task of publication as one of his essential responsibilities. Ordinarily he can expect no payment for this type of service to scholarship; in fact, he may even have to defray a share of the publication costs out of his own pocket.

The manuscript of a scholarly article should be prepared in much the same way that an important course paper is prepared. When ready, it may be submitted to one of the periodicals in the scholar's field, accompanied by a brief covering letter and return postage. If the article is accepted, the author must not expect immediate printing, and he may be asked to make certain changes in the article before the editor deems it publishable. He must be prepared to correct the galley proof carefully; absolute accuracy at every step in this process is vital.

The scholarly book review is a type of writing for publication in which the scholar frequently engages. Reviews help to inform colleagues regarding new publications in the field. A review should explain the thesis of the work reviewed, analyze the materials presented, assess the method by which this presentation is accomplished, and pass judgment on the general value of the work, at the same time indicating the type of reader for whom the book is intended.

18

THE QUESTION

OF ORIGINALITY

How essential is originality in a research project? What are the grounds upon which one may judge whether a piece of research is truly original? These questions appear to perplex some young scholars.

Anything which is not original, of course, cannot really be considered a contribution to knowledge. Every scholar should pride himself upon independence of thought. To pass off another person's ideas as one's own is not only dishonest but also extremely damaging to self-respect. For the true scholar the most highly prized reward of achievement is the exuberant personal satisfaction he experiences in solving a difficult problem which nobody previously has been able to attack successfully, and in thus adding to the stockpile of the world's knowledge a fact or principle never before known, therefore new as well as true. To a person imbued with the real spirit of scholarship, no returns in money or glory could equal his mental elation at the triumphant conquest of some profound and knotty problem and the free gift of that new knowledge to his fellow-mortals.

To be called original, a piece of scholarship must be considerably more than a rehash of other scholars' ideas. One sometimes hears on university campuses a rather barren joke, half believed by graduate students until they manage to learn better: To copy from one person's writings is plagiarism, to copy from the writings of many is research. This misconception, actually put into practice by some

263

young scholars, regrettably stems from a lack of understanding of the real nature of originality. A mere summary of what others have learned or of their opinions with respect to some problem does not provide a solution to the problem. In fact, it constitutes the bare preliminary to research. Learning what others have done or thought about a problem is essential to determine the present state of knowledge on the subject, and therefore always precedes research. But having hunted down all existing studies and comments with respect to the problem chosen, and having examined and summarized all the conclusions reached or the opinions proposed in these sources, the scholar finds himself not finished with his investigation but only ready at last to begin his own search for additional evidence and the formulation of his own hypothesis. An intelligent summary of already existing knowledge on some subject can prove decidedly valuable in extending the student's fund of information and is thus a desirable educative experience, but it should never be confused with real research.

Part of the difficulty in confusing a survey of knowledge with a contribution to knowledge may result from the strong urge felt by many a young investigator to produce a paper and earn favorable recognition for scholarly attainment. There is an old and well-known scholarly disease known as *rushing into print* which affects a considerable number of scholars. The desire to see a piece of work printed and admired (or sometimes the need for a grade and credit in a college course) may cause the scholar to write up his report prematurely, before he can be quite certain of his results — in other words, before he has really carried the study to completion.

Charles Darwin worked for some fifteen years after formulating his theory of natural selection and survival of the fittest before he was ready to publish his discoveries. Even then he probably would have delayed publication had not another investigator of evolutionary biology, Alfred Russel Wallace, arrived at nearly identical conclusions and written an essay on the subject. Wallace, who had previously had some correspondence on scientific matters with Darwin, sent the latter a copy of his essay to read. It was entitled "The Tendency of Varieties to Depart Indefinitely from the Original Type" and was based upon observations made among the flora and fauna of Brazil and the Malayan archipelago. After consulting some of his close friends and scientific acquaintances who knew about his own work in this field, Darwin wisely arranged for the simultaneous publication of Wallace's essay and an abstract of his own projected book. The two reports were read before a meeting of the Linnaean Society on July 1, 1858. Darwin's principal report, the famous On the Origin of Species, appeared slightly more than a year later.

Credit and Cooperation

When two investigators announce identical discoveries at about the same time and especially when each has arrived at his conclusions independently, to whom shall the credit go? In the case of Darwin and Wallace, the theory of natural selection sometimes is attributed to them jointly and spoken of as the Darwin-Wallace hypothesis. Yet the work of Darwin on the subject was so much more detailed and his data so numerous that Wallace's essay seems almost like a mere abstract of the larger study. Both men, incidentally, appear to have been influenced in developing the theory by reading the work of Malthus on population growth. Most people today are likely to associate the theory of natural selection with Darwin alone. Similar confusion exists with respect to identifying the discoverer of ether's usefulness as an anesthetic. In recent years a large number of medical research men, working both independently and in teams, sharing discoveries as they are made, have been conducting studies in the hope of developing a cure or a safe preventive of poliomyelitis; and when it is found, who shall say which of them shall be accorded the credit?

Strictly speaking, the ideal attitude in research considers public service before everything else. The credit for an important new discovery should be regarded as of less moment than the fact of the discovery itself. Perhaps this ideal tends to ignore the ever-prevalent human factor, the natural desire of all human beings for public recognition of their achievements. Years ago it was quite common to see scholars withholding bits of information from one another, out of what might be called professional jealousy. Occasionally two scholars would engage in a race to see which of them could succeed in finishing a study first and publishing his report before the other.

The first one to publish would then receive the credit; the other might be considered an interloper or imitator. We have now grown more mature, and scholars today delight in exchanging information with one another, knowing that such mutual aid furthers the cause of all scholarship. No honest scholar, of course, would accept information or ideas from another without making proper and grateful acknowledgment of the debt in his published report.

As was mentioned in an earlier chapter, the ethics of scholarship dictate that no scholar shall undertake to investigate a problem which already is under investigation by another scholar. No reputable scholar would knowingly violate this principle, though occasionally it may be transgressed through ignorance. The principle, to be sure, does not apply in the case of an unusual or pressing investigation in which the efforts of many investigators have been invited and encouraged. For example, experiments aimed at finding the means of preventing poliomyelitis have been conducted over a period of years in many medical laboratories throughout the United States, not to mention the studies which have been going on at the same time in other countries. Here a special and vigorous campaign has been waged in the hope of securing results as quickly as possible. Public funds have been collected for the support of such research. We have, then, an extraordinary set of circumstances which do not apply to most research projects; there is no violation of ethics when dozens of medical research teams attack, as they have in this instance, an identical problem of such obvious magnitude and and one which so directly concerns the public welfare. A scholar is also justified in taking a problem, even though it has been studied by someone else, if the other investigator has failed to produce results within a reasonable time or has given up his attempts to solve it.

The Dangers of the Premature Report

Rather than exercising an unwise eagerness to rush into print, the scholar should be concerned first of all with the soundness of his work. This nearly always means taking a great deal of time and pains. "Be sure you are right before you publish" is an old but excellent piece of scholarly advice. The young scholar must be willing to spend much more time than he may suppose to be necessary in making absolutely certain that he has found the best solution of his problem, that he has discovered all essential data, that he has not been misled by inaccurate or incomplete observation or by his own prejudgments. Proper assimilation of the vast amount of data usually compiled in the course of any thorough study takes time in itself. The deadline a student must meet in the graduate school or his own very natural desire to be first in the field with some new hypothesis tends to develop a feeling of annoyed impatience with the laborious processes of good research. But research, like genius, owes much to an infinite capacity for taking pains, and the best counsel one can give to an inexperienced investigator is this: *Never be in too much of a hurry.*

The same tendency toward impatience which we often find in the young scholar may blind him to the vital advantage of revising the early drafts of his written report. Revision may well be done several times — and with increasing profit each time. Hardly anyone except a practiced writer can say everything he wishes to say as effectively as possible at his first attempt. Even competent writers of long experience find it essential to revise their writings in order to improve them. How much more beneficial revision must be, then, for the person without much experience in writing or without a special flair for it, especially when he is trying to record numerous and minute details which must be handled with exceeding care and accuracy! Painstaking care in the presentation of research data in the written report can be as vital to the success of a study as the care with which the data were gathered and analyzed in the first place. For most persons the best way to achieve the utmost possible effectiveness in writing the research report is to make an outline of the material first, then to write a preliminary draft of the report, and finally to revise this draft until it satisfies the writer's highest critical standards. The truly original study is the one that has been carefully carried through to completion at every stage, including the final writing.

Originality in the Selection of a Problem

Perhaps a further word needs to be said at this point with regard to the originality involved in the selection of a subject for study. Since the scholar would not be likely to make a really new discovery except by approaching an entirely new problem, originality can be seen to start with problem selection. Although it may be possible to study an old problem in some new way, most investigators find it more satisfactory to attack a problem never before studied. A danger to avoid here, however, is the tendency to pick subjects which are palpably trivial and therefore not worth the time and effort spent in solving them. The value of any problem, it must be admitted, always is a matter of judgment and opinion. A subject which appears trivial at first glance may prove on later examination to have some significance. Nevertheless, many subjects picked by graduate students have the fault of being *obviously* trivial in value, and most of these apparently are picked only because nobody else has previously studied them. Newness in itself should not be the sole criterion in the selection of a problem. In considering any possible topic for investigation, the young scholar may well ask himself whether a particular problem has remained unsolved for the very good reason that it is not really worth solving. A person thoroughly familiar with his field can find plenty of subjects of demonstrable importance needing solution. He should select one of these rather than waste his abilities, in the hope of being original, on matters too slight to justify the time and effort involved. On the other hand, when curiosity truly piques him to learn the solution to some intriguing problem, no matter how trivial it may be, the scholar should be willing to accept the challenge. He should, of course, keep his judgments in perspective and recognize a slight and unimportant problem for what it is.

The Nature of the Doctoral Dissertation and the Master's Thesis

In most graduate schools it is customary to require, as part of the work done to earn an advanced degree, an independent study of an original nature properly conducted by the student, with a report of the procedures and findings written up in the form of a dissertation or thesis. The purpose of this requirement is principally to determine whether the student is able to add original knowledge to his field. Can he sucessfully carry through a major piece of independent research? Many students misunderstand the nature and the purpose of a doctoral study or master's thesis and naively expect members of the faculty to exercise strict supervision over every phase of the investigation. Such is not the case in most good graduate schools. The student is deliberately thrown upon his own resources and must prove his ability to identify a suitable problem, to devise a workable method of solving it, to locate and assess correctly the value and meaning of all pertinent evidence, and to arrive at a logical, defensible conclusion.

The doctoral dissertation or master's thesis ordinarily begins when the student applies to the authorities of the graduate school or the department (often through a major professor) for permission to investigate a certain problem within his field. He may indicate what steps he has taken to assure the fact that the problem is new and that he himself is qualified to undertake a solution. Some universities may ask the student to submit a detailed written outline of his proposal, including a careful statement of the problem and its limitations, a description of the procedures he plans to follow, a tentative hypothesis, an explanation of his reasons for undertaking the investigation and the probable usefulness of its results, definitions of special terms to be used in the final report, a review of the current literature (i. e., research) on the subject, and a brief statement regarding the student's qualifications for the project. Other universities may be content to know only what the actual problem is. In either case, the essential thing to understand is that, whatever the university authorities may ask for in the way of preliminary information, they expect the student to shoulder the burden of proof as to his capability and his plans, as well as to assume the full initiative in getting the study under way. Permission to conduct the study under university auspices does not include any kind of guarantee that the study will prove feasible, that the problem approved will not have to be changed, or that the method adopted will bring satisfactory results. If the problem later has to be abandoned or the results prove inconclusive, the student should not blame the faculty for approving it but only himself. The action the faculty takes is merely to make sure, in granting its permission to proceed, that the student has a real problem in mind and that he seems qualified to investigate it.

Once he has received official sanction to begin the study, the student should not look to his adviser or major professor to tell him exactly what he must do. Except for occasional conferences, he should work, in the main, independently. Some professors are willing to work very closely and for long periods of time with a student and like to keep in direct and continual touch with all the steps in the study. Other professors make no attempt at checking on the young scholar's progress and volunteer no advice, but are always willing to discuss difficulties he may encounter in his investigation and will offer sound advice when consulted. In general, the student should regard his major professor as a "resource person" who can provide aid when the going gets rough but not as one who lays down detailed instructions for the conduct of the study. The doctoral dissertation or master's thesis loses much of its value for the student and can be no true test of his ability if too many of the basic decisions have to be made by a professor instead of by the student himself.

When the student has by hard work and profound thinking completed a significant study independently and has presented it in good form as part of the requirement for his degree, he can be justly proud of his achievement. He can now claim a place among the world's leaders in the advancement of knowledge. He has demonstrated beyond question his power to stand upon his own feet as a thinking man and produce an original work of research. There is, and should be, great personal and intellectual satisfaction in this accomplishment. It is to those who have learned how to solve difficult, serious problems of scholarship independently and who can thus add vital original knowledge to the world's present store that we look for the continued progress of our civilization in the generations to come.

Summary

Originality is the touchstone of all true research, for research means adding new knowledge to the field in which it is undertaken. A rehash of other people's ideas or discoveries does not constitute research.

The scholar of today, in striving for originality, is striving to add new truth to the store of human knowledge; he is not concerned with originality as a means of enhancing his prestige. In the past, scholars frequently vied with one another to secure exclusive credit for making new discoveries. Today, having developed a more mature attitude in scholarship, we have a constant exchange of information among those working on similar studies. No scholar will undertake a problem on which another scholar is already working, in the hope of solving it first and winning the race for publication; on the other hand, if a problem is in the public interest, many scholars may ethically work on it at the same time, in the hope of speeding its solution.

Lack of originality may result from failure to carry a project far enough. An exhaustive survey of the ground covered by others is only the starting point for original work of one's own. Impatience to obtain a degree or to see one's work in print may destroy the value of a study by encouraging a premature report — a report made, that is, before the problem has really been solved or properly written up.

Originality is an important consideration in choosing a subject. The problem, to yield new knowledge, must normally be a hitherto untouched one. The search for a new problem, however, occasionally traps a young scholar into the mistake of choosing a trivial subject not worth his time and effort.

Work done by the student on a doctoral dissertation or master's thesis must be original and independent. He should not expect the faculty to instruct him in his method of procedure, for he is being tested to determine whether he can successfully carry through an original research project. Independent success in research not only provides great personal satisfaction to the scholar but marks him as one who is capable of assuming leadership in the essential and rewarding task of adding to the world's knowledge.

CJ58

SELECTED BIBLIOGRAPHY _____

Albaugh, Ralph M. *Thesis Writing*. Ames, Iowa: Littlefield, Adams and Co., 1951.

Alexander, Carter. *How to Locate Educational Information and Data*. New York: Teachers College, Columbia University, 1950.

Altick, Richard D. *The Scholar Adventurers*. New York: The Macmillan Co., 1950.

Barr, Arvil S., and others. *Educational Research and Appraisal*. Philadelphia: J. B. Lippincott Co., 1953.

Beveridge, W. I. B. *The Art of Scientific Investigation*. New York: W. W. Norton and Co., 1950.

Burtt, Edwin Arthur. *Right Thinking*. New York: Harper and Bros., 1946.

Campbell, William G. *Form and Style in Thesis Writing*. Boston: Houghton Mifflin Co., 1954.

Chapin, Francis S. *Experimental Design in Sociological Research*. New York: Harper and Bros., 1947.

Clark, Charles E. *An Introduction to Statistics*. New York: John Wiley and Sons, 1953.

Cochran, William G. *Sampling Techniques*. New York: John Wiley and Sons, 1953.

Cohen, Lillian. *Statistical Methods for Social Scientists*. New York: Prentice-Hall, 1954.

Cohen, Morris R. *A Preface to Logic*. New York: Henry Holt and Co., 1944.

Columbia Associates in Philosophy. *An Introduction to Reflective Thinking*. Boston: Houghton Mifflin Co., 1923.

Corey, Stephen M. *Action Research to Improve School Practices*. New York: Teachers College, Columbia University, 1953.

Curti, Merle, ed. *American Scholarship in the Twentieth Century*. Cambridge: Harvard University Press, 1953.

Deming, William Edwards. *Some Theory of Sampling*. New York: John Wiley and Sons, 1950.

Dewey, John. *How We Think*. Boston: D. C. Heath and Co., 1933.

Edwards, Allen L. *Experimental Design in Psychological Research*. New York: Rinehart and Co., 1950.

Eells, Walter Crosby. *Surveys of American Higher Education*. New York: Carnegie Foundation for the Advancement of Teaching, 1937. Esp. Chapter IX.

Festinger, Leon, and Daniel Katz. *Research Methods in the Behavioral Sciences*. New York: Dryden Press, 1953.

Freund, John E. *Modern Elementary Statistics*. New York: Prentice-Hall, 1952.

Garraghan, Gilbert J. *A Guide to Historical Method*. New York: Fordham University Press, 1948.

Garrett, Henry E. *Statistics in Psychology and Education*. New York: Longmans, Green and Co., 1953.

Gee, Wilson. *Social Science Research Methods*. New York: Appleton-Century-Crofts, 1950.

Good, Carter V. *How to Do Research in Education*. Baltimore: Warwick and York, 1928.

Good, Carter V., A. S. Barr, and Douglas E. Scates. *The Methodology of Educational Research*. New York: Appleton-Century-Crofts, 1941.

Good, Carter V., and Douglas E. Scates, *Methods of Research*. New York: Appleton-Century-Crofts, 1954.

Hagood, Margaret Jarman. *Statistics for Sociologists*. New York: Henry Holt and Co., 1941.

Hilbish, Florence M. A. *The Research Paper*. New York: Bookman Associates, 1952.

Hockett, H. C. *Introduction to Research in American History*. New York: The Macmillan Co., 1949.

Holmes, Henry W., and others. *Educational Research*. Washington: American Council on Education, 1939.

Huff, Darrell. *How to Lie with Statistics*. New York: W. W. Norton and Co., 1954.

Hyman, Herbert H., and others. *Interviewing in Social Research*. Chicago: University of Chicago Press, 1954.

Jahoda, Marie, Morton Deutsch, and Stuart W. Cook. *Research Methods in Social Relations*. 2 vols. New York: Dryden Press, 1951.

Jenkinson, Bruce L. *Bureau of the Census Manual of Tabular Presentation*. Washington: U.S. Govt. Printing Office, 1949.

Johnson, Palmer O. *Statistical Methods in Research*. New York: Prentice-Hall, 1949.

Johnson, Palmer O., and Robert W. B. Jackson. *Introduction to Statistical Methods*. New York: Prentice-Hall, 1953.

Koos, Leonard V. *The Questionnaire in Education*. New York: The Macmillan Co., 1928.

Larson, Leonard A., Morey R. Fields, and Milton A. Gabrielson. *Problems in Health, Physical and Recreation Education*. New York: Prentice-Hall, 1953.

Lewis, Edward E. *Methods of Statistical Analysis in Economics and Business*. Boston: Houghton Mifflin Co., 1953.

Lindquist, E. F. *A First Course in Statistics*. Boston: Houghton Mifflin Co., 1938.

Lindquist, E. F. *Statistical Analysis in Educational Research*. Boston: Houghton Mifflin Co., 1940.

Lindquist, E. F. *Design and Analysis of Experiments in Psychology and Education*. Boston: Houghton Mifflin Co., 1953.

Luck, David J., and Hugh G. Wales. *Marketing Research*. New York: Prentice-Hall, 1952.

Lutz, R. R. *Graphic Presentation Simplified*. New York: Funk and Wagnalls Co., 1949.

McCall, William A. *How to Experiment in Education*. New York: The Macmillan Co., 1930.

McConnell, T. R., Douglas E. Scates, and Frank N. Freeman. *The Conceptual Structure of Educational Research*. Chicago: University of Chicago, 1942.

McNemar, Quinn. *Psychological Statistics*. New York: John Wiley and Sons, 1955.

Mead, Margaret, and Rhoda Métraux, eds. *The Study of Culture at a Distance*. Chicago: University of Chicago Press, 1953.

Measurement and Evaluation Materials in Health, Physical Education, and Recreation. Bulletin of the American Association for Health, Physical Education, and Recreation. Washington, 1950.

Modley, Rudolf. *How to Use Pictorial Statistics*. New York: Harper and Bros., 1937.

Modley, Rudolf. *Pictographs and Graphs: How to Make and Use Them*. New York: Harper and Bros., 1952.

Monroe, Walter S., and Max D. Engelhardt. *The Scientific Study of Educational Problems*. New York: The Macmillan Co., 1936.

Mood, Alexander McFarlane. *Introduction to the Theory of Statistics*. New York: McGraw-Hill Book Co., 1950.

Northrop, F. S. C. *The Logic of the Sciences and the Humanities*. New York: The Macmillan Co., 1947.

Ogg, Frederic Austin. *Research in the Humanities and Social Sciences*. New York: The Century Co., 1928.

Quirke, Arthur J. *Forged, Anonymous, and Suspect Documents*. London: George Routledge and Sons, 1930.

Remmers, H. H. *Introduction to Opinion and Attitude Measurement*. New York: Harper and Bros., 1954.

Research Methods Applied to Health, Physical Education, and Recreation. Bulletin of the American Association for Health, Physical Education, and Recreation. Washington, 1949.

Robinson, Victor. *The Story of Medicine*. New York: Tudor Press, 1931.

Ryan, W. Carson. *Studies in Early Graduate Education*. New York: Carnegie Foundation for the Advancement of Teaching, 1939.

Sanders, Chauncey. *An Introduction to Research in English Literary History*. New York: The Macmillan Co., 1952.

Schneider, George. *Theory and History of Bibliography*, trans. Ralph Robert Shaw. New York: Columbia University Press, 1934.

Simpson, George, and Fritz Kafka. *Basic Statistics*. New York: W. W. Norton and Co., 1952.

Smith, Henry Lester. *Educational Research, Principles and Practices*. Bloomington, Ind.: Educational Publications, 1944.

Spear, Mary Eleanor. *Charting Statistics*. New York: McGraw-Hill Book Co., 1952.

Storr, Richard J. *The Beginnings of Graduate Education in America*. Chicago: University of Chicago Press, 1953.

Walker, Helen M., and Walter N. Durost. *Statistical Tables: Their Structure and Use*. New York: Teachers College, Columbia University, 1936.

Wert, James E. *Educational Statistics*. New York: McGraw-Hill Book Co., 1938.

Wert, James E., Charles O. Neidt, and J. Stanley Ahmann. *Statistical Methods in Educational and Psychological Research*. New York: Appleton-Century-Crofts, 1954.

Whitney, Frederick Lamson. *The Elements of Research*. New York: Prentice-Hall, 1950.

Wilson, E. Bright, Jr. *An Introduction to Scientific Research*. New York: McGraw-Hill Book Co., 1952.

Young, Pauline V. *Scientific Social Surveys and Research*. New York: Prentice-Hall, 1949.

Zeisel, Hans. *Say It with Figures*. New York: Harper and Bros., 1947.